The Really Useful ICT Book

The Really Useful ICT Book is a practical and easy-to-use guide to give you all the confidence you need to use ICT really effectively, inside and outside the primary classroom. It makes clear how ICT can be taught as a standalone subject, and how it can be used easily and imaginatively to enhance the teaching of other subjects.

Jam-packed with ideas and templates to save you time, this friendly handbook offers an introduction to:

- using ICT inside the classroom – including interactive whiteboards, computer suites, VLEs and e-safety;
- using ICT outside the classroom – including word processors, laptops, data loggers and digital cameras;
- when and how to use a wide range of software and hardware – from spreadsheet packages through to digital photography, e-portfolios and software simulation;
- using ICT in all subject areas;
- practical suggestions for using ICT in cross-curricular topics;
- using ICT to develop teacher and pupil creativity;
- using ICT for assessment and in your professional role.

With an emphasis on developing children's creativity and on progression from Key Stage 1 to Key Stage 2, *The Really Useful ICT Book* is a comprehensive compendium of advice and inspiration for all training, newly qualified and experienced teachers, as well as those in support roles in primary schools.

Jill Jesson and **Graham Peacock** are Senior Lecturers in Education, Sheffield Hallam University, UK.

The Really Useful Series

The Really Useful Book of ICT in the Early Years
Harriet Price

The Really Useful Physical Education Book
Edited by Gary Stidder and Sid Hayes

The Really Useful Maths Book: A Guide for Primary Teachers
Tony Brown and Henry Liebling

The Really Useful Science Book: A Framework of Knowledge for Primary Teachers, 3rd Edition
Steve Farrow

The Really Useful Literacy Book: Being Creative with Literacy in the Primary Classroom, 2nd Edition
Tony Martin, Chira Lovat and Glynis Purnell

The Really Useful Creativity Book
Dominic Wyse and Pam Dowson

The Really Useful ICT Book

A practical guide to using technology across the primary curriculum

Jill Jesson and Graham Peacock

Routledge
Taylor & Francis Group

LONDON AND NEW YORK

First published 2012
by Routledge
2 Park Square, Milton Park, Abingdon, Oxon OX14 4RN

Simultaneously published in the USA and Canada
by Routledge
711 Third Avenue, New York, NY 10017

Routledge is an imprint of the Taylor & Francis Group, an informa business

British Library Cataloguing in Publication Data
A catalogue record for this book is available from the British Library

Library of Congress Cataloging in Publication Data
Jesson, Jill, 1950–.
   The really useful ICT book: a practical guide to using technology across
   the primary curriculum/Jill Jesson and Graham Peacock.
   p. cm.
   1. Educational technology – Great Britain.   2. Education, Elementary –
   Great Britain – Computer-assisted instruction.   3. Information
   technology – Study and teaching (Elementary) – Great Britain.
   I. Peacock, Graham.   II. Title.
   LB1028.3.J47 2011
   372.133′4 – dc22   2010053797

ISBN: 978–0–415–59277–2 (pbk)
ISBN: 978–0–203–81019–4 (ebk)

Typeset in Palatino
by Florence Production Ltd, Stoodleigh, Devon

Printed and bound in Great Britain by the MPG Books Group

Contents

Acknowledgements   viii

Introduction: Finding new ways to learn   1

Part 1: A useful guide to ICT in the classroom   5

1   Creativity and ICT   7

2   Using ICT inside the classroom   15

3   Using ICT outside the classroom   37

4   Assessing children's use of ICT   39

5   Use of ICT in a teacher's professional role   45

Part 2: A useful guide to software and hardware   49

6   Word-processing software in the primary classroom   51

7   Spreadsheet software in the primary classroom   66

8   Database software in the primary classroom   76

9   Branching database software in the primary classroom   80

10 Data loggers in the primary classroom   84

11 Digital cameras, movies and photocopiers in the primary classroom   87

12 Digital microscopes and visualisers in the primary classroom   95

13 Graphics software in the primary classroom   100

14 Simulation software in the primary classroom   107

15   Control technology, Pixies and Roamers in the primary classroom   110

16   Digital audio equipment in the primary classroom   112

17   Hand-held devices in the primary classroom   117

18   Multimedia authoring programs in the primary classroom   119

Part 3: Really useful ideas for using ICT across the curriculum   **123**

19   English   125

20   Mathematics   132

21   Science   138

22   Modern foreign languages   144

23   History   145

24   Geography   151

25   Design and technology   157

26   Art and design   162

27   Music   165

28   Physical education   168

29   Religious education   171

Part 4: Using ICT in cross-curricular topics   **175**

Topic 1   Fabrics and bags enterprise project   178

Topic 2   Looking into the past   180

Topic 3   Our community   182

Topic 4   Learning about animals   184

Topic 5   Plants and growing   186

Topic 6   Famous people   188

Topic 7   Healthy me   190

Topic 8   Sports/Olympics/World Cup   192

Topic 9   Robots/superheroes/monsters   194

Topic 10   Caring for our planet   196

Appendix 1: Attainment targets   198

Appendix 2: Creating templates   199

Appendix 3: Instructions for creating a hyperlinked PowerPoint presentation   202

Appendix 4: E-safety   203

Appendix 5: Glossary   204

Bibliography   209

Index   212

Acknowledgements

We would like to thank the following people for sharing their advice and expertise with us:

Pam Ward at Sitwell Junior School, Rotherham
Dave Shaw at Mundella Primary School, Sheffield
Jack Todhunter at The Newman School, Rotherham
Matt Revill at Foxhill Primary School, Sheffield
and Sheila Sharpe at Sheffield Hallam University.

Introduction

Finding new ways to learn

This book is for all primary-school teachers and student teachers who want to spend more time with motivated pupils who enjoy finding new ways to learn and less time repeating the same lessons in the same ways; it is for experienced teachers who would like to add new skills and ideas to their teaching repertoire; it is for teacher trainees who want to have successful placements by utilising up-to-date skills and differentiated ways for pupils to plan, record and evaluate their learning; it is for all adults in the school who want to see how they can make more use of the IT skills and the hardware and software they already have.

The ideas we propose for computer programs, such as word processors, paint programs or spreadsheets, aim to be more engaging than typing up a best copy, making flood-fill and squiggle patterns or compiling a few block graphs. There are also suggestions for more advanced techniques using digital video, podcasting and multimedia presentations. It is a book to dip into to find new ways to use familiar (and some not so familiar) pieces of hardware and software, or to find ways to employ digital technologies, perhaps in subject areas in which you have never used them.

Part 1 looks at a range of issues, such as the ways digital technologies can be used to develop the creativity of pupils, ways to use information and communication technologies (ICT) both in the classroom and out on field trips and the use of ICT in a teacher's professional role. Part 2 considers the facilities provided by a range of hardware and software applications and how these can be employed in different subject areas.

Part 3 deals with the use of ICT in subject teaching and how the teaching of each programme of study can be enhanced by the use of a range of digital technologies. Part 4 unpicks a selection of generic topics similar to those commonly taught in school. Suggestions are made for ways to use ICT to promote teaching and learning and for ways to adapt these ideas for children in Key Stage 1 (KS1), Lower Key Stage 2 (LKS2) and Upper Key Stage 2 (UKS2).

There are so many exciting ways to develop teaching and learning techniques through the appropriate use of ICT: this book aims to support teachers to extend the creativity, skills and ideas they already have, along with suggestions for ways to develop them in new directions.

Information, communication, cooperation, creation and interpretation (ICCCI)

For most of the last century, education was concerned with helping the population to become literate, numerate and aware of its cultural heritage. In the twenty-first century, our needs have been reappraised, in particular by the Rose Review (2009) and Cambridge

Primary Review (Alexander 2009), and the old goals have been extended not only to include familiarity with *information* and *communication* technology, but to develop *cooperation, creative* and *interpretation* skills (ICCCI) in ways we have not done before.

What is needed now is not just basic literacy but the ability to read and create multimodal texts. Where numeracy was once concerned with basic computation, it is now more concerned with analysis and interpretation. Where knowledge of our cultural heritage was concerned with a basic familiarity with what civilisations produced both in the past and the present, now there is more emphasis on developing a personal creative culture. It is acknowledged that, rather than there being one culture to study, there are many local, ethnic and personal cultures, and that in fact everyone may belong to several small group cultures, whether they are those of the family, the reading group, the club or the school.

In addition to communicating with a teacher, we need to be able to communicate what we have learned to friends through texting, e-mail, blogging and social networking. We need to collect information in wikis, publish it in articles, share it in brochures and on websites, and disseminate it through multimedia presentations that may never be printed, though widely shared online. Societies require people who can cooperate in finding information, sharing ideas and equipment and working together. We are beginning to realise the benefits of a personal creativity for all that is motivating and fulfilling and that may, in some cases, contribute to a local or even national culture. Becta reported in 2010 that 86 per cent of primary-school teachers now make some use of technology with learners in order to be creative. Numeracy, more than ever, requires the ability to interpret data rather than just accumulate or compute them. On a daily basis, people are faced with statistical reports and conflicting data in the media and they are expected to manage online bank accounts, credit cards, investments and budgets.

The teacher's job is now to 'chunk' and challenge. By that we mean that teachers need to break down the skills required for ICCCI into manageable chunks of learning for each individual, and to provide challenges for them to use the skills, first in specific contexts such as:

- creating a graph in order to understand habitats;
- writing a 'welcome to school' leaflet for new pupils;
- finding recipes or kite designs on the Internet to adapt in a DT session;
- logging and interpreting changes in the environment;
- organising a presentation with a group of friends;
- summarising features about the area in which they live in an e-mail to a school in another country;
- creating a personal portfolio of work that demonstrates their skills and achievements.

Waite, in Wheeler (2005), notes that, although many studies have looked at the capacity of ICT to support attainment and ability, few consider how attainment and ability levels may affect students' use of ICT. She points out that poor ICT proficiency may impede learning in other areas, just as a lack of literacy skills might hinder access to other subjects. This book aims to develop skills in IT that can promote learning in all other curriculum areas. Waite goes on to suggest that, 'The expectation of greater personalisation of learning . . . makes it especially important to begin to unpack some of the factors at an individual level which may impact on students' optimal use of ICT for learning' (p. 143), and notes cognitive style, learning styles and the personality of the pupil as factors that all need to be considered by the teacher. In the following chapters, we suggest projects for a range of cognitive styles to suit pupils' many different ways of organising and presenting information, to reflect a wide range of interests and learning styles and to engage personalities that require both open-ended and supported challenges.

An individual's use of ICT will be affected by internal constructs, past experience, preferred learning style for the situation, as well as external classroom factors, such as peer activity. Much is made in some areas of education these days of the preferred learning styles of pupils. Perhaps not enough is made of the fact that these are flexible and may vary with the subject and the situation. There are different forms of ICT to suit all learning styles and all subject areas, and so we need to see digital technologies as much more than word-processing, painting and graphing machines.

This book suggests ideas for e-learning, which is the use of ICT to enhance subject teaching and learning (Potter and Derbyshire 2005), as well as ways to use ICT for real projects to develop IT capability to solve problems.

Digital literacy

Digital literacy is the combination of skills, knowledge and understanding that young people need to learn in order to participate fully and safely in an increasingly digital world. This array of skills, knowledge and understanding is a key component of the primary and secondary curriculum and should be incorporated in the teaching of all subjects at all levels.

(Becta 2010)

Digital literacy is more than the ability to use a computer; it involves critical thinking, collaboration and social awareness. It involves being able to use IT skills effectively, as well as the ability to analyse and evaluate digital information to see if it is accurate, fair and honest. To do this, pupils must be taught about the many facets of e-safety (see p. 203) and about appropriate of digital technology. The Becta (2010) report points out the difference between pupil confidence in using IT, which may be high, as opposed to pupil competence, which may not be so well rounded and advanced. There is much more to responsible and effective use of ICT than the ability to type, reach the Internet and communicate electronically, and the skills of questioning, evaluating and criticality need to be taught in this context at all levels.

With a population that is rapidly becoming digitally literate, there are increasing opportunities to ask questions of a wider range of people, make connections with prior learning, explore ideas, see situations from different viewpoints and reflect on our learning so as to make it more meaningful. Teachers are becoming progressively more skilled in using ICT for creative presentations, effective communication and innovative ways of recording, data collection and statistical analysis. We hope that the suggestions in this book will offer new ideas and insights to both experienced teachers and those training for qualified teacher status.

Please note that some of the websites referred to have been closed while this book has been in production.

Part 1

A useful guide to ICT in the classroom

Introduction

In Part 1, we look at issues common to the use of ICT, both in the classroom and on educational trips. A brief review of relevant literature is followed by a look at how ICT can be used to develop both pupil and teacher creativity. Inside the classroom, we look at the potential that interactive whiteboards (IWBs) have for making lessons dynamic and engaging in new ways. Not all schools use their computer facilities intensively, and computer suites are often the easiest places to find a quiet, unused room in a school. Even the standalone computers can be isolated and unused. In this book, there are suggestions for making better use of both standalone and suites of computers. E-safety has had its profile raised, thanks to the Byron Report (2008), and some of the main points are outlined here. This is followed by sections on how to develop good practice in finding digital information, communicating using e-mail and other Internet facilities. The section on using ICT outside the classroom looks at a range of hardware and software that may be useful on class trips and residential visits or just around the school grounds. The section on assessment tries to simplify the process, showing how ICT can be used for planning further learning as well celebrating success. Assessment should not be excessively time consuming, and developing e-portfolios is a natural development of this work. Finally, we look at the use of ICT in a teacher's professional role and how it can help to reduce the burden of planning, teaching, assessing and record keeping. There are case studies to show how some of these ideas can be implemented in good practice.

1 Creativity and ICT

In this chapter we will explore:

- what we mean by creativity;
- questioning and challenging;
- making connections and seeing relationships;
- envisaging what might be;
- exploring ideas and keeping options open;
- reflecting critically on ideas, actions and outcomes;
- challenges to develop creative skills.

Whose creativity?

Creativity was listed briefly as a skill to be encouraged in the first National Curriculum (NC) in 1989 and was, for some time, subsequently considered mainly in artistic contexts by educators. By the time of the New Primary Curriculum (NPC), which was published and withdrawn in 2010, creativity had been extensively discussed, defined and identified as a key skill to develop in all pupils and in all subject areas. Creativity was given major consideration in both the Rose (2009) and Cambridge reviews (Alexander 2009) and featured in all areas of learning in the NPC. The NACCE report (1999) stated that all of us have the capability to be creative if we are given the opportunity and it defined creativity as '*Imaginative activity fashioned so as to produce outcomes that are both original and of value*'. We may not all achieve the creativity of Beethoven or Einstein, but we are all capable of thinking imaginatively, for specific purposes, to create useful and original outcomes. These outcomes do not have to be artefacts, but may be ideas or processes or systems. Creative outcomes may result in discoveries in medicine, constructions in architecture or engineering, new ways to organise roads or logistics, or advances in artistic fields. In the classroom, this might start as discovering the best way to lay out a brochure using a word processor; finding ways to solve a maths problem with a calculator; using a graphics package to redesign parts of the school grounds; composing a jingle on an electronic keyboard for an advert; using a spreadsheet to organise a budget; or creating a digital gallery of pupils' work for parents and friends to see.

It would be useful to discuss with colleagues what is meant by the term creativity, as many people believe it to be an arts-related skill, most often exhibited by someone wearing a French beret. See research from Bath Spa by Davies *et al.* (2004) to confirm this, or ask your friends to draw their idea of a creative person. Very few are likely to show a computer being used.

In 2004, the QCDA produced materials to help teachers identify and develop the features of creativity in their pupils. The publication, 'Creativity: find it, promote it' (2004), stated that, 'Pupils who are creative will be prepared for a rapidly changing world where they may have to adapt to several careers in a lifetime' (p. 9).

Using the five characteristics of creativity outlined in this publication, this section will look at ways of using the new digital technologies to develop creativity in a range of educational contexts. Of course, ICT is not the only way to develop creative skills, but the opportunities it affords deserve close consideration. The five characteristics of a creative person identified in this publication (p. 10) are:

- questioning and challenging;
- making connections and seeing relationships;
- envisaging what might be;
- exploring ideas, keeping options open;
- reflecting critically on ideas, actions and outcomes.

Questioning and challenging

In order for pupils to learn, they need to be skilled at asking questions. This is a skill to be taught from the earliest days in school, with children progressing from 'how?' and 'where?' to 'when?' and 'why?' and on to 'what if?' and 'how can?'. All questions should be acknowledged as being of worth, and ways to help the questioner to answer them should be identified.

Questions can be answered using the acronym AREST, as shown in the box.

Digital technologies can be used in many contexts, with each of the above techniques, though they may not help to answer every question that a thoughtful child might devise.

In KS1, children posing questions such as 'How do some seeds cling to clothes?' could be helped to find the answer by putting the burrs of goosegrass or burdock under a digital microscope or visualiser, in order to see how the burrs attach themselves to different types of fabric. Challenges such as 'Do I live nearer to school than my friends?' can be answered with a look at Google or Google Street View. Unusual questions such as 'What if there was no blue in the world?' might be checked out by taking the blue out of digital photos.

Children in LKS2 might want to know 'What did the Vikings have for breakfast?', and research using a CD-ROM or the Internet could help to answer this and similar factual

---

Asking someone who might know the answer can be done through e-mail, texting, webcam, skype, video-conferencing, blogging or social networking in an attempt to find someone who has relevant information.

Researching the answer can be done using the Internet or CD-ROMs.

Experimenting to test ideas through practical investigations, possibly using data-logging to record accurately; modelling to try out ideas; or data-handling software to organise and make charts to help analyse the data.

Simulations, when first-hand tests are impracticable, are available on CD-ROMs and on the Internet.

Thinking around the problem, reflecting on ideas, events and discussions and perhaps recording these reflections using ICT to organise mind maps or just notes and lists.

questions. The Internet could also provide some of the prices and information when a class tries to discover 'Which animal would make the best pet?'. They could consider the exercise and cleaning routines and record initial set-up costs and weekly care expenses on a spreadsheet. Charts from the latter could be combined with their research results into a multimedia presentation. To see if a story would be more exciting in the past or present tense, it would be simpler to redraft using a word processor than by hand.

Older primary pupils in UKS2 are usually very motivated when challenged to design their ideal bedroom/playroom or to redesign their classroom to use the space more effectively. This can be done using the computer-aided design (CAD) room-planning programs from IKEA (www.ikea.com/ms/en_GB/rooms_ideas/splashplanners.html) or just standard graphics tools in Word, Textease or other word-processing (WP) programs.

Once familiar with the technology, they might ask, 'What if we left the data logger on all night? Could we use the movement sensor to see if the fish in the tank go to sleep at night?' or 'If we left the sound sensor on all day, what would we find out about the sound levels in different types of lesson?'. You, the teacher, could then challenge them to see 'How could we make a quiet but dull place in school more interesting, or a noisy place quieter?'.

Children who are creative will be curious about themselves and the world. They will want to know the answers to questions, will love to dream up the most interesting and surprising questions and enjoy the challenge of answering them. If a teacher knows all the answers to the questions the class is asking, then the pupils are asking very limited and unimaginative questions.

Making connections and seeing relationships

In order to develop original concepts, it is useful to think laterally rather than linearly and be able to make connections between seemingly unrelated objects or ideas. New products or designs are often invented by associating apparently unrelated objects, using the free-association method promoted by de Bono (1976). Classification systems for plants, animals and rocks have been developed through observation of what items have in common and what makes them unique.

To develop this skill in KS1 children, a teacher could present sets of pictures, using clip art or photos on an IWB, and challenge pupils to spot the odd one out. In the case of a cart, a horse and a tree, there are several possibilities, such as: the cart is the only one not alive; the horse is the only one not made of wood; or the tree is the only one that cannot travel. Children will find other interesting explanations for their ideas. To learn more about

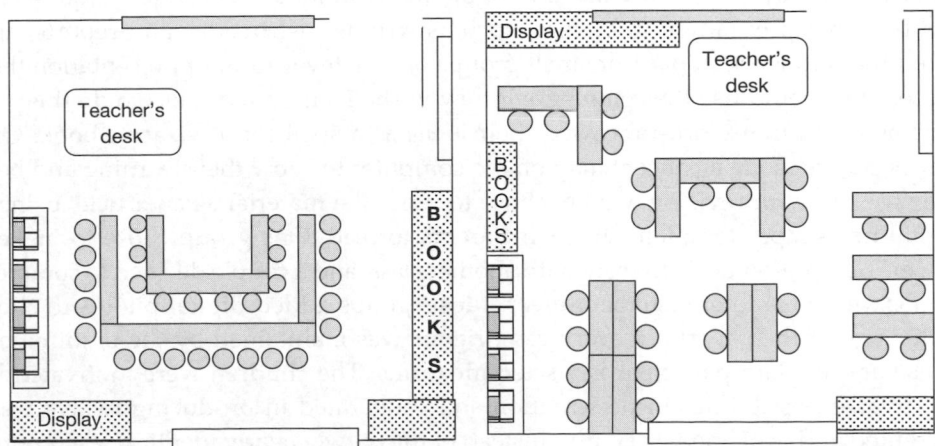

Figure 1.1 Which layout will suit the class best?

a story, for example *The Gruffalo,* and the language it uses, ask your class to make a soundscape for the story, either using a digital music program or else recording percussion instruments on to tape or a digital sound file. This could be added to a reading of the text and turned into a podcast for other classes to share. A class that has recently learned to write simple instructions could use a computer template, with headings and bullet points, to write instructions for a magic spell to make a friend laugh or a recipe to turn their teacher's hair green.

Pupils in LKS2 will find it engaging to communicate their knowledge in novel ways. They could word-process speech and thought bubbles to create cartoons strips to show their understanding of a science concept or a story from RE, or make a digital animated film to record their learning in history or PHSE sessions. Creating analogies and metaphors is another dimension to creative thought, and so the teacher could challenge the class to explain what friendship is like in response to pictures shown on the whiteboard, e.g. a tree, a kitten, a ball, rain, climbing a hill. Answers might be that a friendship is like a tree because it can grow, like a kitten because it is easily hurt, like a ball because it can bounce back when you think you have lost it, like rain because it is refreshing, and like climbing a hill because it can be hard work but worth it. Pupils could create similar puzzles for their friends using clip art, e.g. a school is like . . .; a holiday is like . . .; a story is like . . . These could be added to a class e-zine, virtual learning environment (VLE) or the initial analogy, word-processed as a heading on a wall poster, on which friends can add handwritten ideas.

Older pupils in UKS2 could use concept-mapping software such as Kidspiration to create a mind map to show connections between prior knowledge and recent learning. They could then copy the information and use it to make a digital presentation for parents' evening or a class exhibition. When searching for patterns or trends to answer the question 'How can I make the best parachute for my action figure?', they can use a spreadsheet to record time taken for proto-parachutes of different sizes, shapes and materials to fall, before constructing a final version. They should be taught to present their learning in as wide a range of ways as possible, so that, instead of just writing down what they have learned and completing worksheets, they make digital movies, podcasts, multimedia presentations, word-processed posters and brochures to share with different audiences.

Case study: Using ICT for recording in science

An Advanced Skills Teacher (AST), working with a Year 5 (Y5) class on separating mixtures, taught the subject on a Harry Potter theme. Once the teaching and testing were complete, she asked her class to record their learning for a particular group of readers in a way that would interest them. She reminded them of techniques they had been recently taught in literacy, such as writing instructions and reports, and asked them to work in pairs or small groups on whatever form of presentation they chose. They could use the computers if they wished, and most chose to do this.

Some children word-processed their ideas as a spell for a wizard's book. One pair of pupils made a concept map on the computer to show their learning and help their friends with revision. Others chose to write the material as an article, using a digital newspaper template, for their parents to read. One group chose to make a PowerPoint presentation to share with another class, and a couple decided to complete the task in verse to amuse themselves. Most groups added digital photos to show each stage of their work. In every case, rigour was maintained by the requirement to use and explain particular key scientific terms. The children were motivated by the diverse possibilities in presentation and cooperated in producing twelve well-presented and explained write-ups, instead of thirty-two, nearly identical test reports. Sharing the results was useful revision for all.

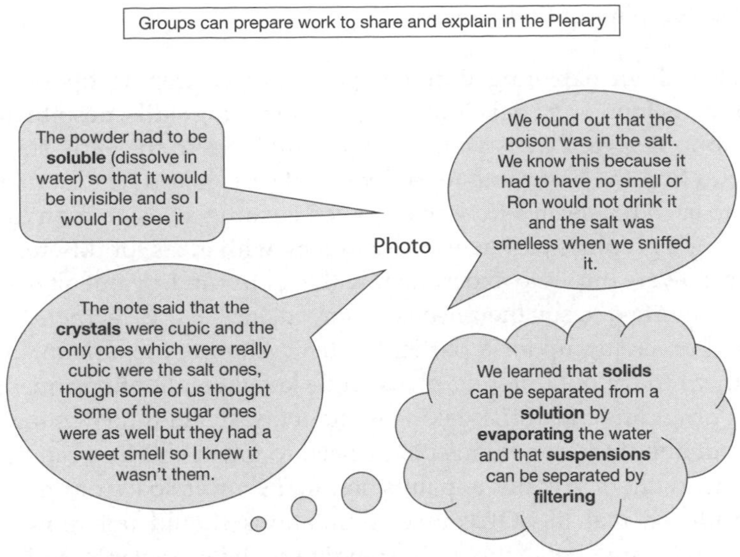

Figure 1.2 What we learned, by Jack, Tim, Laura and Chloe. The final slide from one group's presentation

Envisaging what might be

An important role of education is to help the learner to see things in new ways and from different points of view; to imagine the possibilities of different situations; and to foresee problems and visualise solutions. A higher-order thinking skill to develop is the 'What if?' question.

KS1 children should be helped to imagine and then to see what other places are like and what the people there are doing. A webcam on another area or even another country can show the weather, the time of day, as well as local activity. Nearer home, taking digital photos of their home or school from the perspective of a baby, or of their street from the perspective of a wheelchair user, could help to develop empathetic understanding. The pictures can be added to a presentation, with simple headings or speech bubbles to show what they have found.

Many children find the individual computation of sums stressful. If they can be helped to see them as group puzzles and games through the use of IWB games, then individual learning may be eased and increased. Many different designs can be trialled in a graphics or WP program, so that the artist can try out as many 'what if' ideas as they want, until a satisfactory design or composition is achieved.

Pupils in Y3 and Y4 might take and adapt digital photos to show their different personalities or how, with the addition of some brush strokes to the photo in a paint program, they might disguise themselves. Altering the colour levels of digital photos could show them what the world looks like to a red/green colour-blind person or to an animal that sees colours differently from the way humans do. Creating digital films about bullying, theft or other problematic situations enables children to visualise alternatives in problematic situations and ask themselves 'what if?' when trying out different scenarios.

By Y5 and Y6, children can be challenged to envisage how the playground could be improved and use their research skills to find out about some of the options. They can use Google to find the shape of the school grounds and a graphics package to help add new features to the area. Similar projects will help them to see possibilities and visualise alternatives.

If they use Twitter to tell a traditional tale in 140 characters, what would be lost? What might be clearer? For projects that involve data-handling, they can see how data can be manipulated in charts and learn to choose the most appropriate for their use. In all these activities, digital technology allows pupils to experiment with ideas while keeping all alternatives intact, more effectively than using traditional, hand-operated methods.

ploring ideas, keeping options open

eativity is also about exploring different possibilities, keeping options open until a preferred solution is found and developing decision-making skills, despite the uncertainty that multiple options give. Play is vital for exploring ideas in the early stage of learning, as children try to find the best route for a floor turtle, disguised as Postman Pat's van, to deliver letters to each house on a floor map. When creating a design for a card, bookmark or calendar, using a graphics package lets them play with ideas for different recipients. A WP package empowers pupils to experiment with layouts and try out alternatives that are easily erased or modified to suit their needs. A spreadsheet allows learners to explore ideas when budgeting or saving up for a particular item. Altering the amounts to be spent or saved allows them to try out different plans while keeping all options open.

Simulation programs enable risk-taking without disaster or time wasting. For example, when finding out about the conditions plants need to grow, children can use simulations to try all options, without risk to the plants and in a shorter space of time than it would take to get results in real life. Of course, simulations should not replace all practical investigations, which are vital to the understanding of the way plants really grow and the time growth takes. The measuring jug and weighing simulations on the interactive teaching programs site (http://nationalstrategies.standards.dcsf.gov.uk/search/primary/results/nav:49909?page=1) allow endless experimentation, without spillage or weight lifting, as part of the learning process on estimation and experimentation in measuring.

It is fun to experiment to see how a piece of music would sound using a different tempo or different instruments. Using musical software, and saving different versions, this can be done without spoiling the original composition. Tactical games such as SimCity allow learners to play with ideas, try out strategies, anticipate and overcome problems and modify ideas.

Later in primary education, graphics programs can be used before materials are cut and perhaps wasted when designing the perfect tent or den with a friend. This could even be done with a distant friend, using e-mail or a blog. Groups of friends could put together a wiki on uses for a digital camera (challenge them to find more than a hundred). Older pupils can experiment with control technology to turn lights on or off, raise and lower barriers and make warnings sound in response to instructions. Such activities will generate many problems to anticipate or solve, where creative ingenuity is developed. Word-processing programs can help change a story into a poem, or vice versa, to see the effect. Alternative approaches to simply writing down what pupils have learned can be explored through digital film, digital sound, control technology and graphics programs.

Reflecting critically on ideas, actions and outcomes

Unless we think about what we have done and try to learn from it, our progress is likely to be minimal. Reflection is an integral part of the learning process, as we learn to assess what works and what does not, and there are several ways the use of ICT can help to structure this.

Even young children can be helped to make an electronic portfolio of their learning, which might include scanned images of their creations, photos of them carrying out tests or working in different subjects, and samples of text and graphics created on the computer. These can be easily assembled into a presentation using a program such as PowerPoint. Pupils can type comments about what they found most interesting and most challenging and what they would like to do next. If a teaching assistant (TA) can help with assembling these, the task can be made easier for a large class. An important part of the process is the child choosing which pieces to put into the portfolio and deciding on the comments he/she will add to show peers or parents. Another way to aid reflection is for pupils to record their experiences on tape or with a microphone attached to the computer, to comment on what they have learned and how they would like to progress.

Pupils with greater keyboard control could add speech and thought bubbles to digital text, photos and artwork to review what they have learned and explain the most useful or enjoyable part of a session. Concept maps can be used to demonstrate learning before and after a series of lessons on a particular topic, and reflective comments can be added. Some children write not only book or film reviews, but also reviews of an event for a class e-zine or VLE that their family and carers can read. Word-processing reviews allow for correction of mistakes and rewording of ideas. Few adults would write an article by hand these days, with the editing features of a word processor available, and we should allow pupils the same scope and supports as we use ourselves. However, avoid the temptation to use the word processor to make fair copies of handwritten work. Start and finish the writing using a computer, or start and finish by hand.

For older pupils on a class trip, a digital movie camera could be set up somewhere private so that pupils can take turns to talk to it, Big Brother style, to reflect on what it feels like to be away from home, perhaps for the first time. Podcasts or other sound recordings can be used by children to explain what they have learned and describe what they have done. Podcasting requires descriptive and analytical skills, with no visual clues to aid the listener's understanding. Some schools are now using blogs for pupils to review their learning, to add constructive comments on other people's ideas and to invite feedback from them. This might be for a particular project, or as a regular electronic diary to show progression throughout the year.

Whose creativity?

For creative teachers, it is not hard to make the classroom appear, at first glance, a wonder of pupil ingenuity and originality. There is indeed a place for teachers organising lessons in an imaginative way, whether it is setting up a series of science lesson screens round a Harry Potter theme, or preparing a presentation at the start of a local-studies project that appears to show big business plans to develop a supermarket on the local playground. The danger for creative teachers is that they allow their creativity to dominate the class, so that pupils are not given enough choice, time and space to try out ideas, make and learn from mistakes, and explore further alternatives in our results-led educational culture. It is the teacher's task to allow appropriate challenges, often pupil-led, that will develop a range of creative skills in the pupils, using digital technology where appropriate.

It is important that pupils have the opportunity to develop their creative talents, because it is exciting, motivating and good for their self-esteem. It helps them to develop cooperation skills, to see fresh possibilities and ways round problems, and to deal with situations that do not turn out as expected. The latter should be seen as learning opportunities rather than failures. Creative skills include an openness to new ideas and the ability to search for them, the ability to link past learning to current situations, to see what has happened and to learn from it. The development of creative skills and attitudes leads to higher achievement, which is what all teachers hope to promote in their classes.

The advantages of using ICT to develop creative skills are its accuracy, speed and versatility. Alternatives can be explored, and all choices can be kept until a final decision is made. Different versions can be saved and adapted for particular situations or recipients. ICT is not one technique: it can be visual, oral, aural, graphic, practical, diagrammatic, realistic or imaginative. ICT tools are certainly not the only way to develop creative skills, but they can go a long way towards increasing cooperation and communication, developing imagination and increasing enjoyment, and towards personalising and enriching the learning experience in the busy classroom. Along with the skills of an open-minded teacher, they can help pupils to question and challenge, to make connections and see relationships, to envisage what might be, to explore ideas, to keep options open and to reflect critically on their ideas, actions and outcomes.

Table 1.1 *Some challenges to develop creative skills using ICT*

Questioning and challenging	KS1	What if there were no blue in the world? Use a **paint program** to remove blue from photos. How do some seeds cling to clothes? Use a **visualiser** to look closely at magnified plants and hooked seeds.
	LKS2	What did the Vikings have for breakfast? Use the **Internet** to look for ideas. Use a **spreadsheet**, the **Internet** and a **presentation program** to find which animal would make the best pet. Consider set-up and weekly care costs, exercise and cleaning routines.
	UKS2	What if we left the **data logger** on all night? When is dawn/dusk? If we left the sound sensor on all day, what would we find out about the sound levels in different types of lesson? How can I use the space in my bedroom more effectively? Use a **graphics** program/shop design program to try out ideas.
Making connections and seeing relationships	KS1	Find the odd one out from sets of three pictures – for example, car, tree, horse – shown by the teacher on the **IWB**. Practise instructional writing skills. For instance, use a **word processor** to write a spell to make a friend laugh at my jokes or to make all food taste of chocolate. Create a **soundscape** for a story and add to a **podcast**.
	LKS2	Use a **WP** to create strip cartoons to show learning in science or a story from RE. Explain what characteristics a friend shares with **clip art** pictures shown on an **IWB**. Try a ball, tree, cat, rain, flower. Create similar challenges, e.g. a school is like . . . A holiday is like . . . A story is like . . .
	UKS2	Create a **mind map** to show prior knowledge and recent learning. Take the information and use it to make a **digital presentation** for parents' evening or a class exhibition. Use a **spreadsheet** to record time taken for parachutes of different sizes, shapes and materials to fall. Decide what will help make the best parachute for my action figure.
Envisaging what might be	KS1	Use a **webcam/e-mail** to find out what the weather is like elsewhere. To see maths as games, use **IWB** maths games in teams. Use a **digital camera** to take pictures of the locality from a baby's point of view.
	LKS2	Use a photo in a **paint program** to see what the world looks like for a colour-blind (red/green) person. How could I disguise myself? Alter digital photos in a **paint program**. Using a **music program**, experiment to see how a piece of music would sound using a different tempo or different instruments.
	UKS2	Use a **design program** to explore ways to make the playground more interesting. **Twitter** a traditional tale. What is lost, and what might be enhanced? See how data can be manipulated in a **spreadsheet** chart, or with a different type of chart where appropriate.
Exploring ideas, keeping options open	KS1	Use **turtle graphics** to find the best route for Postman Pat. Create an abstract art design for a calendar/bookmark in a **graphics** program. Use a basic design altered to favourite colours of recipient.
	LKS2	Use a **spreadsheet** to see how long it would take to save up for a special computer game, and how long it would take with a pocket-money increase. Use **simulations** to see the effect of conditions on the way plants grow. Try all options without risk. Use interactive teaching programs to save time and space, e.g. the measuring jug and weighing scales.
	UKS2	Design the perfect tent/den with a friend. Use **e-mail** and a **graphics program** to communicate ideas. Change a story into a poem or a poem into a story using a **word processor**.
Reflecting critically on ideas, actions and outcomes	KS1	Create a **portfolio** of learning with comments on it. Include artwork scanned in, written work and photos of pupils in a range of activities. Speech, thought bubbles and captions can be added by children to say what was easiest/hardest/most interesting/most enjoyable, and what they'd like to learn/do next.
	LKS2	Record their experiences with **digital audio/tape** and comment on them. Use both speech and thought bubbles to show what has been learned and what was thought to be the most interesting/difficult part of a session. Create before and after **concept maps**. Write a review of an event for a class **blog/wiki/e-zine**.
	UKS2	Use **blogs** to help pupils to review their learning and to comment on other people's ideas. Create a Big Brother film on a school trip to reflect on the day's activities and being away from home.

Note: Words in bold can be found in the glossary.

2 Using ICT inside the classroom

In this chapter we will explore:

- interactive whiteboards;
- use of computer suites and standalones;
- developing e-portfolios;
- getting the most from the Internet;
- personalising learning.

Interactive whiteboards

As an introduction to IWBs, we will look at: their features; points to consider when using an IWB; the ways IWBs can help children; use of IWBs in different parts of the lesson; using IWBs with children who have special educational needs (SEN); and how IWBs can be useful for teachers.

Introduction

IWBs have now become a standard piece of equipment in most primary classrooms. Once they are linked to a computer and a projector, the teacher can use them to create and use stimulating and attractive presentations that can help to organise lessons, explain objectives, use dynamic and interactive resources and link to the Internet, as well as other electronic devices, such as a visualiser or data-logging equipment.

> It can be used as an alternative to virtually every other classroom resource, traditional and modern, for example blackboards, flip charts, OHPs, maps, pictures, number lines, 'big books', calculators, and cassette and video players. At a touch, the teacher has access to a bank of resources that would previously have taken years to accumulate and a vast cupboard to store.
>
> (BECTA (2006) Teaching Interactively with Electronic
> Whiteboards in the Primary Phase
> (http://publications.becta.org.uk/download.cfm?resID=25918))

Although research into IWB efficacy is still in its early days, the advantages of an IWB over a wipe-clean board have been detailed by many authorities. The versatility of possible multimodal presentations and its efficiency in supporting planning, resourcing, modelling and interactive working are noted by Smith *et al.* (2005) and Becta (2003). With an IWB, teaching can be made more dynamic and enjoyable, through engagement with audio and visual materials on the screen by both teacher and pupils. 'Pupils are universally enthusiastic about the interactive whiteboards, because of their clear visibility ("We can see!"), the easy access they give to ICT through touch, and the added variety they bring to lessons' (Somekh 2007). Images from a small computer screen can be shared with a whole class, enabling demonstrations of new techniques and a sharing of resources that might otherwise be either too small or shown horizontally on a table, where not everyone has a clear view (Smith *et al.* 2005). Matthewman and Triggs (2004) found that interest and creativity in a lesson were increased through the multimodal approach facilitated by an IWB. Several studies have noted that the 'seamless flow' (Latham 2002) between verbal, visual and other sensory aspects of learning made possible by an IWB enables well-paced lessons, where different aspects of a subject can be integrated (Ball 2003, Becta 2003).

A review of research into the use of ICT in European schools by Balanskat *et al.* (2006) has shown that effective use of whiteboards can improve the pace of lessons and increase pupil motivation and engagement in lessons. There can be more interactivity between the teachers and their classes, as well as between groups of children within the class. IWBs can help improve teacher efficiency through the saving, sharing and reuse of lesson plans and resources and give more direct teaching time in class, as less time is needed to write material on the board.

The pilot study of IWBs in primary schools by Higgins *et al.* (2005) showed that use of IWBs can create greater opportunities for questioning and discussion during lessons, giving children of all abilities and experience '*a richer, higher-quality learning experience*'. As teachers were able to use and annotate resources previously prepared, more time was available for high-quality interaction, and actual teaching time was increased. There were more questions, more open questions, time for longer answers from pupils and almost twice as many evaluative responses from teachers using whiteboards in lessons. The report suggested that there was some evidence that the use of IWBs improves the performance of low-achieving pupils in English, and that the overall impact is greatest on writing. The impact of the use of IWBs was found to be broadly similar for both boys and girls.

Pupils are reported as being very positive about whiteboard use (Balanskat 2006, Somekh 2007). They are used to a high standard of presentation from TV programmes, and the IWB can present information in a similar way, which they find motivating. The typed text is easy to read, and, with the increased pupil–teacher interaction and multimedia features, it is easier for them to pay attention. Pupils like to have their work shown on the board and the immediate feedback they get from this. Higgins *et al.* (2005) show that children learn better when an IWB is used in the classroom, because IWBs are 'engaging and motivating, particularly for primary pupils, and . . . students pay more attention during lessons thanks to the stimulating nature of the presentation'.

Some studies have suggested that the saving and printing of whiteboard screens reduce the need for note-taking (Becta 2003). However, this strategy would not be suitable for most pupils in the primary phase and could just result in a different type of worksheet being produced. Thomas (2003) reports on the use of whiteboards in modern foreign language (MFL) teaching, primarily in the secondary sector, though the lessons learned can be applied in primary teaching as well. Tools that enable teachers to highlight, annotate, drag, drop and conceal parts of sentences or words, as well as the facility to mix visual and aural information, make it easier for pupils to make connections between what they see and what they hear. Somekh *et al.* (2007) found that,

> Although use of an interactive whiteboard in whole-class teaching appears to have relatively little impact on raising the attainment of pupils with special educational needs (SEN), it has a marked impact in engaging their attention and often greatly improves their behaviour.

It was, however, noted that,

> Where teachers had been teaching with an interactive whiteboard for two years and there was evidence that all children, including those with SEN, had made exceptional progress in attainment in national tests, a key factor was the use of the interactive whiteboard for skilled teaching of numeracy and literacy to pairs or threesomes of children.

Overall most of these studies have noted that the use of the IWB helps to support visualisation of complex concepts, as well as the demonstration of skills such as measuring with a protractor and using a microscope. It is useful to introduce new ICT techniques and software, and, although there is initially extra work in preparing the necessary resources, this is seen as an investment for later, as teachers often reuse and share resources through a school intranet or on the World Wide Web (WWW). Effective teaching still requires the use of traditional resources alongside the IWB, so that pupils have practical, hands-on experience to back up IWB demonstrations.

Good teaching is interactive, whether it be between teacher and pupil, between the pupil and a resource such as a computer, or between peers, and so strategies that stimulate feedback from pupils and interaction between them can help children learn more effectively. Interactive teaching helps pupils to demonstrate their thinking through speech or actions, and the visual, auditory and kinaesthetic interaction facilitated by an IWB helps them to explore ideas and to remember what they learn. Slower learners benefit from seeing other children explain their ideas and demonstrate how they arrive at their solutions. Interactive tools allow pupils to move items on screen, copy them to other screens, link with lines and annotate text and graphics. It is not always necessary for the children to interact physically with the electronic whiteboard: the teacher can be a mediator. It may be more time efficient for the teacher to hold the pen to model a particular skill or concept, but, whenever possible, the children should be in control of what is happening on the screen. This is sometimes best done in small-group work. Not all pupil interaction is directly with the screen; it may be verbal interaction between pupils and their teacher as they explain their ideas and direct demonstrations. Individual response can be through wipe-clean boards, which are held up for the teacher to assess the progress of individual children. The high standard of presentation possible is in line with the professional presentations the class are familiar with from entertainment systems at home, and this familiarity can inspire confidence and boost interest. John and Wheeler (2008) note that both Becta and OFSTED prefer the term 'electronic whiteboard', because its use in a classroom does not guarantee interactivity. We are using the term IWB, as this is not only prevalent in schools but is also an aspiration for their use.

Features of IWBs

- Text tools enable text to be neatly presented in a range of fonts, styles, sizes and colours. Some IWB programs do not yet have spell-check features, and so the content needs careful checking for typing errors. Texts can be displayed for shared reading in a way that helps to keep the teaching group together. Screen pens allow for additional text, highlighting or lines to be added to annotate the text, which increases ownership of all that is on screen.
- Shape tools allow the accurate and speedy drawing of a range of shapes, which can be moved and resized on screen. These can be used to organise the screen into different areas, create graphics or hide small selections of text, which can be moved to reveal answers or further information.

- The spotlight and blind tools can be used to reveal small portions of text or one picture at a time, allowing for closer examination and perhaps deduction of genre. See Text-disclosure activities at www.mape.org.uk/activities/discloze/.
- Hyperlinks to websites, other documents, multimedia files, CD-ROMs and DVDs can be inserted for efficient connection between media.
- The camera tool on some programs enables single words or large sections of text or graphics to be copied to new screens. This can be used as a quick form of note-taking.
- A rub-and-reveal facility enables information on screen to be concealed by a block of white or coloured ink, which is then rubbed away to reveal an answer. This almost magical element can add interest to lessons that need this.
- The drag-and-drop facility enables text or graphics to be moved around the screen. This is useful for sorting activities in maths and science and redrafting text in any context.
- Active voting systems provide an additional interactive facility so that pupils can contribute their calculations, votes and ideas to a lesson, while their teacher assesses their learning and their progress and can adjust the teaching to suit individual learners.

The computer is easily linked to a visualiser, a digital microscope, a data logger, a voting system, a digital video camera or scanner, and the results can be shown through the IWB. Photos taken with a digital camera can be shown on screen and annotated. In whatever way these tools and techniques are used, the IWB should promote discussion between all those involved and enable learning to take place more easily than without it. Useful interaction may be verbal rather than physical.

IWB software can be installed on computers that are not connected to a whiteboard, so that resources can be prepared away from the classroom. Presentations can be prepared from text, images, photos, animations, drawings, video clips, sound files and hyperlinks to other files or to the Internet. Items can be grouped and locked to keep them in position. Many clip-art resources and templates come with the whiteboard's software, and further resources are available online.

Points to consider when using an IWB

- Siting the board. The IWB needs to be in a position where there is enough space and at the right height for pupils to use it. If the board is higher than you would wish, make sure that space to write and items to be moved by the pupils are at the bottom of the screen.
- Try to avoid light falling on the board so that it cannot easily be seen. Blinds or even black paper on a section of window can make a huge difference to visibility.
- Enough space is needed nearby for the laptop, visualiser and resources that are not to be used on-screen.
- Avoid overuse of the IWB as a flip chart. Used well, it should be more than a list of notes to structure a lesson. Keep it interactive.
- Take care to ensure text visibility. Consider which font size and colour of text will be most suitable for the class. Red text may be difficult to read by people who are colour-blind.
- Access must enable all children the same opportunity to use the board, and so consideration should be given to individual use, especially for those in a wheelchair or with visual problems. This may be done through use of an interactive slate or voting system that is linked to the screen.

Ways IWBs can help children

Develop literacy skills

The IWB can be used at every stage of a lesson to develop discussion and thinking skills in response to the stimulus provided by the teacher. This might be a picture that is slowly revealed using the spotlight, blind or rub and reveal tools, as pupils deduce from the clues available what the picture is about. The same activity might be used to develop imaginative skills, as they create a story or poem from it. Text-disclose activities, where only parts of a text can be seen, may be used to identify the key features of a particular genre. Oracy skills can be developed in any subject area if the teacher uses the presentation on the IWB as a starting point for this. Hence, a historical simulation of flying through a town in Ancient Egypt, or deductions pooled while reading a map to locate treasure, or a shared exploration of pupils' understanding of structures in science can give more time for class debate than if the teacher had to give the information to them in a less visual and more time-consuming way. The whiteboard is good for brainstorming ideas, which can then be saved rather than deleted when a clear screen is required.

Reading skills are developed through regular interaction with easily read fonts on an IWB, where key words may be highlighted or coloured, and the teacher can focus everyone on the line or words to be studied in the text. Writing skills can be modelled by the teacher using the on-screen keyboard or handwriting tools, and text analysis is shared using the highlight and underline facilities. The camera tool is useful to copy key words and phrases to a new page so that they can be used in another genre, such as a poem or poster.

Develop ICT skills

The most convenient way to teach pupils new ICT skills and introduce new programs is to demonstrate their use on a big screen to the whole class, before individual or group

---

Case study: Using ICT to encourage literacy and oracy

Jack is an experienced teacher in a special school in Yorkshire. He is passionate about using ICT to broaden his pupils' experience of the world and to help them communicate. He uses ICT particularly to help develop oracy and literacy skills and uses a range of stimuli to encourage the children to work with video cameras in small groups, as well as individually on challenging projects. In one case, pupils videoed each other responding to a national news story about their town, when a celebrity chef suggested it was the least healthy place in the country. The discussions on the planning and editing of the film were as important as videoing it. Children with physical as well as learning disabilities have been encouraged to talk through puppets, and pupils film the puppets as they talk to the camera. The results are often a breakthrough in communicating difficult and personal issues. One girl, who found any form of communication difficult, was set up with a video camera on her wheelchair and went around the school videoing her favourite places. This was a major achievement for a child who lacked basic communication skills.

Video-conferencing is an important part of the work at Jack's school, and live discussions with NASA space scientists gave an enormous impetus to the preparation of questions about space flight. More locally, a group of older children went to Haworth in Yorkshire to interview, on camera, residents' responses to the influx of visitors to their town and their views about *Wuthering Heights*. In all projects, the planning and editing processes are as important as the final products.

practice. Data-logging records can be shown on the screen, and points where the loudest or quietest sounds were recorded can be zoomed in on, highlighted and discussed. Techniques to animate a story can be explored so that everyone can see them before paired practice. The construction of charts, the manipulation of graphics, modelling of decision-tree use and database searches can all be shown on prepared screens, which pupils can revise again as required.

Develop cooperative skills

At any point in a lesson, the IWB can aid the teacher in modelling, not just the academic aim of the session, but how to take turns, listen to other people's contributions and share ideas. The class can work in teams to advise their representatives, using the board, which numbers to choose in a maths game. They must learn to pool ideas when choosing the most appropriate words in a class writing session on the board, and cooperate to devise and record plans for a science investigation. Throughout these and other activities, they are learning to take turns and cooperate to achieve a common goal. In the small-group section of a lesson, an electronic planning sheet may be completed by a design group. Using the IWB screen, several pupils can all see their ideas clearly as they are typed by a member of the group. The large screen enables them to have a group experience, and they have to agree on plans and the wording of ideas before the text can be entered. There has to be a high level of on-task discussion to complete this task, so that all are happy with their contribution. 'Enhanced speaking and listening opportunities lie at the heart of good IWB use' (Barber *et al.* 2007).

Develop thinking skills

One of the most productive possibilities with an IWB displaying a piece of software is the opportunity for pupils to try out ideas and see how they work. In literacy, this might involve the group redrafting layouts until a consensus is reached that the chosen format works well. In numeracy, a whole class may be trying to beat the clock to match pairs in a number game, find a solution to a problem or direct one person to manipulate shapes or organise numbers to fulfil a set criterion. When using spreadsheets or simulations, they can be asked 'what if' questions and try out their ideas to check the consequences. Of course, much of this can be done individually on small screens, but the larger IWB allows more than three children to join in. Even if they are not all directly manipulating the board, they can be discussing options, recording ideas in pairs and advising the person who is controlling the tools. They can be involved with predictions and explanations, with analysis and synthesis, and they can be engaged by asking further questions of their own. As Barber *et al.* (2007, p. 44) suggest, 'from the moment they encounter one (an IWB) they want to touch and ask "what happens if I try this?", "why did that happen?", "let me have a go" or "let me be involved" . . . this can enable children to visualise sequences and learn in a way that was not previously available'.

Use of IWBs in different parts of the lesson

Mental warm-up/introduction

When an IWB is used at the start of a lesson, it is important to keep the levels of pace and interest high, and so it might be most efficient for the teacher to be directly interacting with the board, using advice from the pupils to direct her actions. They may, for example, instruct her about which numbers to enter or which items to move. Children can interact verbally and be kept active mentally through the use of number fans or dry wipe boards so that the teacher can assess their understanding. Through use of resources the teacher has prepared on-screen, answers can be revealed using rub and reveal, the screen blind or a spotlight. The surprise element of the random number generator can motivate pupils in many maths activities.

Film clips, aerial photos and simulations can be used to introduce a topic in the most visual way possible. A concept map or number line might be created or annotated to show knowledge at the start of a topic, and the screen can be saved and updated at a later date to show learning at the end of the project. There are many good IWB resources online suitable for lesson starts, but one danger of the Internet is that there are so many of them that much teacher time can be wasted searching for the perfect resource. The IWB may also be linked to a visualiser to project maps or newspaper cuttings or to share artefacts, so that everyone can see the initial stimulus for the lesson.

Whole-class session

In the main part of the lesson, a series of prepared screens that show the learning objective, key words and organisation of ideas and activities can be used to structure the session. This can also be done with the IWB software or PowerPoint, which can also be annotated using the tools in the bottom left-hand corner of the screen (hover the mouse over this area to see them). Avoid using too many slides. The teacher can prepare more than are actually used and decide which are most appropriate, depending on the responses of the class. In this part of the lesson, the teacher is often modelling ways to write, sort, calculate or organise learning. Children can be actively involved through interacting with the board, as well as sharing ideas, although if too many are asked to come from the back of the class time can be wasted and pace and concentration lost (Allen *et al.* 2007). The sound facility can be used to demonstrate correct pronunciation in MFL lessons, play music as a stimulus for art or writing, and enable children to hear news events from the past just as they sounded to those involved. This may be the part of the lesson where the teacher is modelling a skill

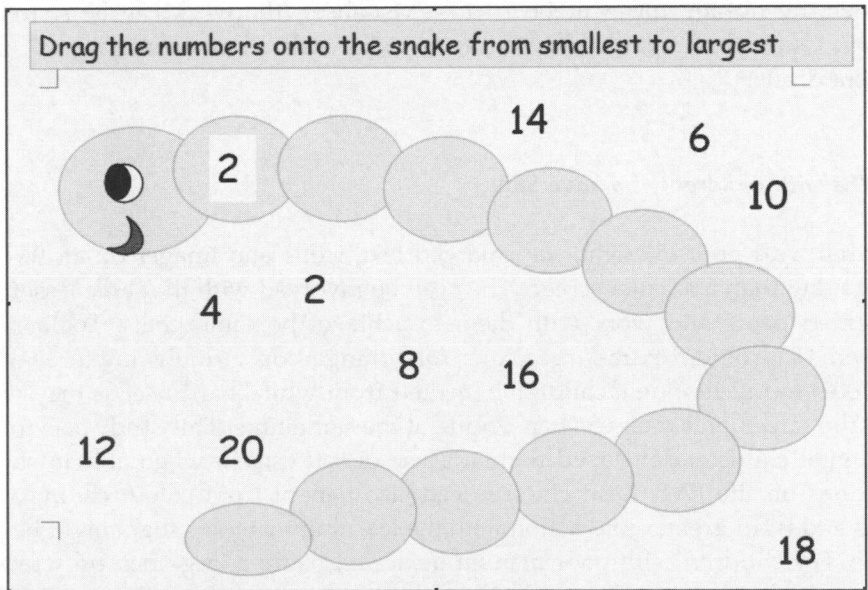

Figure 2.1 Caterpillar interactive screen for small-group work

d asking the class to help them practise it. All writing, calculations, diagrams, charts d other work created in this part of the lesson can be saved as a record of the teaching d learning that have occurred. This work can be recalled for revision or development at a later date.

Small-group work

This is often a time when the board is not used to its full potential, though if it is handed over to a small teaching group, perhaps with a TA in charge, this can be when pupils have the greatest opportunity to interact directly with the board and learn new ideas. A small group, with or without a TA, might benefit from hands-on interaction with the teaching materials in a way they could not do as easily with the whole class present. The teacher can put up an interactive task designed for the needs of a particular group, or a few pupils might want to explore the possibilities of a simulation, practise a maths skill or annotate a text to share with the rest of the class later. Alternatively, the slides in use in the main part of the lesson can be left available for individuals to scroll through, as needed, to inform their group activities.

Plenary

This is a time to summarise learning, give feedback and celebrate achievement. It may be an opportunity to introduce the next stage of learning to be developed in a subsequent session, or a simulation could be used to revise the learning objective with pupils able to move and manipulate options offered on the screen. To conclude a science session, small-group data can be added to prepared charts for the whole class to interpret. Some teachers like to end maths lessons with a motivating game to reinforce learning, and there are many to choose from. If pairs or groups of children have been working on other computers in the group work part of the lesson, then their work can be easily transferred to the teacher's computer and shared with the rest of the class, while feedback is given to those who created it. Immediate feedback is beneficial and motivating for pupils, and it saves the teacher from having to mark work later in the day. If the work is paper based, then, by linking the whiteboard to a visualiser, the work can be shared in the same way. Using the freeze facility on a visualiser will allow comparison of first and subsequent drafts.

Using IWBs with children who have SEN

For children with poor eyesight, the enlarged text, icons and images on an IWB can be more engaging than a smaller screen. They can be involved with the same lesson as their better-sighted peers and work with them to achieve the same goals. Toolbars can be customised to provide extra-large icons for younger or visually impaired children. Carter (2002) found that deaf children benefited from whiteboard use, as they were able to watch the screen and their teacher signing at the same time. This study also found that deaf bilingual children developed a great sense of self-esteem when able to show their presentations on the IWB. Deaf children can also benefit from colour-coding words in sentences and from greater interaction with the learning materials than might be possible otherwise. For children with poor manual dexterity, using a large pen on screen rather than a mouse can give easier access to the programs used, as they simply touch directly what they want. Some types of IWB can even be controlled with a finger rather than a wand, so that pupils interact very physically with the board. Dyslexic children can benefit from a blue (or other colour) screen background to the text they read. This can be prepared for a whole class, without inconveniencing other readers. The font size and style can be changed to suit the class's needs. Voting systems enable the shy and those who lack communication skills to be directly involved with a lesson.

Interactive whiteboards can be useful for teachers

Teachers can use IWBs to:

- prepare reusable lesson plans that are visually engaging and help to organise and structure a lesson;
- share objectives;
- show key questions;
- list vocabulary;
- display diagrams, charts and photos that can be annotated;
- show the organisation of groups or tasks;
- link to audio visual materials on the Internet or through CD-ROMs;
- show a picture (or items with a visualiser) as a stimulus for discussion;
- brainstorm ideas;
- disclose text or graphics slowly or partially;
- use maps from the Internet or those that come with IWB software;
- teach a large group computer, keyboard or Internet-navigation skills;
- teach a smaller group through direct interaction with the board;
- interact with text through highlighting, underlining or annotation, e.g. use the highlighter tool to highlight nouns, verbs, adjectives etc.;
- demonstrate the steps of a maths calculation;
- enable a small group to plan a project or investigation;
- save lessons to show to pupils who were absent;
- share individual or group work completed in a session.

Use of computer suites and standalones

There is a range of ICT provision in primary classrooms, including computer suites, laptop suites and standalone computers. According to a Becta report by Rudd *et al.* (2009, p. 23), 'the vast majority of teachers are enthusiastic and confident about using ICT for teaching and learning, and . . . these levels of confidence appear to be increasing year on year'.

However, anecdotal evidence from observation by university staff visiting schools and trainees on placement in schools does not always corroborate this statement. This could be because only the teachers enthusiastic about ICT responded.

Some schools have full computer suites that are purpose built and shining with educational technology. These suites can be timetabled or booked, sometimes in relation to specific subjects to be taught in them. In some schools, however, much of this is rarely used. Other schools have mobile suites of computers that can be booked, or standalone computers, either in the classroom or just outside it, allowing daily use of interactive technologies and the potential for their use in every session. Too often, the standalones stay alone, not even switched on, or with the same programs open every day, so that familiarity breeds disregard. To get the most from each digital situation, some suggestions for their use are outlined below.

The computer suite

Before a session in an ICT suite, the teacher may have to turn on the computers and access the desired program, depending on the age of the class or the school rules on this subject. It is good practice for the children to do this as soon as they are able. They should also each have a named folder to which they save their work, inside a class folder that can be further subdivided into boys and girls for ease of use. These can be set up by the children themselves at the start of the year and used throughout it, before their electronic portfolio is moved up to the next year group.

As experienced teachers know, effective use of a computer suite starts before the pupils have even left their regular classroom. First, the teacher will make it clear what they will need: only taking a pencil and notebook helps to minimise time-wasting but ensures they have access to other forms of written communication, should the technology break down or the children get stuck in some other way. The order in which they leave the classroom should reflect the order in which they are to arrive and with whom they will sit. It is useful to establish a clear routine for logging on to the school intranet or to a specific program, to avoid the frustration of a whole class trying to log on at once and jamming the system. They should also know what their first task is, and this may involve the pencils and paper brought in, so that organising ideas and planning for learning can start immediately. A sound rule to help communication is that all hands are off keyboards while the teacher is explaining a task, otherwise instructions are missed by those unable to hear for the rattle of keys, and those typing will not be concentrating on what they are being told. Another rule will be needed so that pupils are clear about what they do when they are stuck. To avoid calling out and waving at the teacher, some schools advocate placing a small plastic brick or figure or flag on top of the monitor, so that the teacher can see at

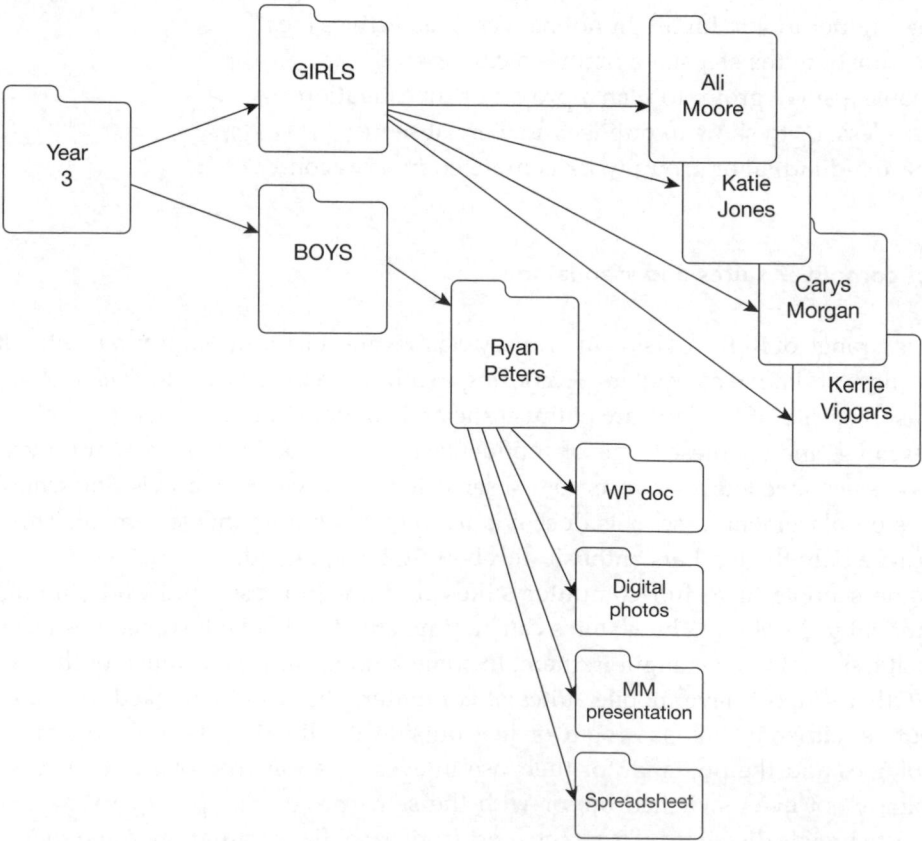

Figure 2.2 Named folder structure

Rules for successful saving

1 As soon as you have opened the program, type your name and save the work to your own folder.
2 Always use your name/initials as part of the file name, followed by the title of the work.
3 Save again at the end of every line or every minute by pressing Ctrl S or Apple S.

---

a glance who needs help next. Pupils should be told what alternative, paper-based task should be attempted, so that there is no excuse for inaction, and this seems to reduce the number of problems, as they are keen to solve difficulties themselves rather than resort to paper and pencil.

Successful saving is a key skill to be taught as early as possible, as the frustrations of losing work can make any writer, designer or problem-solver reluctant to keep trying if their work is regularly lost. The writer has successfully used the rules shown in the box.

Putting the child's name at the top of the work and using their name or initials in the file name help to avoid the mistake of filing into the wrong location and aid recovery when this has happened. Regular saving should just be to update the file and not to keep multitudinous versions. If working with a partner, pupils should create one initial file and then make one Save As file to the second student's folder at the end of the session. If logging out will not permit this, they could e-mail the work to each other, or store a second version on the school intranet to be downloaded to the second folder, or store the file on a data stick and upload it to the second child's file.

It may be advisable for pairs of children to work regularly with each other for a week, term or in a particular subject. ICT use is a great opportunity to develop communication and negotiation skills and is a situation where two heads may well be better than one. On a practical note, this may be essential if there are not enough computers for each child to have their own. If there are enough, paired work by adjacent pupils can still be encouraged.

A routine for leaving the suite should also be taught, and enough time should be allowed to ensure that work is printed only if required; that the pupils have logged off both the school intranet and the Internet; that all folders are closed; that their property is collected; and that chairs and work space are left tidy for the next class.

The laptop suite

Much of the advice above and below will be the same for a suite of laptops. A problem here may be trailing wires to link them to a power supply or, alternatively, making sure they arrive with enough power to keep them working without a flex. With a laptop suite, when recording science investigations, one laptop can be allocated to each investigation group to record their results. This could be done on a table prepared by the teacher. If working on history or geography, each research team can be allocated a couple of laptops to use alongside the reference books and the CD-ROM they have been allocated. For ideas on using laptops outside the classroom see p. 37.

The standalone computer

Using these is somewhat simpler than a suite, as usually there might be only one set of class folders to negotiate, and the standalone can be switched on at the start of the day ready for use, with the most appropriate program ready on-screen. As a general rule, whatever form of recording is being done with pen or pencil by the majority of the class, at least a couple of pupils can be using a computer for a similar activity. For instance, while the majority of pupils are comparing conditions between two localities or periods of time, a pair of pupils could be organising their comparison in a table on the computer, with the advantage that their work can be checked and edited as they go, with support from their teacher or an assistant. (A comment from whoever is helping them, added in italics at the end of the work, can be very motivating.) These children are getting immediate feedback, and the work will not need marking later. While some pupils plan a test, an article or a poster by hand, those using a computer, perhaps with a template, will have the advantages of a tidy layout, spellchecking and other editing features to hand. This can, with their permission, be shown on the whiteboard in a plenary session, and teaching points can be made to the rest of the class. The work that pupils of differing abilities tackle can be differentiated through use of a template, to make it more or less demanding than that attempted by their peers. Another use of the standalone could involve using templates to reinforce or assess learning for particular children, on a similar theme to the work done by the main class. Use of these might take just five minutes or so from a main activity, and a TA could oversee the organisation of pupils coming to the computer and record their progress to share later with the class teacher.

Developing e-portfolios

This section will consider the benefits of electronic portfolios (e-portfolios) and portfolio technologies.

An e-portfolio is simply a digital collection of work by a pupil that demonstrates his/her achievement over a particular period. The work can be audio, video, graphical and textual. A multimedia computer, a scanner, a camera and a software package are all that are needed to create an e-portfolio.

An e-portfolio can take several forms. At the simplest level, it may just be an electronic file containing all the digital work the pupil has produced in the year. To be of any use, this should be organised into folders indicating either subject matter or the term in which it was done. Individual pieces of work can be marked in italics to show attainment against the targets set and to give suggestions for further development. The work and targets should be discussed with the pupil as soon as possible after completion. Where pupils have collaborated on a piece of work, a copy needs to be stored in each child's portfolio.

A more useful e-portfolio is a summative selection of the pupil's work that shows the most interesting and representative evidence of achievement. This should be selected with the child, so that there is an opportunity to consider the progress made during the year, celebrate success and discuss targets for the future. The process of selection is a key part of the portfolio, and the experience of creating it should be motivating for the child. As Barrett (2006) pointed out, this is a way of realising the promise of technology to both improve and showcase student achievement.

A third form of e-portfolio comprises a selection of the work a pupil has done in one particular context, with a commentary on the learning made by the pupil. This could be created using dedicated software such as PebblePAD or a program that incorporates hyperlinks, so that these can be made to a number of pieces of work, stored in the same electronic area, but in different formats, such as spreadsheets and digital film.

Whichever system is used, to make the most of the selection of content, critical assessment and reflection on the part of the pupil are key factors in its value, so that the selection process is a learning opportunity in itself, and the resulting portfolio is more than a digital scrapbook that replicates its paper-based predecessor.

The benefits of e-portfolios

- E-portfolios can have both formative and summative use. They can show parents and the pupil's next teacher about previous experience and attainment, both in ICT and other subjects. Certificates awarded for sport, music or effort can be scanned and kept with other records of achievement in electronic form. If the portfolio is kept by the school, it can be linked, with appropriate security, to the school record-keeping system.
- Selecting material for a portfolio helps pupils to reflect on their learning and set new targets for development.
- Collating evidence of achievement celebrates success. It can be motivating to share these accomplishments with peers and relatives.
- Regular portfolio creation shows progress year on year.
- It provides evidence for teacher assessment and levelling.
- An e-portfolio holds a lot of information, but takes up no physical space (unlike paper-based portfolios), and it is more portable. Pictures, artwork and writing samples can all be scanned in and saved. Reading samples could be audio-recorded if required.
- Collaborative work can be scanned and copied, and photos can be added of practical sessions and can show evidence of fieldwork experience.
- The creation of the portfolio can develop computer and technology skills, such as using a camera/video/scanner.
- A commentary on the work can include explanations about the context of the work.

Portfolio technologies

Desktop multimedia software, such as Appleworks or PowerPoint, allows the user to create hyperlinked presentations of digital work to display in slideshow or web-style formats (see p. 202 for instructions about creating a hyperlinked presentation). Plan the layout on paper before writing the pages, so as to ensure a coherent structure.

Blogs and wikis can be used for pupils to record their achievements in a regular way, with a daily or weekly comment on their learning. Personal webspaces such as MySpace and Facebook, used in combination with image-hosting sites such as Flickr, are already motivating pupils to create personal collections in the public domain in their own time. For some pupils, this will be a development from creating a school portfolio, and these popular sites can really engage pupils and encourage the compilation of creative and personal portfolios. Although less appropriate for recording school achievements, they could be encouraged, with appropriate e-safety considerations, for pupils to develop very personal and individual records of achievement.

Other options include hosting on a school intranet or e-portfolio service, such as PebblePAD. Commercial systems such as PebblePAD and e-folios allow pupils to collate resources and guide them into reflective practice and action planning through a series of prompts. These may be suitable for more able pupils. Whatever option is chosen by the school, it can be very motivating if the completed e-portfolio of work is copied to a CD or data stick, which can be taken home at the end of the year.

Getting the most from the Internet

This section is about helping pupils acquire relevant information from CD-ROMs and the Internet and looks at ways the many facets of the Internet can be harnessed for educational use:

- finding information from CD-ROMs;
- background Internet information;
- finding information from the Internet;
- the benefits of the Internet;
- how to search the Internet;
- problems on the Internet;
- discussion boards;
- social networking sites;
- wikis;
- blogs;
- Twitter;
- texting (SMS);
- school websites, e-zines, e-mail;
- virtual learning environments (VLEs).

Finding information from CD-ROMs

For children in KS1, the best way to learn research skills and acquire information at the same time is through the use of CD-ROMs. These operate like small, self-contained websites, but the material is safe and limited to the required topic. Using a talking book can be a useful start to learning about CD-ROM icons, before progressing to factual CDs and introducing pupils to a glossary, index and the use of keywords in a search. Young children will need to be taught about using the main, hyperlinked buttons on the left of the screen or at the top and how to search for hyperlinks. These may be obvious, through the use of icons or underlined text, or may require searching for until the pointer tool turns to a hand and reveals them.

Background Internet information

Over the last twenty years, the development of the Internet has given us many new ways to communicate. Following the Stevenson report in 1997 (Independent ICT in School Commission 1997), which noted the digital divide across the country, the document 'Connecting the learning society' proposed connecting every school in the country to the Internet, the largest and most rapidly expanding source of information and method of communication in the world. The Internet is much more than a database of information; it embraces many new ways of communicating and sharing ideas, and new ways to do this are being invented each year. The Internet, which was once just a device to allow the military in the United States to communicate, is now so accessible that even infants can log on to their favourite sites, send e-mails and Skype their friends. Material written in genres that have never been paper-based are available to anyone with an Internet connection. It is not even necessary to own a computer, as schools, libraries and many clubs offer the opportunity to anyone who wants it to connect swiftly to the rest of the world. Even our phones connect us to the Internet. Instead of just literacy, we have information literacy, which requires new skills and competencies. We bank, download, share and shop online on the WWW, and pupils need to learn the skills that will enable them to make the most of these opportunities.

The Internet is a global system of interconnected computer networks that use a standard way to link users around the world. It is a network of networks, connecting billions of computers and users through millions of databases and information sources. It links private, public, academic, business and government networks, from small, local ones to huge, international concerns. The Internet supports many information services and resources, including the WWW and e-mail. The pages of the WWW are the most visible part of the Internet and are connected to each other by hyperlinks. They can be uploaded and read by anyone with an Internet connection and a web browser.

Very often, lesson plans include the requirement for children to carry out their own research into topics they find interesting. This can be a good way to personalise learning and engage the learner, but, if the skills for doing this effectively are not taught, it can be a frustrating experience for all concerned.

Finding information from the Internet

The Internet can be a fabulous resource for accessing information and communicating with people worldwide. It also has its dangers, as some people use it for purposes that can be harmful to children (see p. 203 for information about Internet safety). Hyperlinks on the Internet may be blue, or underlined text, or icons, buttons or images. The cursor changes to a hand when it moves over a hyperlink. Each page, although linked to many others, has its own uniform resource locator (URL), which makes it easy to identify. Pages that are of particular interest can be bookmarked in a 'Favourites' or 'Bookmarked' collection on the computer, so that they are easy to find again.

The benefits of the Internet

The benefits of the Internet can be summarised as follows:

- It allows access to a huge number of websites that will enable pupils to collect information for topics of interest, from football to ballet, from Ancient Greece to modern-day Sheffield. There are texts, graphics, charts, photos, films, games and challenges to be enjoyed. It allows pupils to gather information from a huge variety of sources.
- The information can be very up to date compared with a book. The latter usually takes at least a year to write and publish, whereas Internet sites can be created in less than a day.
- The Internet allows access to a worldwide range of museums and art galleries that it would be impossible to visit in person.
- There is up-to-date information about timetables, prices, weather and financial information.
- Through e-mail, it is possible to communicate quickly with people in different areas and even different countries.
- The technological features of the Internet seem to appeal to boys as well as girls, and so some are encouraged to read when they might be reluctant to use books.
- The limited amount of movement needed to access the Internet makes much of the world available to those with mobility problems.

The information that children gain from the Internet can be used to develop their ideas and can be presented to others in a variety of forms, both individually and collectively. It should also be examined critically, and consideration should be given to the intended audience before it is shared.

How to search the Internet

There is so much information on the Internet that, unless pupils are being taught about how to search for it, they should not waste their time browsing ad hoc, but rather should be directed to specific sites of known use. We would not send them into a library to wander round all sections – children, adults and reference – without some direction, and so it makes sense to guide them in an area that is much larger.

Pupils need to be taught how to use search engines to find information. These are database programs that help the user to find relevant pages of information by compiling huge catalogues of information through following links from one site to another, using keywords to identify relevant pages. Another type of search engine is a directory, which searches by using keywords that the site creator uses to describe the site. Google is the most popular search engine, perhaps owing to its simple layout and speed of response. Ask Jeeves and Yahooligans are search engines particularly suitable for children. Ask Jeeves and some other search engines allow for advanced searches, where you can limit the number of results through choosing particular categories as well as keywords. Too many results can be overwhelming, and not very useful. Searches using the words AND, OR and NOT can help to limit results.

- *AND* narrows the search, so that more than one keyword has to be found.
- *OR* widens the search, so that several similar terms will bring up results.
- *NOT* narrows the search by excluding some keywords.
- *+ and -* signs can be used with similar results.
- *"quotation marks"*: put these around an exact phrase or sentence to find it; e.g. "Jane Brown" will find only the people who are called that and not all the Janes and all the Browns, which would give a much larger but less useful result. If you put speech marks round a sentence, even small words such as 'is' and 'the', which are normally ignored by search engines, will be included, e.g. "Is there anyone there said the traveller?".
- *Keywords*: use these with +, - and OR and speech marks to create advanced and useful searches that bring up manageable and relevant results.
- Use the *wild card* symbol * with a keyword if you are unsure how to spell it, and the search engine will look for words with similar spellings; e.g., if you are unsure how to spell a word, such as 'ancient', then you can type the letters you think it has followed by *, i.e. 'anctien*'.
- ~ Search engines such as Google allow the use of a *tilde* (the ~ line above the hash key). This will find synonyms of the keywords you request, e.g. ~numeracy brings up sites with the word 'maths' in as well.

For more advice on ways to create effective searches, type *How to search the Internet* (with and without speech marks) into Google and read the results! The book *Literacy and ICT in the primary school,* by Rudd and Tyldesley (2006), has more detail on effective Internet use than is possible to include here. Internet scavenger or treasure hunts can be written by teachers to help pupils both learn to use searching skills as well as to find useful information for a particular topic.

Before pupils start looking for information they should:

1   list the questions to which they wish to find the answers or areas of interest;
2   list keywords for each question/area of interest.

This will save wading through many pages of information without a focus. They should be taught what to do when they find the information they want. Should they:

(a)   copy it down fully/in note form into a workbook for writing up later by hand?
(b)   electronically copy and paste large chunks of text to edit into their own words at a later date?
(c)   electronically copy and paste keywords and phrases, which they will assemble into their own writing later?

What you decide might depend on the time available and whether they will be able to edit what they find on a computer at a later date. It is a useful skill to learn to copy and paste to another document, but they should always end up with their own version of what they have read, or else they are really stealing someone else's work and presenting it as their own.

Bookmarking useful sites is a skill to teach to save pupils repeatedly hunting for a particularly good site. The latest ways to do this can be learned from an Internet search, as new ways to organise favourites and keep lists of favourite sites, which can be called up on any computer, rather than just the user's, are frequently being updated.

Problems on the Internet

- Inappropriate material: much of the information on websites is not written for children, and it can be discouraging to try to wade through pages of text that are not aimed at the reading age of the child.
- Undesirable material, which may be linked to useful and legitimate sites. (Check sites you recommend regularly to make sure that one is not linked like this. Even the Teletubbies once had a problem here. Beware of words that may have more than one meaning. Even on a protected school site, words such as mould (I wanted information on micro-organisms), webcam (I was after weather rather than live entertainment) and pussy (the pupils were doing a project on pets), brought up unwanted options.)
- Computer viruses: ensure your virus protection and firewall are up to date and do not open e-mails from sources you do not recognise.
- Malware: a type of virus where a hacker takes control of someone else's computer without their knowledge and sends out spam (unwanted junk mail) from it.
- Not all information is accurate or up to date. Anyone can put a web page up, without having the facts or opinions expressed on it checked. Pupils will need guidance to read with caution and to watch out for personal opinions posted as facts. People will also put up websites and not update them. Other websites get taken down, so that links to them do not work. This can be very frustrating for the young researcher. Wherever possible, teachers should check the quality of websites they recommend children should use. Teaching the pupils to evaluate the quality of a selection of websites is a

---

Checklist for evaluating websites

Appearance: How attractive is the site? Consider layout, the use of graphics, colour and charts: what do they add to the site? Is the text of an appropriate size and reading age?

Ease of navigation: Are the hyperlinks easy to follow? Are the links to other sites live?

Interactivity: Are there quizzes, games or a discussion board on the site?

Organisation: Is there a useful set of hyperlinked buttons on the left-hand side/at the top of the page? Is the text well written and easy to follow? Are headings and subheadings/bullet points used well?

Usefulness: Does the site have the information required? Is it accurate and up to date?

Pupils could make their own lists of useful features, grade a selection of websites against them and then justify this grading to their peers. Pupils who are dyslexic or partially sighted may have different criteria from their peers, and teachers should take this into account when recommending websites to their classes. For example, people who are dyslexic sometimes find it hard to read text that is underlined, and so icons rather than underlined hyperlinks may be easier to use.

useful exercise in discrimination. They could use the vowel mnemonic shown in the box to help them assess the relative merits of different websites on a particular project.

- *Time-wasting.* The WWW is so huge that finding the most useful information can take a long time. It is also very seductive, as the perfect picture or piece of information always seems just a click away. If the above suggestions are followed for searching sites and evaluating them, and a time limit is put on all searching activities, then less time will be spent in 'cyber-chasing' and getting lost in the Internet.

- *Plagiarism.* Good practice starts young, and children should understand, before they leave KS2, that copying what other people write and passing it off as their own work is stealing, in the same way as taking their possessions is. It is also of little use to a child to copy, and possibly not even read and understand properly, chunks of text from the Internet. All facts found should be redrafted in their own words, and, if exact phrases or sentences are used, they should be put in speech marks with an indication of who wrote the original text. Ask pupils to write underneath each picture/piece of text which website they have taken it from.

- *Access.* Not all pupils have access to the Internet at home. Other options are to encourage pupils to use computers at the local library or out-of-school club, or to discriminate in their favour in school time, perhaps allowing extra access on class computers or laptops.

Discussion boards

Discussion boards, newsgroups or message boards are Internet forums, which are online discussion sites. Electronic discussion is also known as conferencing. It can be done through electronic bulletin boards, where questions and answers are posted about a particular subject or by a special-interest group. Some groups require people to be registered to be able to see the messages, but it is possible to read the discussions without joining in, and this is known as lurking. There are usually rules for behaviour set for the site, and some of the problems associated with this method of communication are listed on the Wikipedia site (http://en.wikipedia.org/wiki/Internet_forum). Another way of discussing ideas uses e-mail distributions lists, so that all postings are e-mailed to every user in the group. This is called a 'listserv'. The postings are often checked by someone before they are sent on to others, to avoid inappropriate material being circulated. Discussion boards can engage children in communicating about subjects that interest them. Care should be taken that they join only those that are suitable for their age and interests. They may even be able to engage with experts in a field who can fire their enthusiasm for a particular activity. There are some useful safety rules on the Children's Message Board to which users have to agree before they can join (www.crossingbridges.co.uk/forumentry.htm). The BBC has a discussion board site with lots of engaging links (www.bbc.co.uk/cbbc/mb/). Here, children can join in with adventurous challenges, share jokes and enjoy web chats with people of their own age. It is carefully managed.

Discussion boards and e-mail are asynchronous, in that users do not need to be online at the same time to communicate. With Skype or video-conferencing, users do need to be online at the same time (synchronous). Electronic conferences, which use text or audio facilities, can also be synchronous.

Social networking sites

Internet sites, such as Facebook, Myspace, Flickr, Bebo and Think.com, where people can communicate without having to know all the people to whom they write, are becoming increasingly popular. Boys are as keen to engage with this form of writing as girls, and they can be motivating places to practise communication skills, make friends and exchange ideas and information. They are also, of course, liable to misuse by unscrupulous individuals, and pupils need to be aware that the chatty ten-year-old girl they think they are writing to may be a middle-aged man with dishonourable intentions. These sites are, in effect, instant self-publication sites, and pupils need to be taught about what they should and should not reveal about themselves. There are many excellent features on some of these sites that help to give privacy and protection, but not all the onward links from each person's page can be checked for safety. Some websites allow photos to be uploaded and shared, or allow the giving of virtual presents. Smartphones can be used to contact the sites, so that access to e-friends is possible from almost anywhere.

Effective communication is one of the basic skills of a civilised society, and, if these sites enable pupils to develop such skills, they can be of great use. They can encourage people to develop a wider range of interests, share ideas and resources such as digital photos, reflect on the way they present themselves to the world and understand other people's points of view. However, they do have their dangers and can take up a lot of social time.

Wikis

A further form of self-publication and co-authoring, a wiki is a collaborative writing tool on the Internet to which anyone has access and can contribute. This means that the quality and veracity of what is published on a wiki cannot easily be verified. Wikipedia is the ultimate co-authored electronic encyclopaedia, but, because it is a wiki and anyone can post information there, some sections have very little authority. The site managers do try to indicate which entries are validated externally and which are not, but pupils should be encouraged to look at all entries with a critical eye. To show how easy it is for anyone to add items to Wikipedia, you could get your class to write an article about their locality or school and add it to the site, using the simple instructions provided online. They might even be able to correct another entry using local knowledge of facilities or biodiversity. Creating a wiki can be a useful exercise in co-authoring: knowing that anyone can correct or alter your work is a great stimulus to getting it as correct as possible.

Blogs

Another form of self-publication is a blog. This is a personal website that is often written rather like a diary, with comments and reflections on what happens to the writer on a regular basis. It may be supported with photos and other digital graphics. A blog is sometimes dedicated to a particular topic, sport or interest, and many of them comment on the news. They are easy to start using a free tool from a site such as www.blogger.com/.

Twitter

Twitter is a social networking and microblogging (mini blog) website that enables its users to send and read other user messages, called tweets, which are text-based posts of up to 140 characters. Tweets are visible to all by default, though senders can restrict message delivery to their friends list. One of the attractions for children is the character limit, which is a challenge to make the most of, but does not require extensive composition, unlike many literacy tasks in school: it is enjoyable for the reluctant writer to compose in tweets, even though they may not all be published.

> NB: The same security precautions of not revealing true identities or locations the writers frequently use should be applied to all forms of self-publication by pupils.

Texting (SMS)

Texting is the exchange of brief written messages, usually over the Internet or by mobile phones using a cellular network. Originally, the term referred to messages sent using the Short Message Service (SMS), but it now includes messages with image, video and sound content, known as MMS messages. This is the way most young and many adult people communicate today. More people text than post, and boys text as well as girls. A downside is that, with the abbreviations used and the speed at which people text, spelling and grammar may be poor or just unconventional. However, as a medium for instant communication, it is hard to beat and could perhaps be used more in schools. A Becta report by Wood *et al.* in 2006 reported that the fastest growing market of mobile-phone users is pre-teen children, and that the Ofcom Media Literacy Audit (2006) of over 1,500 UK children reported that 49 per cent of eight-to-eleven-year-olds had their own mobile phone. The study found that texting allows children to experiment with language in an informal and playful manner and said that,

> Texting presents children with self and peer-initiated opportunities to engage with print, practise conventional spellings and create alternative spellings and explore their own phonological understanding in a non-judgemental context. Parents and teachers can capitalise on the children's enjoyment of such language play through designing and contributing to such activity.
>
> (p. 11)

Overall, the report suggested that text messaging may support literacy, and that spelling is enhanced by text messaging, because of increased exposure to print.

School websites and e-zines

Most schools have their own websites, on which they display a mixture of school administrative details such as term dates and OFSTED reports, as well as pupils' work. Such sites can be used to good effect to motivate pupils to write for a known audience, rather than just to publish work created for other purposes. Individual classes can create their own websites about a particular project or create an e-zine (an electronic magazine) for themselves, their friends, as well as people they do not know. This is quite easily done using a series of templates from a hosting site such as www.schools.ik.org/. This site gives advice on how to get listed in Google and runs awards for particularly good sites. An e-zine can contain stories, puzzles, news and artwork by pupils and is an excellent way to share school activities with parents and e-pals.

E-mail

E-mail (electronic mail) allows people to send messages to each other electronically and very cheaply, and messages can be sent and arrive almost instantly. Conventions for polite communication called netiquette have evolved to avoid people giving offence to each other. There is a tendency for people to be less formal in an e-mail, and, problematically, while some of the abbreviations used in texting are creeping into e-mails, there can be less effort spent on punctuating and spelling correctly as well. In a school context, it is important not to let standards slip, especially when pupils are communicating with people in different countries or writing to official organisations for information or help.

Pictures, spreadsheets, graphics and other text files can be sent as attachments or sometimes incorporated into the main body of the text. Using e-mail is an excellent way for pupils to communicate with family, friends and organisations, both near home and across the globe. Its speed and ease of use are very motivating for both keen and reluctant writers. If pupils are communicating with children in another school, e-mail is a quick and efficient way to do this.

A one-to-one link is easily broken through pupil absence or lack of ideas about what to say after the initial contact. A way to avoid this is to organise the pupils in both schools into groups of eight pupils and give them themes for communication, such as:

- write about school news;
- write about local news;
- write about national news;
- ask a few questions about the other country and what they are doing in school.

To help facilitate e-mail communication, each pair of pupils in a school writes about their theme, to a similar group in the other school. The group's writing is sent as one e-mail to their partner group in the other school. When they get a reply, each pair writes on another theme, so that they get the chance to write about different subjects each time. It also means they have to keep up with what is going on in the local and national news. The questions they ask may be about data that they need for a project, or just about the lifestyle, local features and facilities in a contrasting place. The use of e-mail gives a real audience and reason to write and may get a faster response than writing for a teacher. Collaborative stories can also engage, as each class or group of pupils sends one section of a story for the other school to continue and return. E-palling can work well if schools are linked through projects such as the Comenius project (www.ideacomeniusproject.com/about.asp).

Virtual learning environments (VLEs)

These online learning spaces are dynamic web spaces where material can be uploaded without using html code, the computer language in which most websites are written. With a school's own VLE, or one provided by a local authority, teachers can upload materials for pupils to help them with homework tasks, as well as post examples of work for parents to see and comment on. A VLE may provide discussion boards, blogs and wikis to which pupils, and sometimes their parents, can contribute and thus continue the learning experience beyond the school day. Clear rules for their appropriate use need to be discussed with pupils, and all contributions are vetted, usually by the class teacher, before publication. Using a VLE, which is a protected area, pupils can be safe from an unwanted audience, and the result can be a dynamic and personal web space that encourages learning and the sharing of ideas by both groups and individuals. A VLE is an environment in which pupils can learn to use web tools and techniques safely to support their learning in all curriculum areas.

Personalising learning

Offering personalised lessons to meet the individual needs of all learners is a challenge Fox Hill School has tried to meet through the use of ICT and new technologies. Setting

---

Case study: Using ICT to involve parents in learning

Dave is a teacher in Mundella primary school. He uses ICT across the curriculum to involve parents as much as possible in their children's education. One way he has done this is through the use of the schools VLE. When logged on to this protected site provided by the local authority, anyone with access rights can see work posted for shared viewing. Parents can admire their children's work and even add comments. The VLE can be used to communicate homework tasks, so that both parents, and children who have been absent, can see what is required. The city in which the school is located is part of the bid for the 2018 World Cup, and the children produced and shared their own video clips on the VLE supporting the bid, much to the delight of their peers and parents. Dave has encouraged his class to take the school's camcorders home to record highlights from their home life for editing and promoting writing skills in school. One interesting result from this involved a girl who was silent in school, who showed that she could in fact talk if she wanted to do so.

Case study: Using ICT games to engage children in their learning

Many children enjoy Xboxes, PS3s, Nintendos and other technologies that immerse them in a virtual, interactive world. Staff at Fox Hill School, Sheffield, use video games as a way into topics being studied. Recently, one class began a cross-curricular topic with the Nintendo Wii game *Rock Band* that developed into a project involving music creation, costume design, geography, maths and other cross-curricular skills. One Y4 class used the Sony *EyePet* game as a stimulus for instructional writing; another class investigated ocean habitats starting from the game *Endless Ocean*. The use of video games as an introduction to topics can be an exciting hook for children. It helps to engage reluctant learners or those who find writing difficult but who can excel at video games, providing them with a much needed confidence boost as they begin a new area of learning. The school has found that games can provide a wealth of exciting learning opportunities, ranging from maths problem-solving using car racing games to exploring strange new worlds as part of descriptive writing in literacy. Creative use of ICT in the primary classroom can help teachers to provide children with stimulating lessons that will engage even the most dedicated computer-game user!

---

differentiated challenges through online learning systems such as Education City, self-assessment method (SAM) Learning and the school's VLE means that all pupils in a class can work on the same learning objective, but with activities pitched to individual needs. This approach allows pupils to take ownership of their learning as they work through differentiated challenges at their own pace.

The staff have developed an extensive intranet of software resources in which pupils can find activities to support their learning at an appropriate level. Mental-maths sessions are personalised through the use of hand-held mental-maths games and interactive response systems. Software is used to support literacy work, with spelling banks, word grids, talking word processors and research tools to help children scaffold their writing. Mini laptops are available in lessons to act as interactive dictionaries and research tools. Children use Ipod Nanos to rehearse and practise sentences before writing them down. Pupil camcorders and recording devices help children record their performances in drama, so that they can critique their own work. These ICT tools also provide the means for more able pupils to explore and extend their own learning.

3 Using ICT outside the classroom

In this chapter, we will explore a range of ICT facilities suitable for school trips and residential visits:

- laptops
- palmtops
- data loggers
- digital cameras.

Laptops

On a residential visit, laptops could be used for the following WP activities.

- individuals/groups using a diary pro forma or blogs, possibly with built-in prompts and questions to help pupils relive the events and learning of each day;
- completing tables with data collected during the day;
- preparation of e-mails, sent home or to school, by groups or individuals;
- preparation of questionnaires for data collection, sometimes best done after the area has been seen for the first time;
- writing up notes, along with downloaded photos from each day, which is best done while the events are still fresh in the memory;
- adding speech bubbles to photos for each day's events.

Palmtops

These hand-held computers can be used for immediate capture of ideas, data or photos on visits and residential trips. If they are used for taking notes to combine with photos and webcam images, this should not be overdone, so that it distances the children from the experience. Some come with GPS, or preloaded keys to aid the identification of birds, plants or small animals.

Palmtops could be used in the field for:

- note-taking, using word banks for those who need them;
- completing preloaded history/geography trails to aid in-depth learning;
- combining photos and maps with annotations;
- recording interviews and turning the data collected into reports;

- connecting to the Internet to gain immediate background information if required;
- identifying plants and animals, using keys that are built in or available on the Internet;
- taking photos (some have a built-in facility for this);
- identifying locations, orienteering and developing mapping skills.

Data loggers

Some data loggers can be battery operated and, on field trips, give pupils the chance to monitor light and temperature levels in sunny and shady places, compare river, pond and soil temperatures, and record noises in the urban and rural environments outside the school buildings. A cable or docking station is normally provided to facilitate a connection to a computer. Some data loggers can use Bluetooth or infrared communication to transfer data.

Digital cameras

These can be used on field trips as visual note-takers, to record the appearance of a building, plant or activity that can then be drawn, identified or written about at a later date. Teachers can use them in advance to make maths, science and art trails to be followed by pupils. Children can do the same for their peers. Sharing a camera between a group of children can be frustrating, as not all have equal access to it, but cooperation skills could be developed while ensuring each child gets a fair turn.

Other ways of using them out of school are as follows:

1   The teacher can take a series of pictures on a trail, and the pupils have to identify where each photo was taken from and take a similar or alternative one of their own.
2   Photographs can be taken to show a range of shadows, illustrating how different an object, e.g. a plant, or a person can look, depending on the angle of the sun and the position of the object photographed. (The results could be used as a visual quiz.)
3   Photographs can be used to record activities to be evaluated after the event.
4   Pictures can be taken to record the beach debris in a beach transect or plants in a quadrant.
5   Colours and textures can be recorded for a digital collage.

Issues to consider are the availability of fully charged batteries and care of the camera: keeping it on a piece of cord around the neck will minimise the potential for dropping or leaving it behind.

4 Assessing children's use of ICT

In this chapter, we will explore:

- why we should assess progress with ICT;
- problems with assessment;
- how to assess pupils' achievement in ICT;
- points to consider when assessing.

> Assessment for Learning is the process of seeking and interpreting evidence for use by learners and their teachers to decide where the learners are in their learning, where they need to go and how best to get there.
>
> (Assessment Reform Group 2002)

There are currently four aspects of attainment in the National Curriculum (1999) for ICT at Key Stages 1 and 2:

1   finding things out;
2   developing ideas and making things happen;
3   exchanging and sharing information;
4   reviewing, modifying and evaluating work as it progresses.

The level descriptions for each level of attainment in ICT can be found at: http://curriculum.qcda.gov.uk/key-stages-1-and-2/subjects/ict/attainmenttarget/index.aspx. These attainment targets outline the desirable progression in each of the four aspects of ICT in terms of the knowledge, skills and understanding that it is expected pupils will have by the end of each key stage.

The level descriptions provide the basis for making judgements about pupils' performance at the end of a key stage, taking into account the way they work, as well as the results of that work in a range of contexts and over a period of time. They are not intended to indicate levels of single pieces of work, but to inform planning, teaching and assessment throughout both key stages.

Why assess?

If pupils are to make progress in their use and understanding of ICT, then their progress needs careful monitoring, and their successes must be recorded, so that plans for the next steps, both in teaching and application of that teaching, can be made. Once children have learned to tap letters on a keyboard correctly and add graphics, it is important to extend their skills to produce more sophisticated work. Formative assessment (or assessment for learning – AfL), which checks what pupils need help with, is of most use to children and their teachers. Summative assessment, which summarises what they can do, is of more value to their next teacher and of interest to parents and local or national bodies who collate results.

Teachers, often encouraged by parents, can be too keen to label a child as being at one particular level. It is fine to let parents and pupils celebrate pupils' achievements, and indicate the overall level at which they are working, perhaps at the end of a key stage, which is the only legal requirement. However, we should be cautious about regularly labelling pupils as a working at a single level. It should be remembered that the term ICT covers a wide range of techniques, and that the skills required are perhaps more diverse than those in any other subject. A pupil may be very skilled in one area, while relatively inexperienced in another. They may be level 3 in one aspect of ICT, but level 4 or even 2 in another. It is not the level but the achievement and understanding that are important.

Regular assessment of any work in school, including ICT, is necessary for effective planning for the next stage of learning. This assessment should not only look at what pupils produce, whether a spreadsheet, a poster or a brochure, but also consider the thinking and practical skills that were required to create it. Assessment of ICT work should look at *how* the children have worked: if they have cooperated with others or striven on their own. It should look at how they explain their ideas and the choices they made for the outcome; it should look at their oral explanations of their comprehension of the benefits and problems of using digital techniques; and it should involve the pupils in their own self-assessment. The process of self-evaluation should be a regular part of ICT use, in a way that lets pupils recognise the progress they have made, celebrates their success and helps them identify the next steps in their learning. Above all, it should be sensitive to their abilities and experience and to the effort they have made, so that they feel empowered to tackle further challenges.

Problems when assessing ICT

There are several problems that are particular to the assessment of ICT work. The first thing to consider when levelling pupils' work is whether it is the ICT or the subject component that is being considered. A poorly presented piece of typed work may contain excellent explanations of scientific understanding. Likewise, a beautiful presentation of learning in history may contain little evidence of historical comprehension, but be an achievement in terms of the text, graphics and charts that have been combined. Separate assessments would need to be made for each subject.

First, with written work, a computer can correct spelling and grammar automatically and make the work look so tidy and professional that it conceals the actual ability and attainment of a pupil in literacy skills. This does not matter if it is ICT, rather than literacy skills, that is being assessed. Second, lack of teacher confidence and expertise can result in over-optimistic assessment of pupil achievement. As the assessment should recognise the process as well as the product, it needs to take place during a class session, where the way the children work can be observed, and time spent discussing the work with the pupil is an essential part of any assessment. As with work in other areas, when pupils are working collaboratively, as they often do in ICT owing to lack of equipment, it can be hard to assess the individual achievement. Finally, it can take more time to assess if the work is not saved to an easily identified location owing to poor file-management skills. If this is the case, then the attainment in other aspects of ICT may not be recognised.

How to assess ICT

Several different strategies for recording assessments are suggested below. *It is not recommended that teachers should try to use all of them.* There are several ways to check on the progress of a pupil's understanding and capability in using ICT: many of them are time consuming and out of date almost as soon as they are made. The key to any assessment is that it should be useful and able to inform the next stage of learning, as epitomised by AfL approaches. Some schools favour a tick list of achievements for each pupil, which is annotated once or twice a term. This, if combined with pupil consultation, can be useful, but is also time consuming when it is considered that such appraisal might also be required in ten or more other subjects. Regular observation, which is part of good practice, will note how pupils tackle a technique and how they apply it, so that, if a sheet with pupils' names and a line beside each is available on the teacher's desk, quick notes or Post-its can be added when appropriate, though not for every child in every session. If just a few notes are added each day, a picture will build up over a term about skills, attitudes and understanding for the whole class, and any blank lines will suggest who to focus on next.

Teacher observation is the most useful way to assess pupils' use of ICT, because the processes they go through can be noted and used for future planning of tasks and groups. Good use can be made here of other adults in the class, such as TAs or learning mentors, or even experienced volunteers, who may be able to make either general or focused reports on pupil progress. If a TA is asked to make five- or ten-minute observations of a group of pupils, while working with another group, she may be able to record on-/off-task behaviour, cooperation, progress with an assignment, attitude and perseverance for several children, without intervention. If asked to work with the group, even more detailed records can be kept, if required, while the pupils are supported in their brief.

Much assessment will just be mental and not need a written record. As soon as it is apparent that a pupil needs help it will be given, and, when he/she has accomplished a target, he/she should be directed to the next goal. If these stages are significant, they can be recorded briefly in note form, but, unless major intervention is required, there is little point in recording every step of either learning or misunderstanding that a pupil goes through to make progress. The child itself is the record of achievement, and, like all of us, they forget and later remember, so that a written record is not always a reliable testimony to what they can do.

Assessment by observation includes listening to children explain their use of ICT, the problems they encounter and the ways they decide to address them. It involves open questioning to check on their understanding and reasoning. Sometimes, specific tasks may be set to test a skill or to give pupils the opportunity to demonstrate their learning in different ways.

Assessment can be made easier by looking at a portfolio of achievement. If this is electronic, then different stages of progression can be saved without wasting paper. Paper-based portfolios tend to concentrate on final best copies, which do not always record the full picture. An electronic portfolio is likely to contain all the work that was not thought worth printing, but that nevertheless has relevance. To make assessment easier, it is vital that pupils are taught from an early age how and where to save their work, and, as file management is a vital ICT skill, their success at this should be noted.

Points to consider when assessing

The following should be noted:

- attitudes towards ICT: are they keen/reluctant in particular contexts?
- the views of the pupils about their work and achievements: what do they find helps/hinders their achievement?

- how well do they achieve against specific objectives?
- what is their file-management capability?
- what is their proficiency in using/combining different media?
- in which contexts do they work well: solo/in groups, and at which aspect?
- what is their application in other subject areas?
- how creative are they with the tools provided?
- how appropriate is their use of text/tables/graphs and graphics?
- what about home use?
- do they have particular interests/abilities?

The above list will not be considered for every pupil in every session, but could contribute to a useful summative assessment by the end of each school year. It would provide a constructive summary for the teacher in the following class, who will need to build on previous situations and achievements. Opportunities for some pupils to use their ICT skills in all curriculum areas should be made, so that it is routine for pupils to use laptops or standalone computers in almost every class session. This is not only motivating for many pupils, but provides a real context to apply skills learned in ICT sessions and opportunities to personalise their learning and be creative in presenting their ideas. Effective formative assessment *for* learning is part of the teaching and learning process. It shares the learning goals with pupils, so that they understand the success criteria and know what to aim for. When using the *must, should* and *could* form of target setting, it empowers pupils to reflect and set their own targets. Useful assessment gives timely feedback, is motivating, and involves pupils in self-assessing and the teacher in adjusting the subsequent planning in the light of the appraisal.

Some ICT programs enable changes to be tracked, or record how often online help is accessed, and browsers can track users through sites they have accessed. However, for the busy teacher, noting all these details would be an unrealistic burden. Tutorial software on specialist applications may offer charts that document progress in particular contexts, but more often record pupils' ability in a specific subject, such as maths, or their ability to use one particular program, rather than any skill in ICT.

Individual records do need to be kept for reporting to parents at the end of the year, and for levelling at the end of the key stage (see Table 4.1). The level descriptions are intended to provide a best-fit guide to attainment, though pupils may be working at different levels in different contexts. They can also be used by the teacher to assess whether the teaching is allowing pupils to achieve at an appropriate level. If little work has been done on control technology, for example, then pupils cannot be given a particular grade for it. Regular formative assessment of all pupils should make it quite easy to ascribe a summative NC level. Much research indicates that effective formative assessment is a key factor in raising pupils' standards of achievement.

Whole-class records can be useful to check on the general level of technical achievement and to note where remedial or extension work is necessary (see Table 4.2).

Table 4.1 *Suggested format for an individual pupil record for ICT*

Name		Year	Class
	Term 1	Term 2	Term 3
1 Finding things out using ICT			
2 Exchanging and sharing information			
3a Making things happen (control)			
3b Making things happen (modelling)			
4a Breadth of study (ability to describe/ discuss ICT experience)			
4b Breadth of study (contexts in which ICT has been used)			
Other relevant information, e.g. home use, file management, attitude and confidence			

Table 4.2 *Suggested format for whole-class ICT record (headings should be adapted to fit context)*

Class	Year	Term			
		Unit of ICT work (e.g. combining text & graphics)			
Name	Keyboard skills	Can save to own folder	Can talk about/explain use of ICT	Can combine text and graphics	Can combine own text and own graphics

A key could be used to complete Table 4.2 on a 1–3 scale to give an overview of class progress:
1 = needs help to do this;
2 = can do well with some help;
3 = can do this accurately without help.

Alternatively, NC levels 1–4 could be used. For combining text and graphics, these would be:
1 = uses ICT to work with text, images and sound and to help share ideas;
2 = uses ICT to help generate, amend and record work and share ideas in different forms, including text, tables, images and sound;
3 = uses ICT to generate, develop, organise and present work. Can share and exchange ideas with others;
4 = can add to, amend and combine different forms of information from a variety of sources. Uses ICT to present information in different forms and show awareness of intended audience and the need for quality in presentations. Can exchange information and ideas with others in a variety of ways, including using e-mail.

See Appendix 1 for the full NC level descriptions.

Teachers need to plan a progression of ICT skills teaching, as well as opportunities for pupils to apply these skills in other subject areas and situations. Pupils should be given challenges to find out information in different ways and to practise collecting data using a variety of methods, and they should be required to communicate with a range of audiences, both known and unknown, in both formal and informal ways, using text, graphics, charts and aural and multimedia methods. They should learn how to control digital devices that record, move and operate other devices. If they are not given open-ended opportunities and the chance to decide when each form of communication is most appropriate, then they will not be able to achieve at an appropriate level. Alongside this, the time to reflect on their progress, self-assess and decide which skills they want to develop themselves will give ownership and help to motivate all learners.

There is no legal requirement to explain a judgement or keep detailed collections of evidence for each pupil. A year-group portfolio of levelled work can be a useful and efficient way of collecting samples, which would be annotated with the context in which they were created. These can be used to help develop teacher judgements about pupil levels and, with moderation from other teachers or even other schools, sound conclusions can be developed about pupil attainment in ICT.

Links to portfolios of examples and advice on assessment can be found at: www. northerngrid.org/ngflwebsite/ep.htm.

5 Use of ICT in a teacher's professional role

In this chapter, we will explore ways you can use ICT to support:

- planning
- teaching
- assessment
- record-keeping
- organising resources.

Planning

If all planning, from annual through to termly and weekly/daily, is drafted and refined on a computer, then, in the long term, much planning time can be saved, as the plans can often be redrafted and reused with modification in new classes or circumstances, from year to year.

Worksheets for a subject can be written to suit the average ability of the class and, once saved, can be adapted, with more challenging work for the more able, or more prompts and vocabulary for learners who need extra support.

Templates, to help pupils planning or reviewing science investigations and DT challenges, can be stored in the relevant folder, along with good examples of completed projects for moderation and sharing with other professionals. Each template can be differentiated and saved for different pupil needs. Templates for book reviews, branching keys, recipes, letters and other writing formats, such as instructional writing or newspaper articles, can be created once and adapted to different contexts.

Lesson plans these days are often constructed as PowerPoint, SMART Notebook or Promethean presentations. Even the simplest lesson can benefit from a few organising screens that convey the date, the objective and the organisation of the lesson, such as the activities for each group and the timings that will be used. Stimulating graphics, web links and videos can be inserted as necessary, which saves time locating them partway through a lesson.

Teaching

The many ways digital technologies can be used to aid teaching are covered in other sections of this book. However, it must be mentioned that ICT should be used when it is the best solution and should not replace teacher explanation, pupil discussion or firsthand

---

Case study: Using ICT for planning and class organisation

Pam teaches a junior class in a school where all planning is done electronically, using templates created in Word. She uses her SMARTboard daily, preparing slides to show the children what she wants them to do and to ensure she has the relevant information and examples ready to hand. She says, 'I don't know how I managed without my IWB for so long! It is so versatile and brings instant meaning to a huge variety of subjects and lessons, as well as "hands on" involvement for the children.' Pam browses the Internet to glean information for her lessons, to research ideas and to collect resources, such as pictures, video clips and music, that are not available in school. She find this an easy way to access information, and, in the long run, it saves her time, as the information can be saved and used again, or adapted or changed as appropriate. In Pam's school, the results of all assessments are recorded using ICT – mainly in Excel – and the school completes local and national tables of data digitally, at the request of relevant bodies. All records are kept electronically and centrally, so that they can be accessed by all staff. This ensures continuity and consistency.

---

experience and experimenting. It is there to aid accuracy, recording and communication and to make distant resources accessible.

Assessment

There has already been a section on assessment of pupils' learning in ICT. However, you may wish to use ICT to assess their learning in other subjects. This can be done by the creation of interactive screens, saved as templates, that provide a challenge in an area such as maths or science. The pupils can complete the test – they usually see it as a game – on-screen, and the results are noted by either the teacher or a responsible adult detailed to keep a check on the activity, help if pupils get stuck and call the next child when the computer is free.

Record-keeping

Many schools have now invested in commercial systems or use centrally produced systems for assessment and record-keeping. They help to keep track of pupil progress in each subject

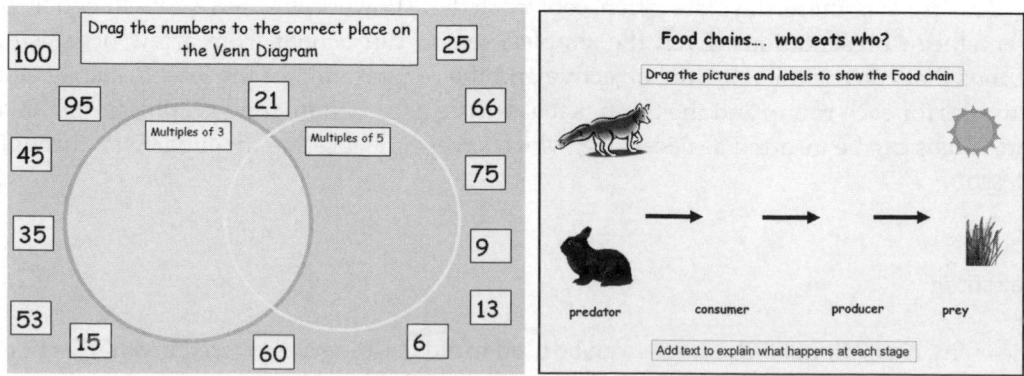

Figure 5.1 Examples of interactive screens to be used as assessment tools

and to plan for personalised learning through such assessment. Specially designed systems, such as SIMS or RAISEonline (www.raiseonline.org/About.aspx), can help to simplify record-keeping. These systems might be supplemented by some teachers who like to keep digital notes on individual pupil progress, which are updated either once or twice a term, or on an ad hoc basis. Such records could be updated from notes, observations recorded on Post-its or a Dictaphone record if this is found to be more helpful. Subsequently, these notes can be cut and pasted to further personalise an annual record of achievement for each pupil.

Stationery for class records, such as subject assessment, need only be created annually, with the pupils' names copied from an electronic register. Lesson objectives and pupil attainment can be added on a printout for those who prefer to keep paper-based records.

Photos of pupils' work, particularly in subjects such as drama, dance and PE, can allow for a speedier and more detailed record than a written description can provide. Digital photos of work in all subjects, especially art and design and design technology, save space in the class and can allow children to take work home much sooner than if it has to be kept for an end-of-year assessment. A secure system for finding each child's work needs to be in place, so that trawling through hundreds of pictures at report writing time can be avoided. If the photos are kept in folders accessible to the class, then pupils will be able to incorporate them into their own records and evaluations.

Contact with parents involves the annual record of achievement, which is at least typed, and often computer-generated from appropriate phrases as well. In some schools, pupils' work and even their homework may be made available to parents on the school's VLE or intranet. This is another way for the teacher to use ICT to develop parental involvement.

Case study: Using ICT across the curriculum

Jane is a teacher who uses a wide range of ICT with her Year 1 class. She uses IWBs routinely to involve and stimulate the children, but is very aware that this resource should not be overused, and that using a small number of screens is often more effective than using a great many.

When the children arrive at the start of the day, they register their attendance by moving a digital photo of themselves or just their name, from one side of the IWB to another. Big books are shared on the screen, either from CD-ROMs or websites or by using a visualiser, and children see how it is possible to find out information from different sources. Pupils use the IWB to practise letter formation, both over and under given examples.

A word processor and a paint program are used to make captions for class displays and to express pupils' ideas, and both are used in a focused manner, so that pupils who get less experience of this type of activity at home sometimes get priority. Children record their class activities with a digital camera and make personal books with the pictures to show parents what they do in school.

The class Pixies (a type of floor turtle) are programmed by pupils to follow routes and carry out missions, so that, in a range of ways, children can develop ideas and make things happen. The class walls are adorned with examples of cards, stories, poems and charts, many of which have been created with the help of a relevant program as pupils learn to exchange and share information. Regular teaching time is spent in reviewing this learning and talking about the ways these electronic tools have helped pupils, and when it is better to use other ways to write, draw and send messages. They talk about their use of digital technology at home, in the street and on holidays as well.

Where parents are then able to add a comment about their child's work, remotely or on a visit to the school, this can help to motivate both the child and the teacher.

Organising resources

Although digital organisation can seem the perfect answer to piles of unsorted paper, beware of overusing this facility, especially when searching the Internet for that perfect lesson. Keeping too many resources in a poorly organised filing system can waste much teacher time. Digital organisation of class work should only be used where it saves time, or increases accuracy or efficiency. The final word of warning must, of course, be to back up regularly to an external hard drive, CD-ROM, school intranet or, at the very least, to a data stick that is not kept with the computer, in case both are stolen or damaged simultaneously.

Part 2

A useful guide to software and hardware

This part looks at the most commonly available software and hardware in schools and how these tools can be used by teachers and pupils to aid teaching and learning. There is an introduction to each type of equipment and ideas for ways it can be used creatively in the primary classroom to meet National Curriculum targets and engage and motivate learners. Many teachers will be very familiar with the particular equipment that their school has purchased and already have considerable skills in these areas, but we hope that you will be able to find new ideas for your abilities here. Each chapter outlines a progression of skills and projects across a range of subjects, from Year 1 to Year 6. Of course, this progression should be adapted to the needs of your pupils and your school – it is not intended as a fixed curriculum or a complete list of all possible activities. You may find that activities suggested for one age group are appropriate at other stages as well.

The chapters are:

6 Word-processing software in the primary classroom
7 Spreadsheet software in the primary classroom
8 Database software in the primary classroom
9 Branching database software in the primary classroom
10 Data loggers in the primary classroom
11 Digital cameras, movies and photocopiers in the primary classroom
12 Digital microscopes and visualisers in the primary classroom
13 Graphics software in the primary classroom
14 Simulation software in the primary classroom
15 Control technology, Pixies and Roamers in the primary classroom
16 Digital audio equipment in the primary classroom
17 Hand-held devices in the primary classroom
18 Multimedia authoring programs in the primary classroom

The four ICT skills listed in the QCDA document have been used in each of the following chapters to show how the software and hardware outlined can help towards the acquisition of these essential skills.

• Find and select information.
• Create, manipulate and process information.
• Collaborate, communicate and share information.
• Refine and improve work.

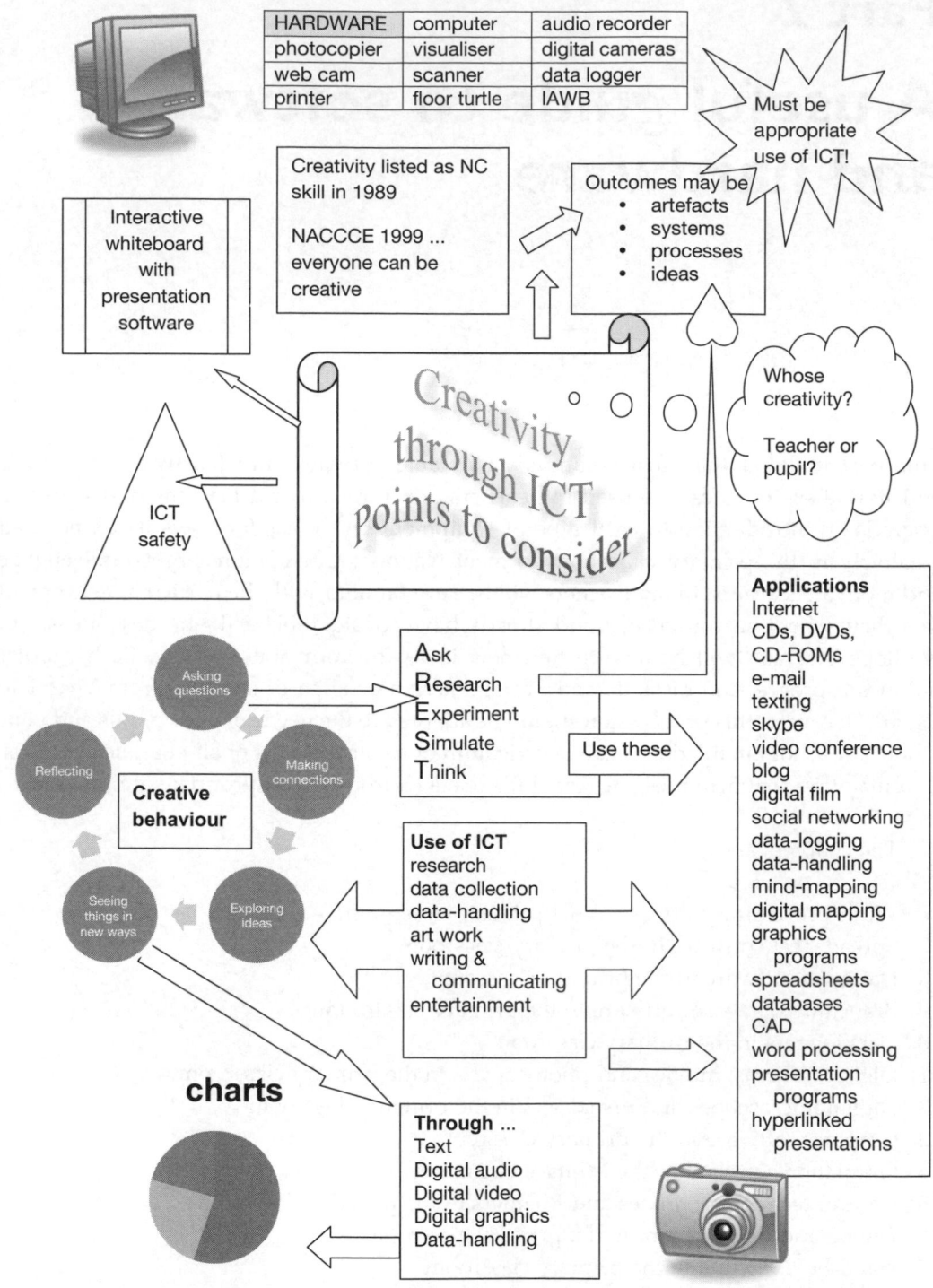

HARDWARE	computer	audio recorder
photocopier	visualiser	digital cameras
web cam	scanner	data logger
printer	floor turtle	IAWB

Must be appropriate use of ICT!

Creativity listed as NC skill in 1989

NACCCE 1999 ... everyone can be creative

Interactive whiteboard with presentation software

Outcomes may be
- artefacts
- systems
- processes
- ideas

Creativity through ICT points to consider

Whose creativity?

Teacher or pupil?

ICT safety

Asking questions

Making connections

Reflecting

Creative behaviour

Seeing things in new ways

Exploring ideas

Ask
Research
Experiment
Simulate
Think

Use these

Applications
Internet
CDs, DVDs, CD-ROMs
e-mail
texting
skype
video conference
blog
digital film
social networking
data-logging
data-handling
mind-mapping
digital mapping
graphics
   programs
spreadsheets
databases
CAD
word processing
presentation
   programs
hyperlinked
   presentations

Use of ICT
research
data collection
data-handling
art work
writing & communicating
entertainment

charts

Through ...
Text
Digital audio
Digital video
Digital graphics
Data-handling

6 Word-processing software in the primary classroom

Introduction to word processing

A word processor is a program that enables text and graphics to be entered, stored, retrieved, redrafted and reformatted. Some of the features of a word processor are also found in desktop-publishing programs, such as Microsoft Publisher for adults or Black Cat's Pawprints for children. In addition, presentation programs such as PowerPoint have many WP features. WP is the most commonly used software, not only in schools but also in the wider business world, and it is one of the most versatile aids to electronic communication. The skills of creating and editing text are intimately concerned with communicating to different audiences through digital media such as e-mail, multimodal texts and websites. It is advantageous for children to learn to type accurately as soon as they are able to do so.

Since word processors were introduced into schools in the 1980s, there has been much debate about how they can contribute to children's learning in the primary school. They have many organisational features, such as the ability to cut and paste text and create lists and headings, while their potential for importing charts, graphics and data from other sources can make them invaluable when pupils are drafting and redrafting texts for different purposes or adapting them for different audiences. However, there has been a tendency to use computers just as machines to produce tidy work, with little teacher input to help children use them to develop their writing skills (Mumtaz 2001, Mumtaz and Hammond 2002).

Pupils should be shown how to use word processing and organisational features to make their work visual and engaging. The use of headings, subheadings, bullets, alignment, arrows, text boxes, speech bubbles, labelled diagrams, imported charts and photographs help to make writing more interesting for the writer and attractive for the reader.

The Mumtaz survey in 2001, of pupils in Years 3 and 5, also found that the most frequent computer use in school was WP, which pupils often found boring. The survey suggested that schools might build more on what is familiar and enjoyable. Research summarised by Becta (2003) indicated that writing development can be accelerated and enhanced by access to WP programs. It has been noted that WP programs can support reflective writing and improvements to pupils' reasoning ability (Deadman 1997). Hayes and Ge's 2008 study of computer-supported collaborative learning found that using computers enhanced the writing process by making early ideas visible for personal and peer reflection, and that this supported negotiation and knowledge building between those involved. Hayes and Ge (2008) found that students who worked with computers, as opposed to paper and pencils, had significant gains in their writing performance. In addition, the students who used computers were more motivated to write than the pencil and paper group. At primary level, Harrison *et al.* (2002) found a statistically significant impact of ICT on the Key Stage 2 English tests. From these surveys, it appears that the key advantage of using word processors effectively in the English curriculum is that it promotes greater engagement

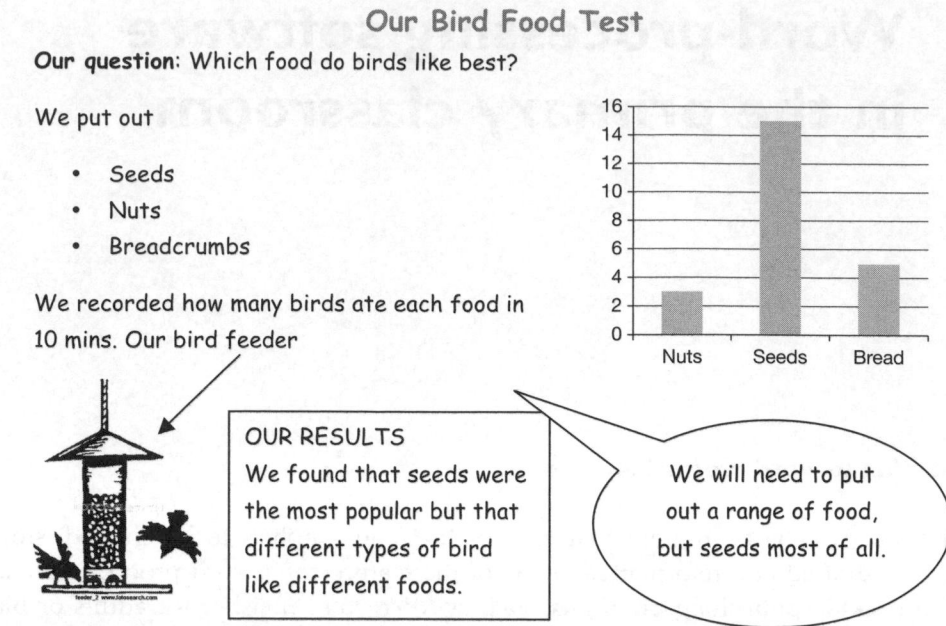

Figure 6.1 Word-processing features

with the subject through the drafting and redrafting process, by allowing opportunities for reflection and analysis and by developing the higher-level thinking skills necessary to communicate ideas.

McCormick and Scrimshaw (2001) point out that teachers need to understand that successful use of ICT depends on many factors, including the way pupils work in the classroom away from the computer: the traditions pupils build up as they interact with their peers and their teacher and in other classroom situations will affect their ability to use a computer effectively. The main reason for using a word processor should always be that the writing process is enhanced, so that the content of the text is better organised and expressed than if it is done by hand. Another reason for word processing is that it is possible to present work for different audiences in particular ways: plain text can be made into posters, charts, tables or even cartoons, where appropriate, to engage the reader. A spellchecker may help children to identify and correct misspellings, while what is most motivating to some reluctant writers is that the appearance can always be neat and easy to read. The features of some word processors aid inclusion and empower those unable to form letters by hand, through voice-recognition software and touch-screen technology. Word processors enable all writers to have perfect letter formation.

How word processing can help children

Editing text

A word processor allows children to plan, draft, revise and edit original text before transferring it to other formats. Most professional writers need to write several drafts of a text before it is published. We must allow children the same facilities, so that even the shortest text is composed with the best possible arrangement of the most appropriate words. Whether they are writing an invitation, a set of instructions, an e-mail or a brochure, they need regular access to word processors to clarify their ideas and amend drafts as required.

National Curriculum requirements, 2009

As part of the 'essentials for learning and life' (ICT capability), children learn how to:

- **Find and select information:** When searching for information on CD-ROMs or the Internet, it is convenient to copy and paste key words and sentences into a WP document for further editing and use. Doing this saves laborious copying by hand before recopying into a final format. A hand-held or audio recording device could also be used to take notes for word processing at a later date.
- **Create, manipulate and process information:** Word processors enable pupils to create and alter information as many times as they need to gain the effect they require. Through word processing, the same information can be reformatted to suit different audiences. Word processors can save time and, in desktop-publishing packages, create professional results through combining text, tables and graphics in different layouts.
- **Collaborate, communicate and share information:** Using word processors allows pupils to collaborate on writing tasks, either simultaneously, if working on the same computer, or at a distance, through e-mail. They can share ideas, merge contributions and edit each other's work, while retaining original versions for further use.
- **Refine and improve their work:** A word processor allows pupils to check spelling and grammar and alter layout and content to improve the work, without laborious rewriting.

Obtaining words from word banks

Many word processors for children such as Clicker, Black Cat, TextEase and 2Simple have a word-bank facility that allows the teacher to prepare words likely to be needed, ready for use on a separate portion of the screen. These words can be dragged from the bank as required, which saves time and avoids the misspelling and subsequent correction that can be so dispiriting for a young writer.

Presenting work to different audiences

An account of a school trip can be adapted as an article in the school magazine, simplified and pasted into a presentation program such as PowerPoint to share with parents, or reformatted as a thank-you letter to the people involved.

Enabling group/shared writing to be presented in a unified style

Collaborative writing can help to develop ideas, speaking and listening skills, as well as writing. Anthologies of pupils' poems, collections of recipes or inventions, booklets or brochures designed by groups of pupils can have a consistent appearance in a common format and with readable text. On any topic, whether scientific, historic or geographical, groups of pupils can research and record their learning on one aspect of the topic and combine their cumulative study into one record of learning for others to peruse. Groups might find out about different aspects of Tudor life or a range of minibeasts and then pool

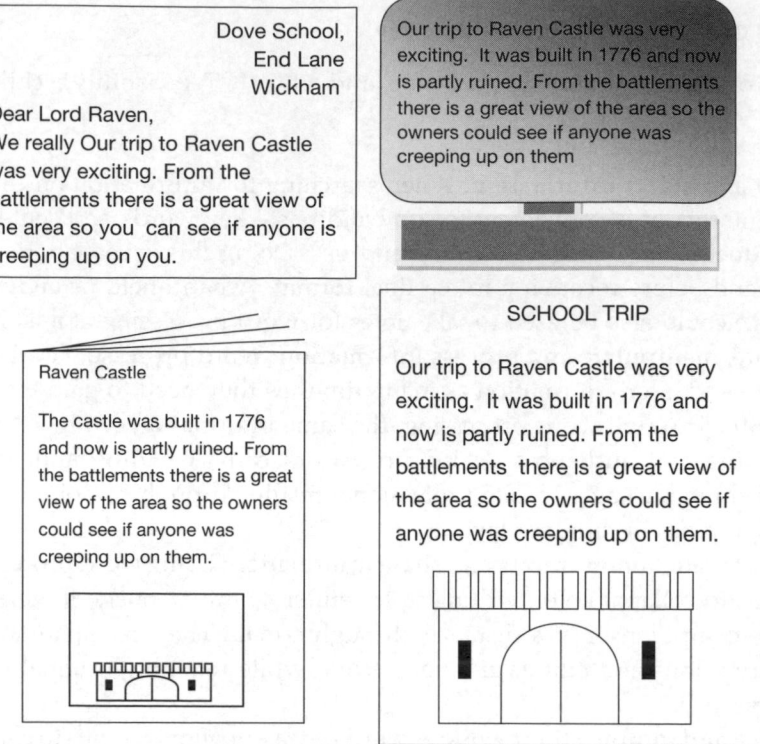

Figure 6.2 Pupils' writing can be adapted for different purposes using a word processor

their work as an attractive and useful classroom resource. This could be printed as a class book or kept as a hyperlinked presentation (see Appendix 3). Through the use of a WP program, every child's contribution can be equally well organised and presented.

Checking work

Even adult writers can make mistakes. Children need to check their writing before publishing to blogs, e-mail or online stories and web pages. This can save embarrassing mistakes. Publishing to blogs or other Internet sites gives reluctant writers a real audience, including their parents, and this can be very motivating.

Checking spelling independently

One of the aims of the teacher is to enable all pupils to become independent and critical reviewers of their work. The spelling and grammar checkers on a word processor go some way to developing this independence, as long as the pupils realise that they may have to choose from several similar words, and that not all their mistakes can be corrected in this way. Having a thesaurus or dictionary always to hand can help pupils to develop a wider vocabulary.

Formatting text and layouts

Text will appear more interesting and inviting if it is formatted in such a way that it engages the reader's attention. Using text boxes, tables, speech bubbles and other layouts can assist with this. The formatting features of a word processor, such as bullets, numbered lists, columns, tables and text that can be altered in font size, colour and style, can help young writers to consider the order and content of their writing. Newspapers are written in columns, factual books use headings, subheadings and bullet points to organise the content, while fiction books use a wide range of font styles, speech bubbles and layouts to keep the reader's attention. The word processor enables children to use similar facilities, which necessitate thought and discussion about the content of each section. Speech bubbles (or callouts on a PC) have a great attraction for children, as many of the texts they enjoy chunk the content in this accessible format. Speech bubbles are an encouraging way of engaging reluctant writers, and this method of recording in any subject can ensure adequate detail, if given keywords have to be used.

In the example in Figure 6.4, the speech and story line have different areas, to reinforce the difference between these types of text.

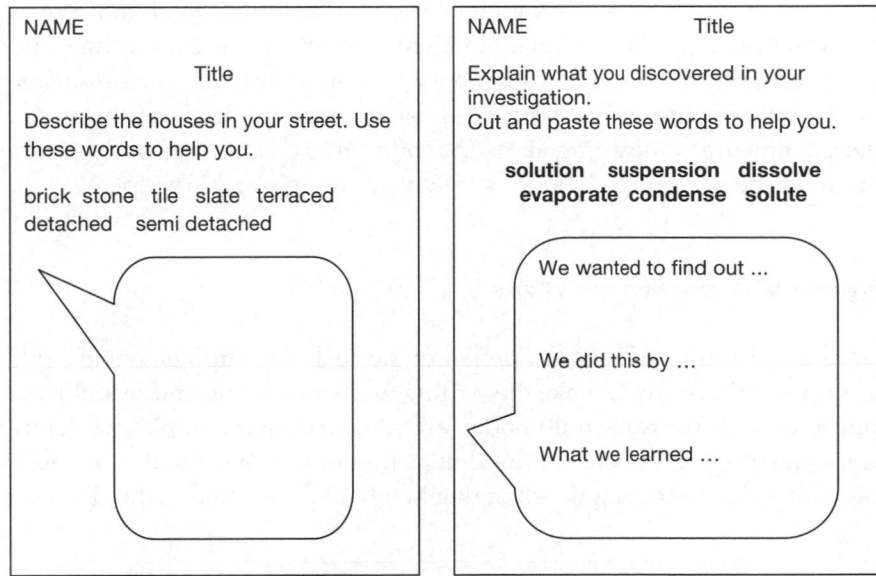

Figure 6.3 A KS1 template and a template for an older reluctant writer

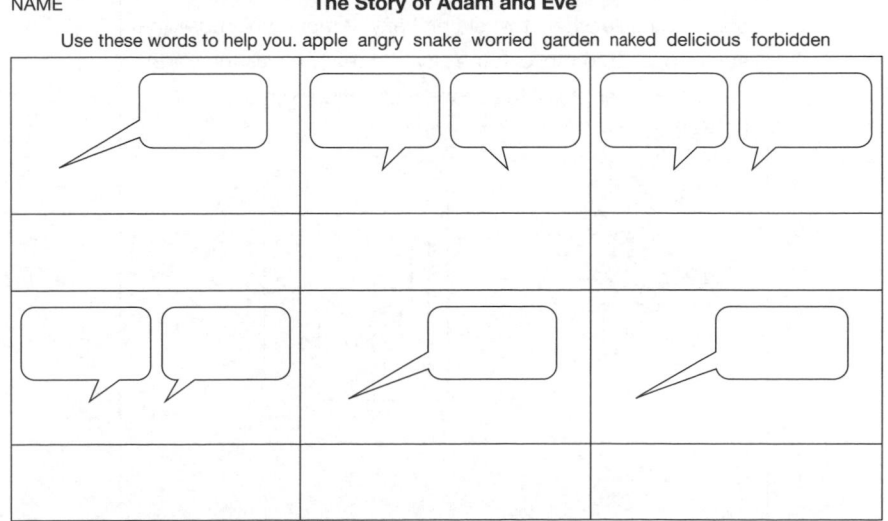

Figure 6.4 An example of a template created by the teacher. The speech bubbles can be added or deleted as required

Writers can progress from single to multiple speech bubbles, and from using the teacher's template to creating their own layout. Artwork can be added by hand after printing, or copied and pasted from a simple graphic created by the child. This type of recording can ensure rigour, by specifying the vocabulary to be used, so that very detailed and imaginative written work can result from these simple prompts. (See Appendix 2 for details on creating such templates.)

The way a text is laid out can affect the style, word count and organisation of the content. Some layouts demand a formal style of writing; a cartoon layout will require a more informal and even a colloquial style and content. Tables need to have as few words as possible to make their meaning clear, while a rhyme scheme pro-forma focuses on another set of skills.

Reinforcing/practising skills where personal handwriting is not essential

It is essential for children to develop a legible style of handwriting, but, if this is not the focus for a lesson, using a WP template to identify parts of speech, through underlining or colouring particular words, may be a more appropriate way to practise such skills and is easier for the teacher to check. Templates using drag and drop to rearrange a text or record ideas in any area of learning allow the children to concentrate on the content of the text, rather than the sometimes laborious task of creating a legible script.

Combining text with graphics and charts

We live in a graphically rich age, where so many texts are supplemented with photos, diagrams, graphs and charts to make the writing more interesting and readable. From Key Stage 1, pupils are able to create multimodal texts. An account of a pupil's work on shadows will be more meaningful if photos of the child acting as a human sundial are added to the text, along with a chart showing the changing height and direction of the shadows. Sound

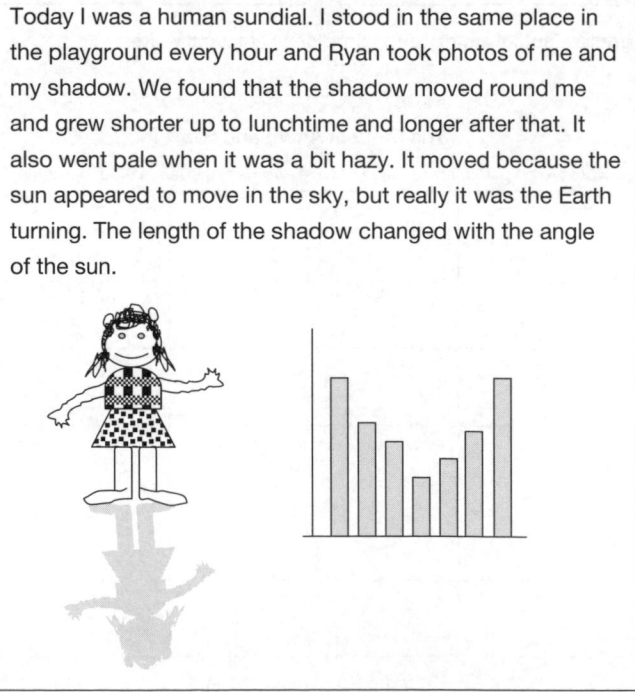

Today I was a human sundial. I stood in the same place in the playground every hour and Ryan took photos of me and my shadow. We found that the shadow moved round me and grew shorter up to lunchtime and longer after that. It also went pale when it was a bit hazy. It moved because the sun appeared to move in the sky, but really it was the Earth turning. The length of the shadow changed with the angle of the sun.

Figure 6.5 A human sundial

clips can be added to electronic reports about a visiting musician, music the class has made or sounds recorded round the school while looking for the quietest places to read a book in peace. Video files can be inserted into screen-based texts to create digital posters or multimedia presentations.

Hearing their work read back to them

Some word processors for children have a sound facility that allows them to hear what they have typed. This can be a useful aid to identify poor spelling or missing or repeated words. Although the software will not be able to pronounce every word needed correctly, it can help to flag up common errors, which the children can then correct themselves, promoting independence.

Splitting the screen

This is a useful facility in programs such as Word, when making notes from screen-based texts and when checking for consistency in a document. A split screen enables source and work to appear close together for ease of reference and note making. To access this, hover the mouse at the top of the right-hand margin, just above the scrolling arrows. A split-screen icon will appear, allowing the writer to drag down a new portion of screen, so that the start and later portions of the text can be seen separately. (The copy-and-paste facility needs to be used with care here, to ensure that notes rather than full sections are copied – see the section on using the Internet, p. 30). It also makes it easier for two children to combine the best features of separate texts they have written by electronic copying and pasting, which saves much time. The split-screen facility enables the writer to check for consistency across a document.

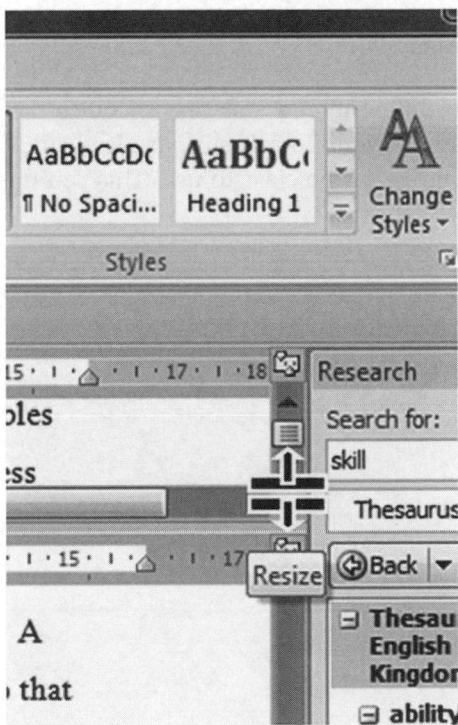

Figure 6.6 The split-screen icon

Producing non-paper-based outcomes

Not all text will end up on paper. Many texts are not intended to be printed, just read electronically. There is little point in laboriously creating a good script by hand, if it is then to be transcribed to a computer for sharing with others, or published on the web. If children's writing is designed for web pages, e-mail, e-zines, multimedia presentations or as data in computer databases, it might as well be composed digitally if it is to be read digitally.

Motivating reluctant writers

The editing facilities on a word processor enable children with poor writing skills to produce an attractive and carefully checked piece of work independently, which can give them the necessary confidence to attempt quite complex work. Pupils can concentrate on just one aspect of writing at a time, the content, and the machine can help them modify the appearance and check spelling and grammar when they are ready to do so. This can be particularly motivating for boys, who may feel they have an affinity with machines and technology.

How word processing can help teachers

Modelling the writing process

Along with the use of an IWB, the teacher can model the whole process of drafting, checking, redrafting and formatting a layout. This will need to be done many times in different contexts. Using the WP and handwriting facilities of whiteboard software, it can be done both in handwriting and in a typed font. Pupils can interact with the teacher's text, make suggestions and improvements and share the editing and redrafting.

Scaffolding children's writing

This can be done through differentiated task sheets. Once the children start their own writing, they will need differing amounts of support. It is quite a simple matter to create a writing frame for the majority of the class to use. This can then be adapted and saved,

NAME

Our Science Test

We want to find out

We will do this by

We will keep these variables the same

We will change this variable

I predict that

Figure 6.7

with differing prompts, and can support a range of abilities and individuals (see Appendix 2 on making templates). This can save much teacher time and enable personal support to be given where it is needed.

Sharing and annotating texts with the whole class

The annotations can be shared with the whole class on an IWB, with the pupils doing the interacting as much as possible. Work done by individual pupils in an independent part of the lesson can be shared with the rest of the class in the plenary. This can save hours of photocopying and many trees.

Preparing work for pupils

Prepared screens can be used by the whole class, small groups and individuals, to investigate spelling and punctuation rules through highlighting and annotation. These might be for reinforcement or assessment activities and are easily differentiated for children at different ability levels.

Providing word banks

Subject-specific lists can extend vocabulary and increase independence in writing.

Providing access to electronic and interactive texts

There are many online texts that are not available in paper-based formats. For example, text from websites and other electronic sources can, subject to copyright, be pasted into a WP program, so that the features of the texts can be displayed and discussed.

Features of WP packages

The features listed below can be used by primary children to develop and share information. There are many more that might be used for particular purposes.

bullets and numbered text	capitalise with shift key
combine text and images	cut, copy and paste (for drafting and redrafting)
find and replace	format layout
format text (font, size, colour and style)	grammar checker
header, footers and columns	help facility
import from other applications	hyperlinks
link to Internet	page size and orientation
print	shapes, arrows and callouts
sort/alphabetise	speech*
speech bubbles/callouts	spellcheck
tables	split screen
text boxes and arrows to create diagrams	templates (for teacher use)
type, delete and undo	thesaurus
word count	word banks*

* Available on some educational WP packages

Word processors used in schools might be the industry standard ones, such as Word or Claris Works, or specialised, child-friendly programs, such as TextEase, Black Cat, 2Simple or Clicker, which have features specifically designed for use by children. These include software that will read the children's text back to them and word banks to help widen vocabulary and aid spelling. Such word banks can have relevant words added by the teacher to suit a subject, a group of children or even an individual.

Progression in WP activities

Not all the features listed above can be introduced at once, and so a progression of skills and techniques has to be devised, such as the one suggested in Table 6.1. Some children will find that these features present challenges; others, with more experience of home computer use, may be able to use many more than those suggested for a particular year group.

These lists are just a guide for structuring the relevant skills, to ensure all have been utilised by the end of KS2. The activities do not necessarily need to be completed in the sequence outlined. For example, using the help facility, which is suggested as the last skill to acquire in KS2, might be needed much earlier. Nor do the activities listed indicate the amount of discussion and negotiation that is essential to make the writing process dynamic and creative. In every case, reading should accompany the writing process, with discussion about ways to improve or develop the text.

The exercises can be done with a whole class in a computer-suite session, or with small groups using standalone computers while other children complete similar pencil-and-paper- or resource-based activities. The suggested progression is a minimum list of progression: if children need to import a spreadsheet in KS1, rather than in the UKS2 classes, and can do this with help, then they should do so. The suggestions do not cover all the features of word processors: others can be taught on a need-to-know basis. The use of templates in many of these activities helps to ensure differentiated support and challenge for children of differing expertise and experience. Use of lower-case-letter stickers can make the keyboard more accessible to those just starting to read and type. Keys that are not needed could have blank stickers to cover them.

Figure 6.8

January	I hope to make a snowman
February	Valentine's day party
March	I go on holiday
April	New lambs at the farm
May	My birthday

Figure 6.9

	My Week
Monday	I went swimming after school
Tuesday	Tom played football with me at play time
Wednesday	I got all my sums right and had fish fingers for dinner

Figure 6.10

Table 6.1 *Progression in WP activities in KS1, Lower KS2 and Upper KS2*

KS1	
Skills and techniques	*WP activities for KS1, including cross-curricular ideas*
Use word bank to create sentences/label pictures (including use of templates to create text with drag and drop)	Drag words that describe familiar objects to match a picture of the object. In history, this might be words to describe old and new toys; in science it could be words that describe the property of a material or an object. Drag words from word bank to make sentences. Read what has been written. *Drag words to label diagrams/photos/computer drawings that have been copied and pasted into the WP program by the teacher. *Drag words to complete sentences. *Match beginnings and ends of sentences taken from a familiar book, e.g. children drag words to complete familiar rhymes/make nonsense rhymes.
Type/delete text accurately	Type names and labels for people, personal possessions, classroom objects. These could be used to help keep the classroom tidy. Labels about pictures or models the children have made would be a relevant context for WP activities. *Certificates, book reviews, science investigations, letters, invitations, could all be scaffolded with templates (see Appendix 2 for examples). *Create a passport, club card or other personal ID. *Write captions for pictures and photos. *Add speech to callouts prepared on a template by the teacher and add them to photos/artwork on the wall. *Alter one line of a given poem at a time to create a new poem. (This will need to be done after a session where the features of the original poem are discussed and alterations are explored.)
Use shift key to capitalise	*Pupils correct a piece of text that lacks capitals. *Create lists of things to do on days of the week, events for each month or a gift list for friends (see Figure 6.8).
Add words/numbers to a table/template	*Add words/sentences to diary template in a table (see Figure 6.9). *Complete a timeline in a 2-column table, with the year in column 1 and significant events such as starting school, holidays and loosing teeth in column 2. *Add facts about shape properties to a table about them. Use tables to record the results of tests and investigations in science or history.
Alter font size, style and colour	*Add words to a 'Wanted' poster and alter font to suit each section (see Figure 6.10). *Alter each line of an advertisement, invitation or events poster to suit the content.
Combine text and image	*Drag and drop pictures from a picture bank, e.g. on Textease. *Use insert facility to add clip art to work. *Use insert facility to add photos to work. Copy and paste digital artwork from paint program into writing and add text to explain ideas.
Copy and paste words/ pictures	If templates are provided with specific vocabulary to be used, pupils should be shown how to cut/copy and paste the words to save time and ensure accuracy. Adding pictures to their work is very motivating, especially if this involves photos of themselves, or their own artwork created in another application or scanned in if done by hand.
Use undo	One of the most liberating facilities on a word processor is the undo facility (Ctrl Z). Knowing how to use this from an early age can prevent frustration when a child's work accidentally disappears, or when the last word needs to be deleted in favour of a better one.
Use, bullets, screen layout and headings to organise and link ideas	Write simple instructions, with headings to list stages and bullets to list items needed. Write a simple brochure, with contents, headings and bullets to organise. Create reports and articles on class events and investigations.
Use WP to amend, save and print work	Use the speech facility (if available) to hear work read back. Correct mistakes identified. Use the underlining facility to identify which spellings need correcting. This could be completed by using word lists around the room, or asking another child or adult for help. Save work to a personal folder. Print work, with permission from teacher.

Lower KS2

Skills and techniques	WP activities for LKS2, including cross-curricular ideas
Cut, copy and paste sentences and blocks of text	Copy and paste from digital texts to make notes. *Cut and paste a list of instructions to improve the order. *Cut and paste events in a story/historical text to show the correct order. Cut and paste pupil's own text to improve meaning. Make a page of tickets/vouchers to be photocopied for an event. Paste repeating lines in a text, such as a poem/story.
Insert callouts, text boxes, illustrations, moving images, hyperlinks and sound	*Annotate a map – local/regional/national – with arrows and text boxes or speech bubbles to show items of interest/indicate points of view (see Figure 6.11). Label diagrams in all subjects with arrows and text boxes, e.g. the water cycle, parts of a mosque, a historical artefact, parts of a plant or animal. *Create cartoon strips to record learning in science/history/RE/other subjects (rigour ensured by requiring keywords to be included). Insert sound files, digital images, moving images and hyperlinks into pupils' writing to create multimodal texts and multimedia presentations.
Format layout including bullets, numbering	Create brochures, booklets, articles, e-zines, for a specific audience such as parents, local tourist information or younger child.
Sort/alphabetise	Group names/teams to be put in alphabetical order. Who is quicker, child or computer? Put a list of inventions in alphabetical order and order of invention. A short published poem can be turned into a list of words, which is then alphabetised. Pupils can then see, not whether they can reconstruct the poems, but what they can do with the same group of words. This relieves them of the need to find the words and allows them to concentrate on creating something new with them (an idea from the poet Trevor Millum).
Find, change and spellcheck	*Alter the tense in a story from past to present to make it sound more immediate and action-packed. *Change dull nouns and adjectives to scintillating ones, possibly through use of a template using the word *nice* too often. Change the names in a story to make it about a pupil/someone else. Use the spellchecker, selecting the correct word rather than the first option given.
Use word count	Write poems/articles/riddles to a short, specific word count, e.g. tell pupils they have exactly 30 words to write a poem on a particular subject. Using the word-count facility will help to ensure each word is considered carefully.
Create and use tables	Use for recording in science (see Figure 6.12a). Make simple time charts in history (e.g. see Figure 6.12b)

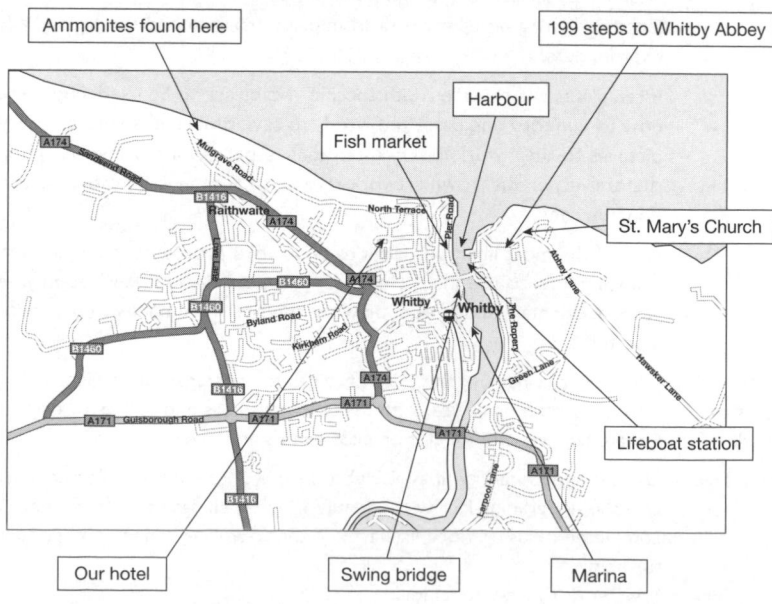

Figure 6.11 Labelled map of Whitby

Upper KS2

Skills and techniques	WP activities in UKS2, including cross-curricular ideas
Alter margins and orientation	Create posters and certificates using a range of paper sizes and in landscape and portrait view.
Import data from other applications such as spreadsheets	This can be done to create reports, multimodal texts and multimedia presentations in every subject.
Format text and layout to suit different subjects and different readers	*Adapt factual reports to create newspaper articles or presentations. Add children's artwork and photos to poems. Turn adverts into persuasive text. Create a range of multimodal magazine, e-zine and web layouts suited to the reading age and interest of the intended reader.
Use a digital thesaurus	*This could be used in conjunction with a 'find and replace the dull words' activity. Look up synonyms using thesaurus. *Alter a given poem using the thesaurus. Create a poem/story/article using the thesaurus.
Use lines and shapes	These can be used to add diagrams to a text, or to create flowcharts that will need annotating, for example to show the stages in a planned production line for an Enterprise project. Google *Rotherham Ready* to find out more about these. *Shapes with a text infill can be put together to create board games, perhaps to record learning on how to deal with hazards and problems. (Some local authorities use a crucial crew day of simulated problems and accidents to teach about ways to cope responsibly. Making board games to record this learning creates an enjoyable challenge that results in games for a wet playtime.) (See Figure 6.13.)
Insert hyperlinks, sound and movie files	Stories told from multiple points of view or with multiple-choice scenarios are fun to create with hyperlinks. (See the multimedia section for details, Appendix 3.) Hyperlinks can also be used in non-fiction texts to refer the reader to the glossary, index or another section. Sound and movie files, e.g. from a trip to a church or temple, can add interest to a multimedia presentation, which can also be shared on the school website.
Create templates	Children should learn how to prepare their own stationery templates, starting with a letter-writing template and progressing to tables for collecting data, creating their own science recording templates or a template to write limericks, with the repeating lines and numbers of syllables shown. They could even plan a template for writing a thank-you letter.
Use help facility	Give pairs of pupils specific challenges such as: Find out how to alter the page margins, add page numbers or change the colour of a hyperlink. They could then teach another pair of children how to use each new skill.

Note: Activities marked * might involve the use of a template (see Appendix 2)

	Car 1	Car 2
distance travelled on hard floor in cm	250	340
distance travelled on carpet in cm	87	120

Figure 6.12a

1950	Grandpa born
1951	Grandma born
1970	Grandparents married
1974	Mum born
1976	Dad born
2005	I was born
2010	I started school

Figure 6.12b

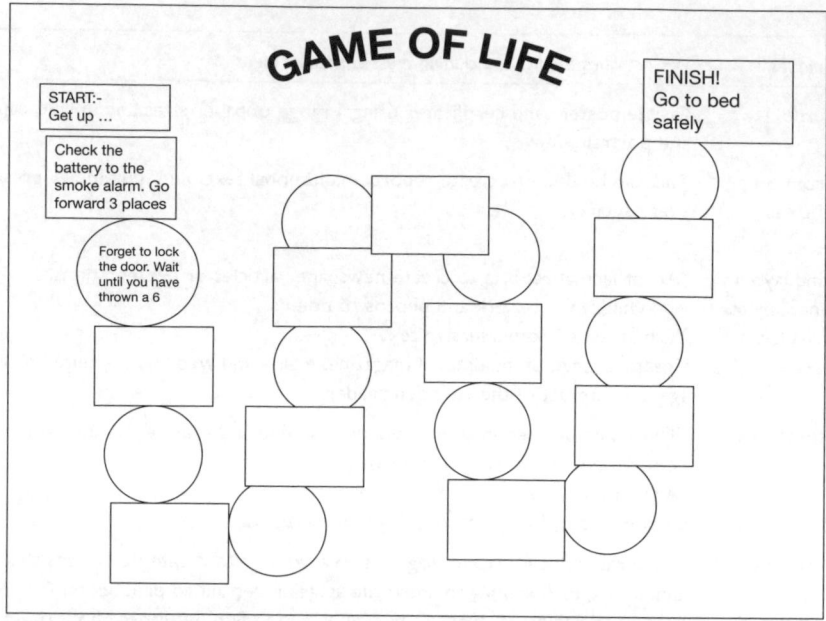

Figure 6.13 Game of Life Template

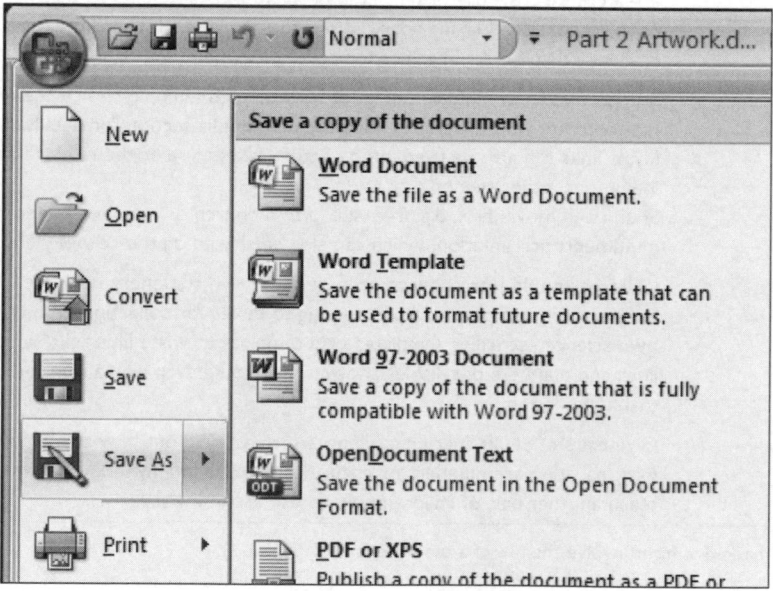

Figure 6.14

WP templates

To create a template in a WP program, create the layout you want, with tables, headings and text required (it should always have the word 'Name' in the top left-hand corner, or it may be hard to trace the writer at a later date). Then, choose '*Save as . . .*' and choose the template option (see Figure 6.14). Make sure the document is saved in a folder where you will easily find it, and not in a general template folder on the computer set up by Microsoft or another manufacturer.

It can be very useful for young children to have a writing template always ready, in Comic Sans or Sasoon, font size 18, with the features shown in Figure 6.15 ready to be altered by the child.

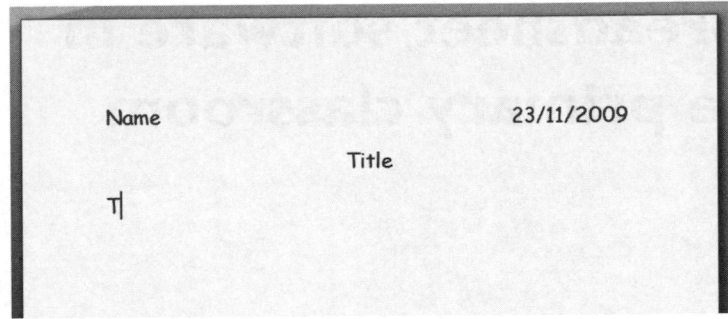

Name   23/11/2009

Title

T|

Figure 6.15

Problems with word processors

An initial problem for a child using a word processor may be simply finding the right keys. Your school will need to decide whether touch-typing sessions or keyboard games are the best way to help with this. Certainly, practice will breed familiarity, and you may be able to devise homework tasks for children to complete on their own or on local library PCs that will help them to improve their typing speed, if this is a problem. For example, creating greetings cards or bookmarks using patterns of letters and numbers might be an enjoyable and skills-based homework to help with keyboard skills. There are several websites that children can use to practise their typing skills and, with the NC emphasis on accurate typing, it might be useful to organise some structured skills training for this, using, for example, www.sense-lang.org/typing/ and www.bbc.co.uk/schools/typing. These sites have tutorials, games and tests to help develop keyboard skills.

As teachers, we can build on pupils' home experience of computer use, as well as compensate for its lack. We must take advantage of the widespread availability of home and library-based computers and help to compensate for the digital divide. If pupils who have them at home can be encouraged to use them for WP with attractive homework challenges, those who do not have them may be given more time in class or a homework club. Once familiar with the keyboard, children may value appearance over content and spend too much time experimenting with fancy fonts or colours. If clear guidance is given about only doing this for a few minutes at the start of a session, or once the text is completed, then this need not be a barrier to using word processors. WP can be done in many programs, including presentation software such as PowerPoint.

An overlay keyboard is a specialized keyboard with no preset keys, so that each key can be programmed with different functions. The overlay can consist of any combination of words, symbols or even pictures. They can be used to simplify the keyboard for young children or for those with a special need. An overlay keyboard might simply reduce the number of available keys for typing, which can be useful for the young or inexperienced.

Reading word-processed documents

Electronic texts require different reading skills from paper-based texts. Some of these skills can be acquired by playing computer games, watching adverts or programmes on TV, by browsing the Internet or using other online web environments. Readers must be able to switch rapidly from one font or background page colour to another, follow hyperlinks and access moving images and sounds. Karchmer (2001) suggests that the facilities of these electronic texts, such as animated graphics, video and hyperlinks, necessitate the development of new literacy skills, such as ensuring that text is visible and arranged in ways that encourage onscreen reading.

7 Spreadsheet software in the primary classroom

Introduction to spreadsheets

A spreadsheet program enables text and numbers to be stored, altered and, in some circumstances, displayed as charts or graphs. Spreadsheets are tables of information. They allow the user to manipulate the information in a variety of ways. Spreadsheets are available for all levels of ability and experience. Textease, 2Simple and Black Cat are three suites of programs that contain easy-to-use spreadsheets. However, even the industry standard, Excel, can be changed by teachers to make it easy for infants to use. Spreadsheets are important, content-free software programs that can assist across the curriculum in every subject. Using spreadsheets allows children to handle large amounts of information and use it to see patterns and draw conclusions.

Spreadsheets can do a great deal of the low-level work of making graphs and charts from the data they have collected in science, history, geography or maths. Allen *et al.* (2007) show how it helps children spot inconsistencies in data at an early (and easily alterable) point. This helps children to focus much more on the underlying learning. For instance, infants charting how many layers of different papers stop light from passing through them might gather their data in a table of results using a spreadsheet. The children could easily sort the papers into least opaque and most opaque using the sort button at the top of most spreadsheet pages. They could then chart their results into a simple bar chart (see Figure 7.1). The chart and table can easily be pasted into a word processor document saving a long winded transcription.

Type of paper	Number of layers made it opaque
Tissue	14
Black sugar	1
Yellow sugar	2
White writing	4
Greaseproof	6

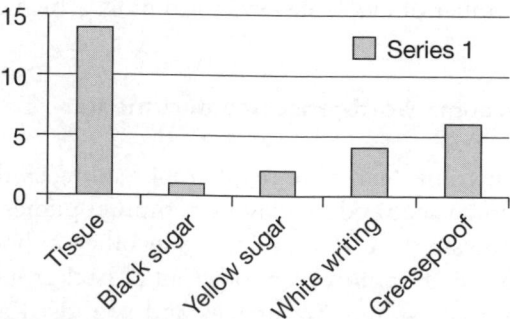

Figure 7.1

National Curriculum requirements

As part of the 'essentials for learning and life' (ICT capability), children learn how to:

- **Find and select information:** When using spreadsheets, children need to check that the data support or disprove their ideas. For instance, they can find out about the different calorific values of a range of foods and then select only the ones they wish to use in their menu.
- **Create, manipulate and process information:** When using spreadsheets, children will find averages of sets of data, for instance, when charting the distance travelled by a car off a ramp.
- **Collaborate, communicate and share information:** When using spreadsheets, children will use the charts and graphs produced to explain their ideas to other people. For instance, the speed at which differently insulated containers cool can be entered on to a spreadsheet and then shared between different groups.
- **Refine and improve their work:** When using spreadsheets, children can add to and refine their data. For instance, they can add new data about the number of worms in a patch of flowerbed over a period of several weeks. The changes can be charted on the spreadsheet. In another instance, children can make a spreadsheet about the cost of food for a party. These data can be altered to take into account changes in the type of food and its cost.

How spreadsheets can help children

Asking questions

Spreadsheets give opportunities to ask 'what if?' questions (Hall 2010). These can be as simple as asking what will happen if we sell books at different prices in the Christmas fair. In this example, the children have set up a formula that predicts how much money is made if books are sold at different prices. The question, 'What if we sold two more at 50p and two fewer at 20p?', is easily answered. See Figure 7.2.

Jarvis (2003), writing about using spreadsheets in humanities teaching, highlights several advantages that spreadsheets afford. He points out the ways in which spreadsheets make graphing and charting easy and accessible. Jarvis also shows that spreadsheets can be used to enhance a variety of cross-curricular topics. He mentions the ways in which heights of mountains and associated weather can be displayed on spreadsheets to aid understanding about factors affecting weather.

Selling books

Price of books (in pence)	Number sold	Total (pounds)
10	5	0.5
20	8	1.6
50	3	1.5

Figure 7.2

Sorting information

Children can sort information using spreadsheets in a variety of ways. They can group similar entries together: for example, grouping all the entries about girls and boys separately, or grouping animals with a certain number of legs together. Figure 7.3 shows the original data collected at random, the table sorted alphabetically and the table sorted according to the number of legs. All manipulation can be done in seconds.

Information about the children in the class can be sorted. For instance, if information about hair colour was collected in a simple table, then children could be grouped according to that characteristic, and the children could ask questions about what the data show.

Ranking information

By placing the entries into numerical or alphabetical order, children can manipulate their data and ask questions about them. For instance, the children could be gathering information about the distance to premiership football grounds or tourist attractions such as zoos. The data for distance could be obtained from www.multimap.com, and the list could be manipulated to rank the attractions in order of distance from the school. Similarly, the distance from home postcode to school postcode could be calculated using the same website. The resulting data could be ranked to show the person who lives furthest from school and the person who lives closest. Adding the time taken to complete the journey by each child would provoke other questions and ideas for ranking the data.

Information from science activities such as the distance travelled by different toy cars off a ramp could be ranked.

The following are examples of how data can be ranked at different levels.

How many legs does it have?

The original data table		Data sorted alphabetically (not helpful)		Data sorted by number of legs (useful)	
ostrich	2	bee	6	slug	0
human	2	beetle	6	worm	0
cow	4	cat	4	eagle	2
crocodile	4	cow	4	human	2
bee	6	crocodile	4	ostrich	2
wasp	6	eagle	2	sparrow	2
beetle	6	human	2	cat	4
sparrow	2	lobster	14	cow	4
eagle	2	ostrich	2	crocodile	4
spider	8	scorpion	8	bee	6
scorpion	8	slug	0	beetle	6
woodlouse	14	sparrow	2	wasp	6
lobster	14	spider	8	scorpion	8
worm	0	wasp	6	spider	8
slug	0	woodlouse	14	lobster	14
cat	4	worm	0	woodlouse	14

Figure 7.3 How many legs does it have?

Filtering information

Spreadsheets can filter information so that users only see items in which they are interested. For instance, if the children collect information about the pets that the children in the class own, they can filter the information so that only the children who own a particular pet are shown.

Spreadsheets used with a filter can often work in much the same way as a database. In fact, there is little to be gained by using fully-fledged database programs such as Pinpoint or Black Cat's Information Workshop rather than a spreadsheet. Databases tend to be difficult to set up and awkward to alter, whereas spreadsheets are easy to amend and use. For instance, the children could use the *Yellow Pages* to compile a spreadsheet of restaurants in the area; it could record the name, location, postcode and telephone number, type of food and whether it does takeaway. The filter facility can be used to view only the restaurants that match the filter criteria. The filter is made active by clicking the small arrow at the side of a column's heading. To make a successful spreadsheet/database try, as far as possible, to fill each cell of the spreadsheet.

The filter and sort buttons are in the 'Data' tab on the toolbar.

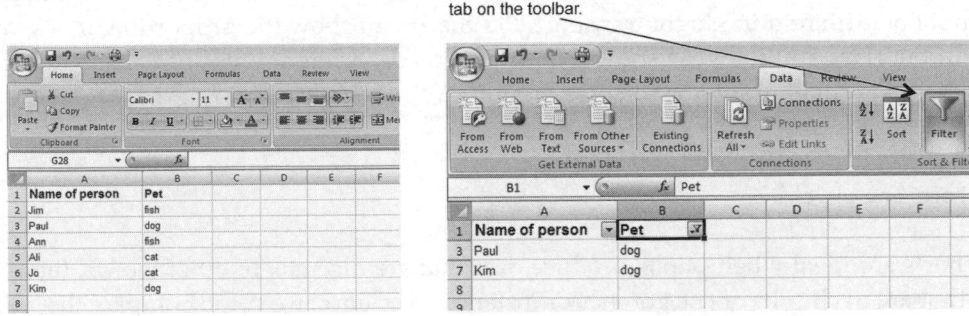

Figure 7.4 Filtering information

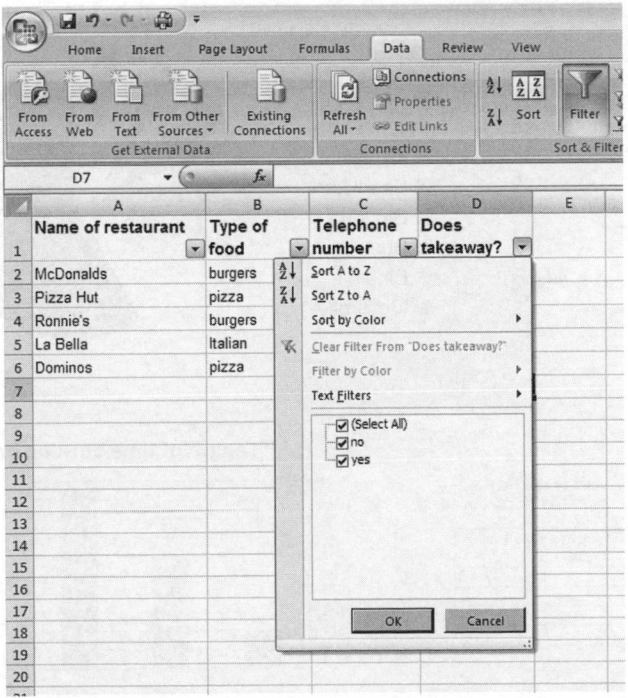

Figure 7.5 Filtering information

Other spreadsheets that could act like databases include data gathered on:

- children in the class – hair colour, height, shoe size, pet, favourite TV programme;
- animals – legs, carnivore or herbivore, covering (e.g. feathers, scales);
- favourite TV shows – type of show, start time, star of the show;
- countries – continent, language, capital, name of highest mountain, height;
- favourite books – title, author, suitable age, number of pages, whether it is illustrated.

Displaying information in charts

Pie charts

Using data from spreadsheets to create bar charts, pie charts and line graphs is one of the main advantages of spreadsheets. Pie charts in particular are easy to produce from data on a spreadsheet and are highly informative. Pie charts are almost impossible for primary-age children to draw using a protractor, pencil and paper. Pie charts can be drawn showing the proportion of blackbirds that were seen, or the proportion of children who travelled to school on different modes of transport. Pie charts can show the proportion of boys and girls in the class and they can show the proportion of different types of vehicle that pass the school in a five-minute period (see Figure 7.6).

Bar charts and pie charts

Bar charts are ideal when pupils produce data that are discrete. In other words, these are data that are in chunks or categories. For instance, in science, we could compare the length of time that a candle will burn in a small, medium or large container. The size of container is a category, and we cannot envisage a scale that includes smallish medium containers. Compare this with line graphs (see below).

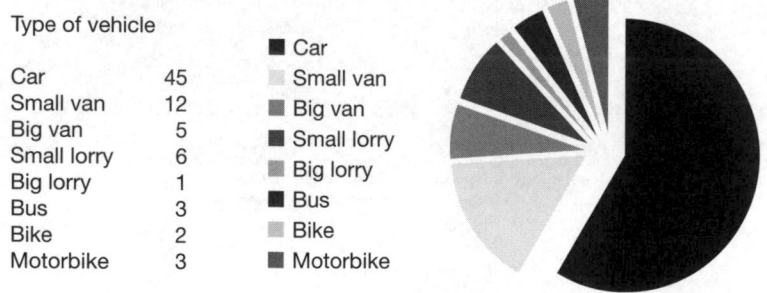

Type of vehicle		
Car	45	■ Car
Small van	12	▨ Small van
Big van	5	■ Big van
Small lorry	6	■ Small lorry
Big lorry	1	▨ Big lorry
Bus	3	■ Bus
Bike	2	▨ Bike
Motorbike	3	■ Motorbike

Figure 7.6

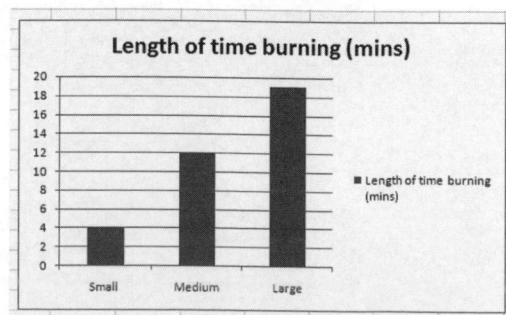

Figure 7.7

Bar charts like this can be produced from spreadsheets in a variety of contexts, such as:

- the heights of mountains;
- the lengths of rivers;
- the lengths of monarchs' reigns;
- the speed of cars.

Displaying information in graphs

Line graphs

Line graphs are ideal when the children produce data that are continuous. In other words, data that are on a scale such as temperature, time, area, distance or mass are continuous data. For instance, in science, we could measure the capacity of jars and measure the length of time that candles will burn in each jar. Both sets of data are continuous (see Figure 7.8).

Manipulating data

Spreadsheets can help the children by doing calculations on data. The 'equals' sign is the most important symbol when using spreadsheets to manipulate data. Pressing the 'equals' sign tells the computer the pupils are about to ask it to work on a formula. For instance, formulae can be set up to calculate the average from a column of numbers. To do this:

1 tap the 'equals' sign;
2 click on the word 'AVERAGE' or type the word 'AVERAGE';
3 drag over the numbers to average.

Children will also enjoy using spreadsheets to plan their pocket-money purchases and savings. They can use the spreadsheet to show their income over several weeks, plus what they spend. They can ask 'what if' questions, such as 'what if I spend half as much on comics – how long will it be before I can afford that new computer game?'.

Here are examples of how data can be manipulated at different stages.

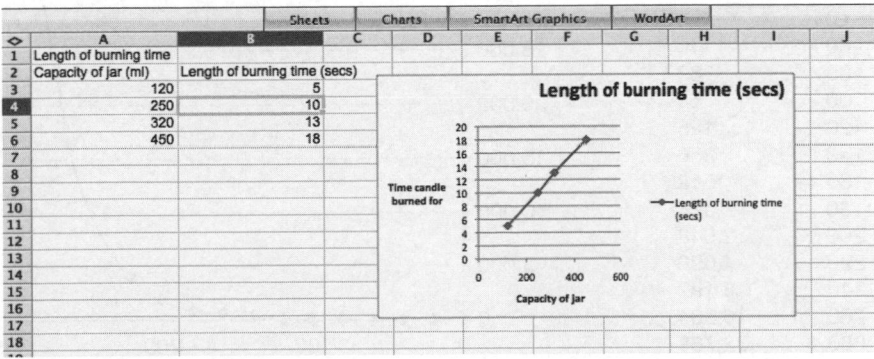

Figure 7.8

	A	B	C	D	E	F
1	Cost of 80g flour in pence	Cost 1 egg in pence	Cost 70g butter in pence	Total cost to make five buns in pence	Selling price of five buns	Profit on five buns
2	5	20	20	SUM A2:C2	Enter price in pence	=E2–D2

Figure 7.9

Modelling business and enterprise

Spreadsheets are used extensively in business to model real life before it happens. A business that is embarking on a new venture will want to see what happens to profit and loss, depending on how many items are sold and how much it costs the business to make them. Many schools are involved in real-enterprise education, where the children produce goods and services for sale. Use spreadsheets to model the costs and income. Figure 7.9 is an example of a simple spreadsheet. Children can see how this operates and what happens when different selling prices are entered.

Modelling changes using spreadsheets

Spreadsheets can be used to show dramatic changes in population using simple formulae. If we suppose that a human population of two people doubles in each generation, and we assume that generations are twenty years apart, the results are sobering and dramatic. After 200 years (ten generations), the population has risen a thousand-fold, and, after only twenty-five generations, the number of people in the population is over 67 million!

To create this spreadsheet (see Figure 7.10):

1 Type the word 'Years' into A1 and type the word 'Population' into B1.
2 Type '0' into A2 and type '=2' into B2.
3 Type '20' into A3 and type '=B2*2' into B3.

Years	Population
0	2
20	4
40	8
60	16
80	32
100	64
120	128
140	256
160	512
180	1,024
200	2,048
220	4,096
240	8,192
260	16,384
280	32,768

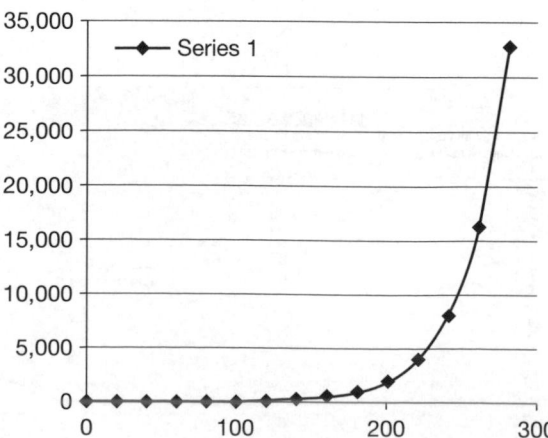

Figure 7.10

4 Highlight the numbers in the 'years' column and drag down using the autofill option (it is the small cross in the bottom right of the cell).
5 Highlight B3 and again use the autofill to drag and paste the formula.
6 Highlight the titles and columns and click 'Insert'; then choose a scattergraph.

This simple table can model the growth of bacteria (they double every 20 minutes, in ideal circumstances), yeast and greenfly. In fact, any breeding population can be shown like this. There is a tale that, in Persia, a wise old adviser was offered a gift by the shah. The adviser said that his majesty had merely to pay him one grain of wheat on the first square of a chess board, then two grains on the second, four on the third and so on, doubling until he reached the final square. The ensuing gift bankrupted the exchequer – try it and see!

Combining text with graphs and charts

One of the great advantages of using spreadsheets is that they can easily be pasted into WP documents to produce well-presented work that combines tables, charts, text and graphics. For instance, in a project on Egypt, the rainfall and sunshine amounts for London and Cairo can be compared. The data can be entered into a spreadsheet, and the children can produce their own charts and graphs. The BBC weather website has several very useful sources of information.

Motivating reluctant learners

Designing and making their own simple spreadsheet are an easy way for pupils to carry out calculations, model reality and draw attractive and colourful charts and graphs. This allows learners to focus on the underlying learning about history, maths, geography or science, rather than on the mechanics of the basic calculations.

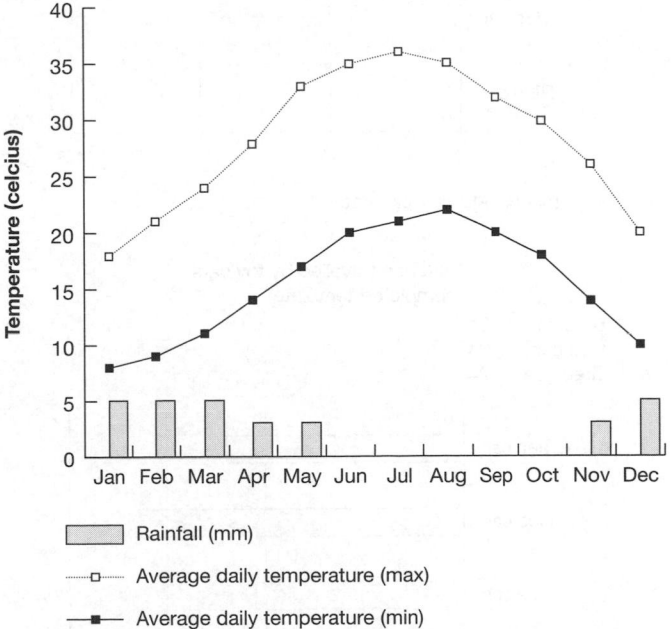

Figure 7.11 Average temperature and rainfall in Cairo

Source: BBC Weather

How spreadsheets can help teachers

Keeping records

Class marks can be recorded, averaged and graphed using spreadsheets.

Improving efficiency and differentiation through using templates

Templates are especially useful when dealing with spreadsheets. They enable the teacher or gifted and talented pupils to design and make a spreadsheet that the class can use to record their work or to produce graphs and charts. To produce a template in a spreadsheet program, create the intended layout with the headings and text required. (It should always have the word 'Name' in the top left-hand corner, or it may be hard to trace the child who produced it at a later date.) Then choose 'Save as . . .' and the template option. Make sure the document is saved in a folder where the children will easily find it, and not in a general template folder on the computer, set up by Microsoft or another manufacturer.

One special feature in a spreadsheet template is the ability to produce a blank template with a blank bar chart, ready for use, if the spreadsheet table is set up without data and the bar chart axes are prepared. Figure 7.12 shows the template, and Figure 7.13 shows the completed table. The child can save the newly completed chart, and the original remains unaltered. Templates with differentiated levels of support and complexity can be saved for children of different abilities or experience.

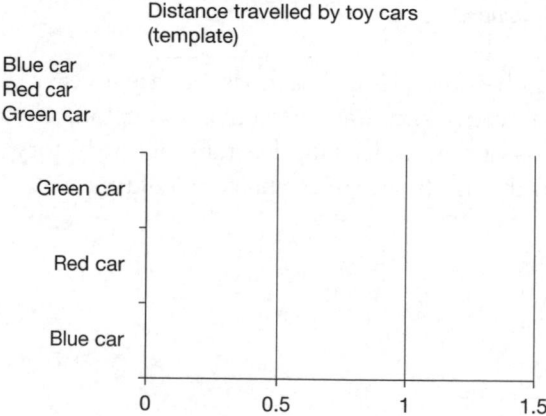

Figure 7.12 Template for pupils to add toy-car data

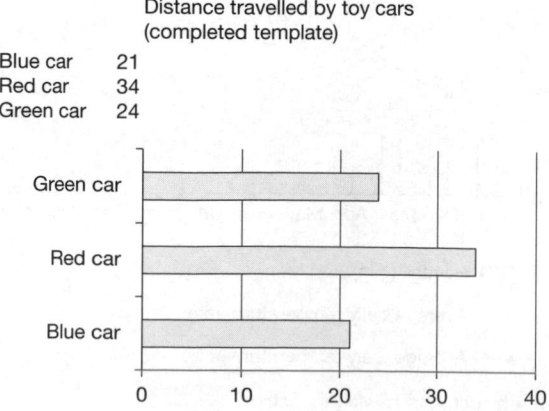

Figure 7.13 Chart to show distances travelled by toy cars

Table 7.1 *Progression in spreadsheet activities in KS1, Lower KS2 and Upper KS2*

KS1

Skills and techniques	Spreadsheet activities for KS1, including cross-curricular ideas
Make simple tables	Use a simple two-column table to record what happens in a scientific experiment. Record information in a table about the way children travel to school.
Make simple pie and bar charts	Make a bar chart using data about favourite food. Make a spreadsheet about the characteristics of pets. Draw a pie chart of boys/girls or who prefers dogs/prefers cats.
Sort data	Use the sorting data buttons to rank the size of children's handspans. Rank the results of scientific experiments, such as the distance travelled by a car off a ramp. Sort simple two-column tables about children's heights.
Rank data	Rank the children's names in alphabetical order, then reverse the order. Vary this by ranking according to surname in alphabetical order.
Use formulae	Create a simple table of multiplication calculations. (In column A, type a list of numbers. In column B, type the words 'multiplied by'. In column C, type a list of numbers. In column D, type =A1*C1. Highlight cell D1 and drag down to paste the calculation in each cell of column D.)
Model business activity	Use the spreadsheet program to show the income from selling different numbers of biscuits.

Lower KS2

Skills and techniques	Spreadsheet activities for LKS2, including cross-curricular ideas
Rank data	Rank the price of different sweets and chocolate brands.
Sort data	Sort tables so that similar items of data are listed close together, such as books of similar length or interest level as voted by readers.
Filter information	Make and filter information in a spreadsheet about the books that are popular in the class – ask the children to plan the headings.
Draw pie charts	In geography, draw pie charts that show the proportion of people who live in different countries of Europe.
Use formulae	Use the average facility to calculate series of averages from a science investigation.
Model business activity	Extend the spreadsheet above to calculate costs and compare them with income to work out profit.

Upper KS2

Skills and techniques	Spreadsheet activities for UKS2 including cross-curricular ideas
Rank data	Rank world cities in order of population.
Sort data	Gather data together that highlight similarities such as the rainfall in different locations.
Filter information	Filter a sheet with information about the characteristics of dinosaurs.
Draw pie and bar charts	In geography and history, draw pie charts showing the types of shop in the local shopping area compared with types of shop in the town centre or out-of-town site. Compare this with historical data from Kelly's Street Directories, which can be accessed at: www.historicaldirectories.org.
Use formulae	Make a series of comparison spreadsheets based on the KS1 stage idea above. How many times taller than the children is a tree, an elephant or a giraffe?
Model business activity	Build a more complex spreadsheet that takes into account costs of fuel and rental of the kitchen when calculating the costs and profits of a business.

8 Database software in the primary classroom

Introduction

Databases are collections of data. The data about each object or event are collected in a record. For each record, data are arranged by category, such as eye colour. These categories are called fields. Figure 8.1 is an example showing records of the children in a class, with fields about their eye colour, shoe size and favourite food. Databases have become a very important part of modern life. A huge amount of data about each of us is held in gigantic computer systems. Road vehicle tax information, CRB checks, NHS records, store loyalty cards etc. all contain information about us. Discuss with older children whether it is a good thing that the government and shops have so much information about us.

Databases and spreadsheets have many features in common, and it will be an individual choice about which of the two types of software a teacher feels is best. For the majority of data-handling, spreadsheets are simpler to create, easier to use and more straightforward to interpret. Databases allow slightly easier and more sophisticated searches of the data than are available with spreadsheets. For instance, the children can write simple sentences such as, 'Show all entries that have height greater than 1.5 m', and the database will carry out the filtering. Constructing a database makes children concentrate on the features that are measurable, important and recordable. For instance, in science, when compiling a database on farm animals, children would focus on features such as number of legs, tail or not, body covering.

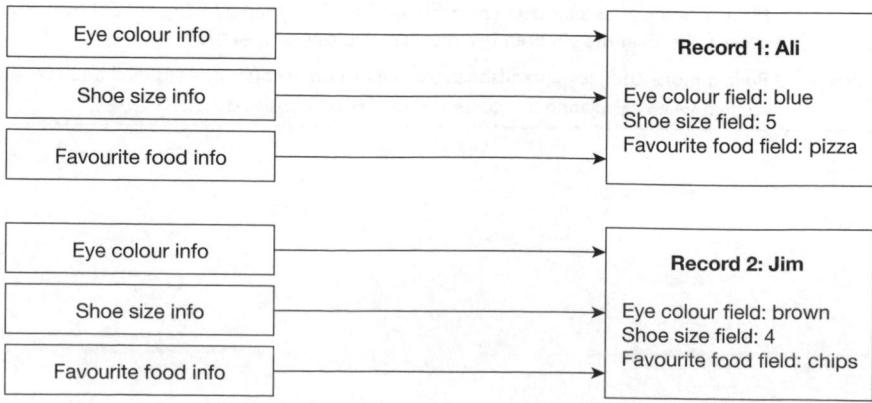

Figure 8.1

National Curriculum requirements

As part of the 'essentials for learning and life' (ICT capability), children learn how to:

- **Find and select information:** When using databases, children need to check that the data support or disprove their ideas. For instance, they can find out about the different calorific values of a range of foods and then select only the ones they wish to study.
- **Create, manipulate and process information:** When using databases, children will find averages of sets of data. For instance, when charting the distance travelled by a car off a ramp, they can compile data and compare the distance travelled by different cars.
- **Collaborate, communicate and share information:** When using databases, children can use information about different world religions, such as does the religion have one or many gods? In a different area of study, children in one school could keep data about the weather over a week and compare it with a school in a different part of the country or a different part of the world.
- **Refine and improve their work:** When using databases, children can add to, and refine, the information they record. For instance, they can continue to add information to a database about class library books as more people add information to a database that contains information about the author, length of the book, reading difficulty, what type of book it is and the score readers give the book.

How databases can help children

Grouping and sorting data

When researching the history of their area, children are able to create and complete databases using information from censuses completed in the surrounding area. A comparison with local, present-day information gathered informally by the class would reveal many contrasts. For example, the 1891 census of most areas of the country would reveal that the majority of men worked the land or dug coal or other minerals. The pupils can use a database to ask questions about the data such as, 'How many labourers were there in our area?' or 'How many people lived in the workhouse?'.

Recording data

Each record looks like a table of information. Figure 8.2 is an example created to record information about the physical characteristics of children.

Most databases allow you to see the data as a summary table (see Figure 8.3).

How databases can help teachers

Keeping records

Databases can allow teachers to keep records of children's personal details, such as age, address and phone number. This is usually done centrally by the school secretary, on a local authority database. Note that, in this context, a spreadsheet may be used as a database.

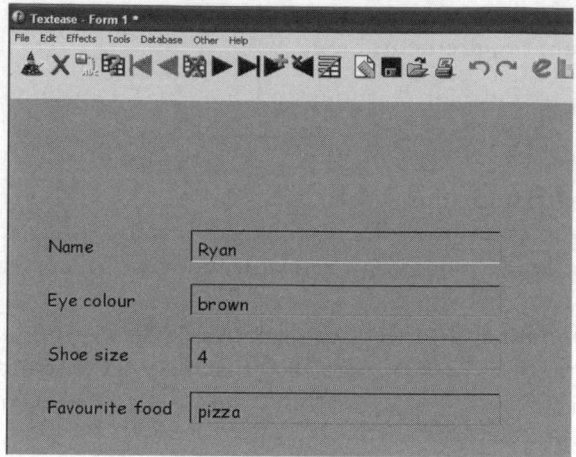

Figure 8.2

	Name	Eye colour	Shoe size	Favourite food
1	Ryan	brown	4	pizza
2	Katie	blue	3	ice cream
3	Dylan	green	4	fruit
4	Carys	blue	3	ice cream
5	Charlie	brown	2	fruit

Figure 8.3

Tracking pupils' progress

In some schools, teachers use a database to help track pupil progress against nationally set standards and to work out which pupils they wish to target to improve the school's SAT rating. Ethically, this poses problems for many people, as pupils may be targeted for help more for the benefit of the school than for their own benefit, and it can result in undue pressure being placed on a small number of selected children.

Table 8.1 *Progression in database activities*

KS1	
Skills and techniques	*Database (DB) activities for KS1, including cross-curricular ideas*
Add to an existing database	The teacher creates a database that records the physical characteristics of the children in the class. The children add to this database. Gather data on pets, including fields such as number of legs, does it have a tail and type of body covering.
Interrogate the database	The children interrogate the database with simple questions, such as, 'How many animals/children have black fur/hair?'. The DB will show all records that are equal to black fur/hair.

Lower KS2	
Skills and techniques	*Database activities for LKS2, including cross-curricular ideas*
Create a simple database about books	Create a database that can be used in the classroom about books and stories. The fields might be: Is the book exciting? Is the book aimed at boys, girls or both? Is it easy to read? Does it have illustrations? In each case, the importance of using standardised entries will need to be emphasised. For instance, if one child completes the fields about whether the book has pictures with the word 'yes', and the next one types 'lots', then the database, when sorted, would not recognise the two entries as both meaning that the book is illustrated.
Interrogate a database	Search a minibeast database to find minibeasts that have 6 legs and live in damp places.
Create charts	Sort data and create charts to help answer questions, e.g. about the types of building material used in different localities.

Upper KS2	
Skills and techniques	*Database activities for UKS2, including cross-curricular ideas*
Add fields to a database	Add further fields to a database the pupils are given.
Sort records in a database	Sort a database of inventions to find those before or after a certain date, or those that happened in the UK and those in other countries.
Create a database designed to record associated data. Children choose the fields for the data	The children could create a database about the weather. This might include fields such as: temperature at 9 a.m.; temperature at 3 p.m.; amount of rainfall; amount of cloud cover; reading on barometer; strength of wind.

9 Branching database software in the primary classroom

Introduction

Branching databases are also sometimes referred to as keys or binary databases. The software can be used in one of two ways. The first is when the user has an object that they do not recognise. By answering the computer's questions about the object, the user can name the unknown object. This is using the computer as an expert system in much the same way as a naturalist will use a key to name a leaf, a flower or a small animal. Doctors increasingly use branching databases to help them narrow down a disease they might be presented with. Branching databases have even more potential for learning when children construct their own. They have to devise simple questions that divide a group of objects. Young children should do this on paper until they understand the principle.

Devising their own keys means that children have to pay attention to the important features of sets of objects. In addition, they have to frame questions in a very precise manner. 'Is it big?' is not a useful dividing question, but 'Is the bird bigger than a sparrow?' is likely to be a good dividing question in a key about birds. Branching databases have many uses across the curriculum, but it is in helping to teach science that they are particularly useful. Branching databases frequently appear in SATs, where children are required to name an unusual plant or animal using the database.

When designing their own branching database, children are required to look at objects in considerable detail and decide which features are important.

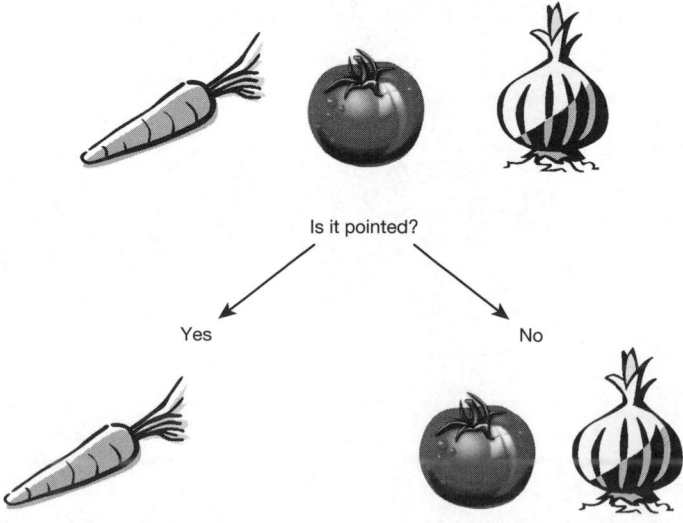

Figure 9.1

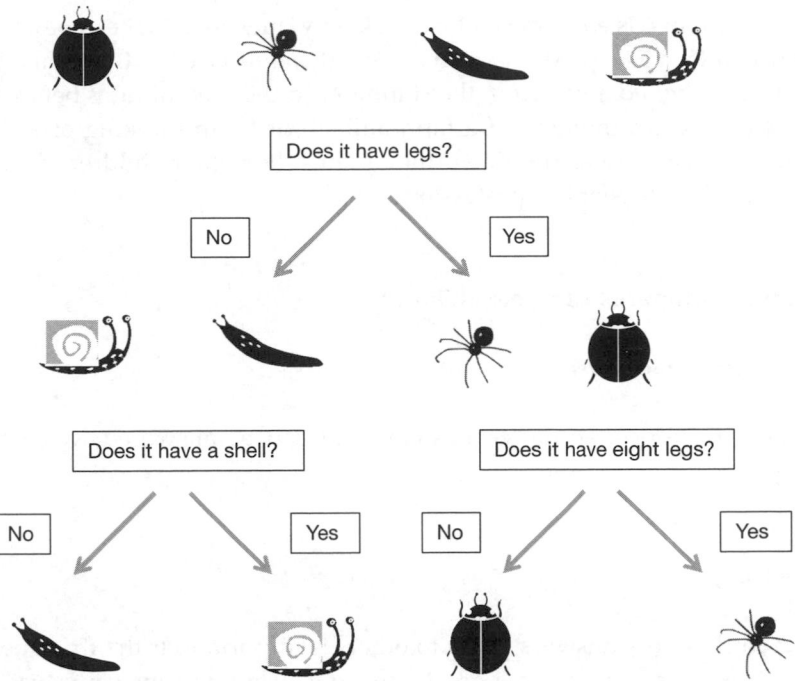

Figure 9.2 Minibeast branching database

Branching databases promote the ability to think logically and answer structured questions in a particular way. They make children focus on the important aspects of the object and distinguish these from the unimportant features. The most important aspect of using branching databases is that the child becomes the expert, and the computer is merely the repository of the information. The child teaches the computer, rather than the other way round.

National Curriculum requirements

As part of the 'essentials for learning and life' (ICT capability), children learn how to:

- **Find and select information:** When using branching databases, children need to focus on the most important aspects of appearance or function. For instance, when creating a branching database to sort a group of different fruits, the children will have to devise their own questions to check that the data support or disprove their ideas. Another time, they might find out about the different calorific values of a range of foods and then select only those they wish to study.
- **Create, manipulate and process information:** When using branching databases, children will have to devise questions that produce sensible divisions.
- **Collaborate, communicate and share information:** When using branching databases, children will need to work in groups to produce large and comprehensive databases.
- **Refine and improve their work:** When using branching databases, children can add to and refine their data. For instance, they can add new objects to the set of objects they are dividing.

The main challenge is ensuring children ask only questions that can be answered 'yes' or 'no'. Many children ask questions such as, 'What colour is it?', rather than, 'Is it green?'. A little practice is needed away from the computer in the few minutes before break, with the teacher saying 'I am thinking of a farm animal' or 'I am thinking of a number' and coaching the best way to narrow down the options. For older children, you could play 'twenty questions' with people's professions.

How branching databases can help children

Phrasing productive questions

The importance of asking accurate questions that can be answered 'yes' or 'no' needs emphasising.

Listening carefully

Listening carefully to the answers given to others is important. If the first question asked is 'Is the number you are thinking of greater than ten?', and the answer is 'yes', then there is no point in asking if the number is less than five.

Paying close attention to physical characteristics

Deciding which features to focus on with questions is important. For instance, when making a branching key to identify different rocks, the children will have to focus on particular features, e.g. the presence of crystals, whether there are grains, or if the rock is heavy for its size.

Table 9.2 *Progression in branching database activities in Key Stages 1 and 2*

KS1	
Skills and techniques	*Branching database activities, including for KS1 cross-curricular ideas*
Use a very simple branching key to identify the odd one out	Make sets of three, where two are clearly related, and one is the odd one out. Find a question that will sort one item from the other two items.
Use a ready-made branching key	Use a branching database from Black Cat, Textease or 2simple to sort materials or minibeasts.
On paper, create a branching key of up to six real objects	Write the yes/no-question branching key on paper. Then produce a similar branching key on a computer.

Lower KS2

Skills and techniques	Branching database activities, including for LKS2 cross-curricular ideas
Use a branching database to identify one item from a set of up to six	Use a branching database with up to six items to identify one item from its picture.
Children devise their own branching key	Create a branching key using simple items such as pets.
Ask questions using yes/no answers and a simple branching database with items that are high contrast	Make a database to sort items, such as African animals or fruit and vegetables, that are both familiar and with a high contrast.
Add two new items to a database that already contains at least six items	After creating and using a database about, for instance, favourite TV shows, children then add a further two items.

Upper KS2

Skills and techniques	Branching database activities, including for UKS2 cross-curricular ideas
Children use a branching database to identify a completely unfamiliar object	Identify one plant from a branching database. The only clue held by the children is an unnamed picture of their target item.
Children devise their own branching key	Children devise their own keys using sets of their choosing. For instance, they can devise a branching key of minibeasts. This is used by other children to identify unknown minibeasts. Users of the branching key add further examples of minibeasts to the branching key, adding a new question when the existing key does not recognise the new animal. Branching databases or keys are used extensively by naturalists to sort and name specimens.
Use a branching database to identify numbers	Differentiated maths activities using a branching database are easy to arrange. Give less experienced children three numbers below 10. Ask them to sort them with questions such as: Is it less than 6? Is it even? Is it the number of sides that a square has? Older and more experienced children could be challenged to sort their set of numbers with more creative number questions.
Ask yes/no questions about items with similar characteristics	Create a branching key that relies on subtle differences between, for example, rock specimens.
Use a branching key on a hand-held device	Use a hand-held device on a field trip to identify plants and animals, e.g. Wildkey.
Add three new items to a database that already contains at least twelve items	Build up, and add to, a complex branching key that incorporates, for instance, information about most of the pupils in the class.

10 Data loggers in the primary classroom

Introduction

A data logger is a device that detects temperature, sound, movement and light in the environment. It consists of a box that is plugged into a USB port and a sensor that is plugged into the box. The changes that the sensor detects are recorded by a continuously changing number display, as a table or, more usually, a chart or graph.

Data loggers perform readings with very little input from the user. A data logger will automatically produce a graph of results that is fairly straightforward for children to interpret. Figure 10.1 shows the graphs produced by a data logger that has a light detector and temperature sensor connected. These graph lines are from a south-facing wall during the school day. Interpreting the graph is an important part of the investigation.

How data loggers can help children

Concentrating on the underlying science

Data loggers can help children to concentrate on the underlying science, rather than just making a series of routine measurements. The graphs generated by the software give an instant picture of what is happening. If the data logger is set to record as a can of hot water is cooling, the graph it produces tells that story of the drop in temperature with great clarity. A data logger left overnight in the classroom, with sound and light sensors plugged in, will give the bare bones of a story. When did the lights get turned off? When was sunset? What caused that sudden spike in sound at about midnight? At what time did the cleaners come into the room?

By automatically detecting, recording and graphing changes in the environment, the data logger removes the need for children to take a series of readings, record them and spend a long time drawing a graph. These repetitive activities can sometimes appear to be the point of the lesson, where, in reality, the real science activity, the interpretation, begins only once the charts are drawn. For example, when children are comparing the rate at which different volumes of hot water cool, the repeated temperature readings take up a great deal of time and concentration. The data logger will patiently record readings of temperature in four containers for as long as required.

Figure 10.1
Data loggers can record light, temperature and sound levels. Some will record movement as well. They can use built-in sensors or external probes for recording data from places that are too small for the whole data logger. They can be used remotely or connected to a computer

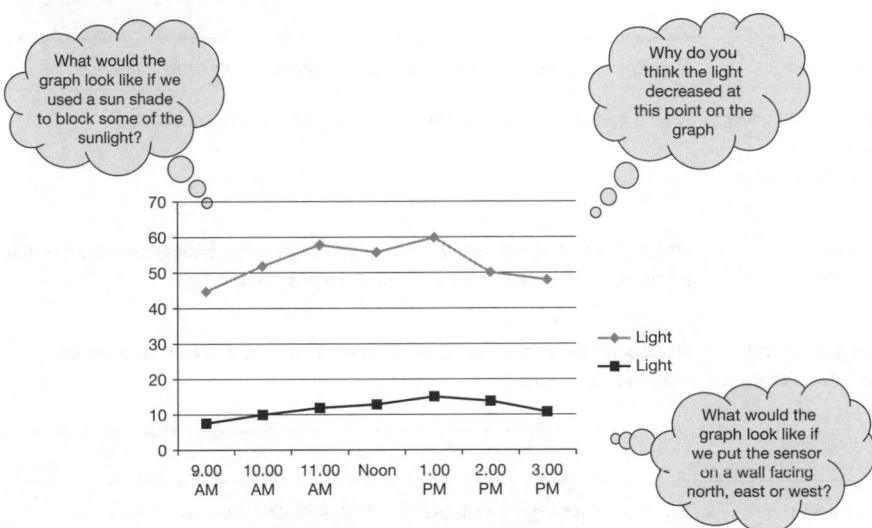

Figure 10.2 Light levels recorded during the day in two different places

---

National Curriculum requirements

The National Curriculum (1999) requires that children should make systematic observations, including the use of ICT for data-logging (KS2/Sc1/2f).

As part of the 'essentials for learning and life' (ICT capability), children learn how to:

- **Find and select information:** When using a data logger, children need to select the changes that they want to record. For instance, they can find out about the changes that happen in a cooling can of water, or the changes in light let through by different fabrics. Children need to be able to make choices about activities with data loggers that are likely to yield interesting results.
- **Create, manipulate and process information:** When using data loggers, children will be able to convert the data into spreadsheet columns. This allows the data to be manipulated and changes to be made.
- **Collaborate, communicate and share information:** When using data loggers, children can share data with other members of the class. Children can use the charts and graphs produced to explain their ideas to other people. For example, the amount of light that passes through different fabrics can be shown in tables or charts using the data logger.
- **Refine and improve their work:** When using data loggers, children can add to and refine their data. They can repeat their tests and compare the different tables and charts produced using the same procedure.

Taking snapshot readings

In addition to taking a series of readings, data loggers can be used to take snapshot readings. For example, children can use a light detector to record the amount of light allowed through by different fabrics. This can be part of a project on making the best curtains for a dolls' house.

Table 10.1 *Progression in using data loggers from KS1 to KS2*

KS1

Skills and techniques	Suggested data-logging activities for KS1, including cross-curricular ideas
Collect data and describe and compare observations and findings (Sc1/2h)	Use a light sensor to find the brightest place in the classroom.
Sort and group information using ICT (Sc1/2h)	Use temperature sensors in tins of ice to see what happens if they are left to warm up in the classroom until all the ice is melted.
Explore light and sound and how we sense them (Sc4/3c)	Use sound sensors to compare home-constructed earmuffs made using different materials.

Lower KS2

Skills and techniques	Suggested data-logging activities for LKS2, including cross-curricular ideas
Capture, record and analyse data, using a range of instruments, including sensors (Sc1/2f)	Compare the insulating properties of different materials.
Offer simple explanations of findings (Sc1/2i)	Place the sound sensor at different distances from sound source and generate a chart to show how rapidly the sound detected declined.
Identify and group materials using properties (Sc4/3b)	Incorporate tests on materials using data loggers, including opacity.

Upper KS2

Skills and techniques	Suggested data-logging activities for UKS2, including cross-curricular ideas
Use equipment and tools, including ICT, to make work more effective and efficient (Sc1/2e)	Use the light sensor to detect light passing through different fabrics as part of an investigation into fabrics.
Make and record accurate measurements and detailed observations (Sc1/2c)	Compare the experience of making manual observations of temperature with those made by data-logging devices.
Decide the best approach to use (Sc1/2k)	Include consideration of the automatic qualities of data-logging when deciding how to capture and record data.

11 Digital cameras, movies and photocopiers in the primary classroom

Introduction

Digital cameras are now a standard piece of equipment in many primary classrooms. They have advantages over traditional film cameras in terms of cost and the ease with which the images can be transferred to a computer, manipulated with graphics software and used in a range of documents. Other advantages include the facility to display images on an LCD screen just after they are taken, the capacity to store thousands of images on a single, small memory device and the ability to delete unwanted images to release storage space. Some cameras can record video with sound and perform simple image editing as well.

The use of digital photography in primary education makes learning more enjoyable and personalised, as pupils can include their own artwork or copyright-free images, which can be instantly inserted and modified. Digital cameras can be easy to use and encourage creative exploration and innovation. Photos that are taken digitally can be shared electronically with a wide audience. They can be printed, sent via e-mail, inserted into documents and uploaded onto websites and online albums.

With even the simplest software, digital images can be changed in colour and size or altered electronically to create special effects. Multiple images can be taken at negligible cost, so that the photographer does not have to get each shot right first time. There is no penalty for mistakes, which encourages creative experimentation and risk taking. Where the desired effect is not reached with the camera, software can crop, adjust colour and brightness and compensate for lens distortion.

Visual literacy is increasingly recognised as a skill that pupils need to acquire, and using images they have taken in their work is one step towards this goal. Visual images of any kind enhance communication and help to share experiences: sharing a picture can be quicker and give more detail than trying to explain something in words. Communication can be enhanced by use of images in addition to words, as an image can, as the saying goes, paint a thousand words. An inspection of ICT in primary schools in 2005 recorded that, in the best practice seen, images from the school's digital cameras were used effectively to stimulate discussion and promote language development. Prensky (2007) says, 'It is hard for me to imagine a tool better able to help education than each student having in their hand a camera, especially one that can transmit the pictures they take anywhere.' He suggests many uses for digital cameras, including the idea that photos (and videos) can allow us to see ourselves as we are when we talk and get useful feedback. 'When you give the children a camera there is almost no interruption to workflow' (Brennan 2010).

Points to consider when choosing a digital camera for use in school

Does the camera need to take movies and stills?

Cameras that record both movies and stills are suitable for taking short movie clips rather than full movie production, depending on the size of the memory card. They are fine for short recordings on field trips, for PE and drama evaluation or for recording experiments in science. If movie making is likely to be a regular goal, then a dedicated digital movie camera may be required.

Camera size and resolution

You will need to consider the age and manual dexterity of the children who will use the camera. Very young children may work best with the chunky, easy-to-grab and safe-to-drop type, of which there are several on the market. However, the quality of the pictures is not always high with these, especially if they are sold more as toys than recording devices. The control buttons should be large enough for the children to use and well spaced, so that they aren't pressed accidentally. Smaller cameras may require more careful handling, but the resolution of the pictures is usually higher. Camera resolution and, therefore, picture quality are measured in megapixels (MP). Pictures taken at low resolution are suitable for adding to e-mails or web pages, but they may appear grainy when printed out. If pupils need to make 5" × 7" prints, a camera with a resolution of 2 MP or more will be adequate; for printing 8" × 10" photos, a camera with a resolution of 3 MP or more will be required.

Viewfinders

The most versatile cameras include both a regular, eye-level viewfinder and an LCD screen. An LCD screen helps pupils compose their pictures, as well as view them immediately, and they are easier to use at high or low angles or in places where the child's head and the camera will not easily reach. However, these screens are hard to see outside in bright light and can be damaged by mishandling.

Zoom lens

Most mid-price cameras include an optical zoom lens, which gives a wide choice of composition when framing a shot, allowing both wide-angle and telephoto shots. Many models also include a digital zoom, in which the camera software, rather than the lens, enlarges the image. As this leads to pictures of poorer quality, first consider the camera's optical zoom rating. A lens with a rating between 3× and 5× should be suitable for most schools' needs.

Built-in flash

A built-in flash is a useful tool for taking pictures indoors and in other low-lit areas. It can also be used outside to illuminate objects in the foreground that are not well lit.

Storage media

Digital photos are stored in the camera on either memory sticks, SmartMedia cards or CompactFlash cards. To transfer the photos to the computer, the memory stick has to be inserted into a USB port on the computer, while memory cards must be inserted into a card reader, which may either be part of the computer or an external card reader that plugs into a USB port. The more photos a card will store, the more it costs, and a high-capacity memory card can store hundreds of photos. Although one high-capacity card gives more memory for your money, it may be less convenient for a class sharing a single camera. Consider instead buying several smaller cards and one or two media readers. Then, once one group has finished taking pictures, they can remove the media card and pass the camera to the next group. Some cameras can even store photos on regular floppy disks or CD-ROMs, which allows pupils to load their own disks onto computers without the need for a media reader. Some printers, such as those in commercial outlets, can print straight from any of these devices. The most common file format for storing image data for still photos is a JPEG (the Joint Photography Experts Group standard). There are many file formats for storing digital movies, including AVI, DV and MPEG.

Remember that not all images need long-term storage. After a walk to identify and digitally record shapes in the school grounds, the images may need to be seen only a couple of times before deletion.

Power supply

Digital cameras have high power requirements. Three types of battery can be used: the first is the standard, off-the-shelf, one-use battery, most commonly lithium AA. These are quite cheap but quickly used up, especially if an LCD screen is used for taking photos. Second, some people prefer to use rechargeable lithium AA batteries. Third, there are proprietary batteries made to the camera manufacturer's specifications, which are rechargeable up to 500 times. They are expensive to buy but last longer than other rechargeable batteries. It is best to have spare batteries of any type, so that there are always some fully charged and ready for use. Rechargeable batteries should be allowed to run down completely before recharging, or the capacity of the battery to recharge fully will be reduced.

Storing digital films and photos

Digital images take up a lot of space on a hard disk, so that it may be more practical to back up all useful images on to CDs or an external hard drive. Saving to an organised filing system, so that the required images are easily found, and backing up to CDs or other external devices are techniques that need to be taught and should form a regular part of classroom practice.

Good practice when using digital cameras

Anyone working with children and cameras needs to consider the school's policy on taking and displaying images of children. Written consent is normally sought from parents at the start of the school year, and so the use of digital images may vary from child to child. Never publish personal information or pupil photos on the Internet or a classroom web page.

To obtain the best results and to minimise risk of damage to the camera, teach pupils some basic camera skills and remind them regularly about safe practice. They will need to know about planning a composition, zooming, or panning on a movie camera, and, crucially, about keeping the camera still to avoid blurry shots. They could devise their own list of good-practice rules, but those suggested below would be a good start for the teacher.

1 Always use the neck or wrist strap when carrying a camera, to minimise the danger of dropping it.
2 Do not touch the lens or LCD, as fingerprints spoil the picture quality.
3 Never use a flash close to someone's eyes. This is unpleasant and could be dangerous.
4 For good-quality pictures, hold the camera steady for two seconds before and after taking each shot.
5 Avoid using the LCD screen for composing most pictures if you have a viewfinder, as this uses up the battery very quickly.
6 Turn the camera off and store it in the camera case when it is not in use.

Creating films

Creating films can be very motivating for even the most reluctant learner, as it involves active learning. Films can be made using either dedicated movie cameras, such as Digi-blue, which has its own editing software, or using movie cameras where the editing is done with generic editing software. PCs have Windows Moviemaker to edit films, and, if it is not on your computer, it can be downloaded for free. Macs have iMovie editor. These programs allow film creation on a simple timeline to which stills and move clips can be dragged and then edited. When considering which software to use, price, simplicity of use and the memory available on the computer need to be considered. Further advice on choosing equipment and making movies can be found from the BECTA publication 'Using digital video in teaching and learning' (2003/04), available at: www.mmiweb.org.uk/publications/ict/UsingDigitalVideo.pdf.

National Curriculum requirements

As part of the 'essentials for learning and life' (ICT capability), children learn how to:

- **Find and select information:** Pupils can collect images of people, places and objects to use in all subject areas of their work.
- **Create, manipulate and process information:** Photos can be composed, altered and combined digitally with other media for particular effects. Discussion about this should accompany each stage, to evaluate the value and effect of each process. Pupils should be helped to look critically at the digital images that surround them to assess their intended effects.
- **Collaborate, communicate and share information:** Photos can be used to make information more accessible and to communicate ideas and feelings in articles, artwork, stories, brochures and multimedia presentations. They can be attached to e-mails and inserted into intranets, e-zines and web pages.
- **Refine and improve their work:** Children should be helped to look critically at digital images they have created and find ways to improve both their composition and use.

To obtain good-quality clips, you may need a tripod to avoid camera shake and a good quality microphone, as the one on the camera may not be adequate. External microphones are good for recording dialogue and minimising external and operating noise. Additional lighting may be needed for indoor shots. For further information, see the hardware section of the Becta CD-ROM, *Teaching and learning using digital video*.

How digital cameras can help children

Digital cameras can help children to:

- develop their observation skills;
- gain an understanding of perspective;
- develop their creativity and self-expression;
- try out ideas, revise and make choices;
- collaborate on visual projects;
- create personal character photos of themselves;
- create portfolios of their work;
- improve techniques in PE, gymnastics and dance;
- solve problems to do with recording and illustrating their work;
- develop ideas in role play, e.g. when on a mission as a roving reporter or someone collecting evidence and points of view for a development scheme;
- revise and consolidate learning experiences;
- illustrate written work, including stories, articles, reports, brochures, blogs, e-zines and e-mails;
- create stop-frame animation films where separate images of an object are combined into a sequence to give the appearance of continuous motion;
- record science experiments so as to review what happened when considering their results.

How digital cameras can help teachers

Digital cameras can help teachers to:

- record children's progress, e.g. when working on science investigations;
- keep records of bulky or temporary constructions made by pupils;
- collect coursework evidence in dance, drama or PE;
- record events, activities and school visits to help with follow-up work (if made into a slideshow, a CD copy could be given to each pupil as an end-of-year present);
- make albums, presentations and wall displays of pupils' work for sharing with parents;
- create resources.

Table 11.1 *A progression of ways to use digital cameras in Key Stages 1 and 2*

KS1	
Skills and techniques	*Digital camera activities for KS1, including cross-curricular ideas*
Gather and sort information	Photograph shapes around the school building: circular inspection covers, rectangular windows, triangular eaves.
Explain ideas	Talk about shapes seen and how the camera helps them to see and take the pictures.
Develop fieldwork skills	Take digital photos of features around the school and create a display linking these to the relevant places on a map of the school. Drawings and labels made by the children could be added as well.
Gather information	Film examples of pushes and pulls round the school. Add text/voice-over to create a short presentation about these to share in an assembly.
Store and retrieve information	Take pictures of pupils throughout the year to illustrate how they grow. This is best done outside in full light, with pupils against a wall and with another object in the photo, or a mark made on the wall, so that differences in size through the year can be easily seen. Add commentary about how the data were gathered and what has been learned.
Use ICT to develop ideas	Create stop-motion movies of small items moving to create a picture or building using paperclips, pipe cleaners or construction kits.
Share ideas by presenting them in a variety of forms	Use digital photos and WP text to create a class book about themselves, what they like to do and events they have taken part in during the year. Make a digital version on a CD-ROM to send to each child's home at the end of the year.
Present their work effectively	Add digital photos of science experiments to reports of their results.
Review, modify and evaluate work in progress	Take digital photos of themselves to show their characters, review which locations and stances and props show this most effectively and retake where necessary.
Develop art and design skills	Use digital photos as images in repeating pattern designs.

Lower KS2	
Skills and techniques	*Digital camera activities for LKS2, including cross-curricular ideas*
Develop empathy and imagination skills	Take digital photos of a location from a beetle's point of view, with the camera on or near the ground. A mini tripod would help with this.
Develop creative imagination skills and self-expression	Take digital photos of themselves for development in art and design sessions. Copy into a paint program and add details such as clothes or background or clip-art images the child might be holding (see Fig 11.1). Print a photo they have taken of themselves, cut it out and add to a paper-based collage to tell a story or show something about their character. Copy a digital photo of themselves into a paint program. Use the eraser tool to rub out all but the head. Draw a new body, based on a real or fantasy animal or person, to represent their alter-ego (see Figure 11.2).

Figure 11.1

Figure 11.2

Skills and techniques	Digital camera activities for KS1, including cross-curricular ideas
Develop art techniques pioneered by professional artists such as Andy Warhol and David Hockney	Use multiple images to create photos of people or places as a collage. View the artist's work first and discuss what the technique adds to the pictures. For Andy Warhol-type collages, paste one picture several times into a document, with each version tinted a different colour in a paint or graphics program such as Photoshop. For David Hockney-type pictures, take many photos of one location/person, print and collage together. Can the children develop other ways to use their digital photos? Discuss what the multiple images add to the single-image presentation.
Develop fieldwork skills	Use cameras to record learning and remember details on school trips, e.g. the architecture of a church, the layout of a rock pool or the types of plant seen.
Consider other people's points of view	Add speech bubbles to photos of an event with either humour or particular information as a focus. This can be very illuminating for school visits, science experiments and records of visitors to the school.
Develop art and design skills	Pupils take a full-face photo of themselves and print out head and shoulders, A4 size. Fold a sheet of A4 paper in half down the centre and cover half the portrait with it. Complete the drawing of the face, using the photo to locate the major features. Remove the photo, unfold and complete the portrait.
Communicate with others	Send photos of themselves and the locality to penpals and e-pals. Create a slideshow presentation of a visit or other learning experience to show to peers/parents. Captions and speech bubbles can be added to each photo. Film a school drama about the temptation to steal or tell a lie. Create stop-frame animation films, where separate images of an object such as a small plastic figure are combined into a sequence to give the appearance of continuous motion. Use this to turn a story they have written into a film or advert. Create a local-area display for visitors to the school. Each group of pupils could take photos of different aspects of the area. Add maps and captions to create an informative display. Add pictures to a hyperlinked presentation for visitors to browse at leisure. Hyperlinks from a map of the area will take the viewer to different sections of the presentation. If printed with one slide to a page, this can also be made into a book about the locality.
Collect, review and organise data	Collect distance and close-up pictures of trees in the locality to show details of leaf, trunk, flowers and seeds where possible. Add pictures to a database, where they can be sorted according to tree shape, leaf shape, deciduous/evergreen. Use to decide which trees would be best to add to the school grounds.
Develop knowledge and understanding of places	On a field trip or local walk identify the locations of surveillance cameras. Map them and discuss the value of each in its location and what local people might feel about them. Discuss where pupils feel other cameras might be sited. Note the location of mobile-phone masts and discuss what they add/detract from our culture.
Prepare information	Improve digital photos by cropping, enlarging/reducing and altering the brightness and contrast in a simple editing program.
Organise and reorganise information	Take digital photos of objects from unusual angles and pictures of their own 3D artwork. Organise into a virtual art gallery, according to subject matter, in a hyperlinked presentation. Reorganise into a brochure for the gallery, with text to explain the views of each artist.
Share and exchange information	Use digital photos and film to create a CD-ROM about the school/locality for e-pals Attach compressed digital images to e-mails.
Share quality information in a way that is suitable for the audience	Use claymation to create stop-motion film where a clay or plasticine model is altered every few shots to create the appearance of continuous motion. Use this to tell an updated version of a religious or historical story. Create a weather forecast using still and filmed images and presentations to camera. This could be done for any country studied.
Review, modify and evaluate work in progress	Use digital film to record work in dance, drama, games or gymnastics. Review film to see how to improve techniques.

Upper KS2

Skills and techniques	Digital camera activities for UKS2, including cross-curricular ideas
See things in new ways	Use the macro setting of a digital camera to take images of small details of larger objects. Use as a 'What is this?' quiz. Images are printed then swapped in a session for other pupils to write descriptive text/poem about the shapes, textures, colours in the image, what it might be and where the photo was taken. Modify an image of themselves in a paint program to appear as if in a Tudor painting. Then create a story about themselves in Tudor times.
Develop observation skills	Complete a scavenger hunt with a camera. Pupils have to take photos of a range of objects to help them become familiar with a locality. They might be required to take photos of items such as: • three round objects, three triangular shapes; • a stone inscription; • a shop sign that does not use words; • the softest thing they see; • the most unusual thing they see.
Develop photographic skills	Take and digitally enhance photos and submit to a school photographic competition to be judged by the youngest and oldest classes, or a local photographer. Have a competition for the best caption for some of the pictures.
Use appropriate technologies and skills to present work to an audience	Create a photo story. Download Photostory 3 from http://download.cnet.com/ Photo-Story-3-for-Windows/3000-12511_4-10339154.html. This program puts photos into a slideshow, lets you add music and zoom and pan across the pictures to give the impression of a moving film. Titles, narration and music can be added to personalise the presentation, which is played through Windows MediaPlayer.
Develop fieldwork skills	Create a history/treasure trail of an area using photos taken by pupils. Print as a brochure. Leave spaces for readers to answer questions that are set. Take digital photos of plants in the wild for identification back in class.
Develop knowledge and understanding of places	Add photos of the area to the Geograph website (www.geograph.org.uk). This project is collecting representative photos of every area of Britain.
Prepare information	Use digital photos to create a school brochure for new pupils. Talk about what pictures add to a brochure, story or report. Use storyboards to work out how to film and edit a dance
Organise and reorganise information	Convey key scenes from books and plays or poems, using a video camera. Use framing, sound and position of camera to convey mood and to express characters' feelings. Take and use digital photos in a virtual tour of an area. Upload to the school/class website.
Share quality information in a way that is suitable for the audience	Create news reports on current issues, such as bullying and environmental disasters. Make a movie for a younger class that shows particular skills in DT or science sessions.
Review, modify and evaluate work in progress	Make TV adverts about products pupils have created. Show to a *Dragon's Den* panel for evaluation and modify in the light of comments received. Use digital images as part of a portfolio of work.
Develop art and design skills	Collage photographic images together in a program such as Photoshop or Paint Shop Pro and enhance using the software to create particular effects.
Collect and record data	Film interviews with visitors to the school about their jobs or experiences in WWII.
Develop presentation skills	Add digital photos and charts to a hyperlinked presentation about topic work done in school. Take digital photos to illustrate personal projects and achievements. Save in a hyperlinked portfolio.

12 Digital microscopes and visualisers in the primary classroom

Introduction

Optical microscopes, which require children to look at objects through an eyepiece, present many children with difficulty in focusing. In addition, it is difficult to point out items of interest, as only one person at a time can see the image. Digital microscopes, on the other hand, connect to a computer or use a built-in viewing screen, allowing children to see the magnified image without squinting down an eyepiece. The image can be shared with the teacher or the whole class. There are several brands of digital microscope available on the market, including the Celestron, which is a standalone device with a built-in screen, the Intel QX-3, which only works when plugged directly into the computer via a USB, and the Motic Digiscope, which can be used as a standalone microscope or can be plugged into a computer for the image to be displayed on a screen or interactive whiteboard.

In several respects, the use of digital microscopes has been superseded by the advent of cheap and powerful visualisers, and so the rest of this section will concentrate on these versatile pieces of equipment. A visualiser is a live camera, mounted on a stand, that can be connected to a computer and whiteboard to display magnified images of both 2D and 3D objects. Snapshots of items and short clips of video can be taken and stored for later examination. Another advantage of the visualiser is that the connection between the image on the screen and the object is more immediately obvious.

Visualisers combine the most useful features of overhead projectors and digital microscopes, but with more features than the former and a higher magnification than most digital microscopes available in schools. To be most effective, the visualiser should be permanently connected to the computer and whiteboard, so that it is always available and becomes a routinely used piece of classroom equipment. Visualisers can be connected to any multimedia projector, interactive whiteboard, PC monitor or TV, and can be projected on to any wall or flat surface to provide a large visual impact in lessons and demonstrations. Most are easily portable.

The visualiser can project information from sheets of paper, books, maps, overhead-projector transparencies, children's artwork and even X-rays. Scarce resources, such as a single copy of a book, can be viewed by the entire class. The visualiser can show any 3D resource used in practical sessions, such as maths and science, or artefacts for history, geography and RE sessions. Resources that are too large to fit on the visualiser can be filmed beside it. Items projected can be moved round, so that all sides can be seen, and labels can be added beside particular features. The camera head can be rotated to get different views of an object as it is moved under it, so that pupils get a real feel for the object displayed. It is still desirable for pupils to be able to handle the objects themselves at some point in the lesson. Images can be saved on the visualiser or to a PC, where they can be added to

IWB software for use in a SMART Notebook or Promethean flipchart. When images are saved using the visualiser software, the screen can be split to show the saved image and a new one beside it. Some allow the storing and recall of several images without saving them to the computer. Displaying small items on a large screen greatly increases the involvement of a class, particularly pupils at the back. It helps pupils engage visually and then interactively, through questioning and annotation. Teachers in the Test Bed project (Becta 2007) reported that the image quality of resources on a visualiser is better than those that are scanned or projected. A visualiser enables pupils to view non-digital resources in high definition. Objects can be illuminated from above or below, and images can be mirrored to show reflective symmetry. The top part of some screens can be frozen to display a session title, date or learning objective. Use of a remote control means the teacher does not have to stay by the board, but, when he/she does, he/she need not be standing in front of the whiteboard and sometimes obscuring it, but can be located to one side as the visualiser is used.

Images from the visualiser can be inserted straight into any software application, such as Word or Powerpoint, that has the facility to insert from scanner or camera. Some visualisers can capture and save moving images as well as static ones. Their cameras can be swivelled through 360° to show live action of people in the room. This could be useful to show a pupil speaking from the back of the class, to help the pupil feel more involved and to show who is talking without everyone else having to turn round. It also means that the visualiser camera can act as a webcam for video-conferencing or Skype communication. Windows Movie Maker can be used with the visualiser to record digital videos and edit the files to create high-quality teaching and learning resources. Open Windows Movie Maker and select the 'Capture from video device' option, and the visualiser will be recognised as the video input device. You can also link the visualiser to video-conferencing software or applications such as 2Simple 2Animate, where images from the visualiser can be used to create animation sequences.

There are generally few problems with visualisers other than the initial cost of setting them up and the cost of the lamps, which have a long but finite life. To get the most from this equipment, staff need adequate though not extensive training and need to have the equipment to hand on a daily basis. Bracegirdle (2009) records that some schools are saving whole lessons recorded by the visualiser and storing them on the school's computer network, to be used by pupils who have missed a session or those who need help with

---

National Curriculum requirements

As part of the 'essentials for learning and life' (ICT capability), children learn how to:

- **Find and select information:** Children at KS2 should be taught how to make systematic observations using ICT. Visualisers and digital microscopes can help with this.
- **Create, manipulate and process information:** Images can be kept for use in other applications.
- **Collaborate, communicate and share information:** Pupils should cooperate and share information they have gained. They might e-mail to other schools the images they have collected of wildlife in their area.
- **Refine and improve their work:** Pupils could compare the advantages of microscopes, both standard and digital, with visualisers and assess which are most useful in a range of situations. They should assess what each could add to their work.

homework assignments. However, for most teachers, the use of a visualiser will enhance their current practice, rather than change it.

How visualisers can help children

Visualisers can help pupils to:

- share their work with the rest of the class, by projecting their picture, their maths book or a piece of writing;
- give feedback to peers, to help with both peer and self-assessment against set criteria;
- show certificates, trophies and items of interest to the whole class in a show and tell session, without risk of damage;
- see X-rays of broken limbs, both in negative and positive modes;
- create stop-frame animation films using prepared backgrounds and small figures, such as Lego or plasticine ones;
- assist sight-impaired pupils with larger visuals;
- present their own 'mantle of the expert' session, complete with artefacts, diagrams and pictures;
- engage with a lesson through a range of easily seen artefacts, maps, texts, pictures and charts. The thrill of seeing hugely magnified insects, flowers, crystals, knitted fabric and wrinkly skin should not be underestimated. The images can be stored and referred to later.

How digital microscopes and visualisers can help teachers

Digital microscopes and visualisers can help teachers to:

- save time and money on photocopying and reduce lesson preparation, as single rather than multiple resources may be required;
- demonstrate intricate skills to an entire class, such as how to use a ruler or protractor, without the teacher's body obscuring the view, as can happen when using whiteboard software;
- share resources, such as plants, seeds, insects and the movement of small animals, in science (NB: make sure they are not projected for too long, so that they become distressed);
- display anything that a teacher would normally hold up at the front but fears the children can not really see very well; it is possible to zoom in and focus on objects at high magnification, making it possible for everyone in the class to see even the smallest artefacts and details;
- show jewellery and coins in a history session or project maps in geography;
- demonstrate small-scale processes, such as dissecting a flower;
- make small books into big books instantly;
- exhibit good work by individual pupils (with their permission) and give feedback. In a plenary session, the whole class can check the work against the success criteria, praise what has been done well and suggest future targets;
- display the words of songs for communal singing;
- compare items such as different types of fabric, text or picture on the visualiser using the zoom facility; one item can be put on the screen, with its image frozen; the screen can be split into active and inactive screens, and the first image displayed beside a second item for comparison;

- video class activities; this could be useful if pupils learn rhymes for MFL or times tables; these can be replayed for revision at a later date, or even while they are entering the class for a session, to get them off to a quick and focused start;
- take a snapshot of a document instead of scanning it;
- capture lessons on a PC, store them on a school's computer network, and reuse or upload them on to a VLE to give near-live presentations;
- create e-portfolios of evidence by taking images of pupils' work and pupils at work.

Table 12.1 *Ways to use visualisers in activities in Key Stages 1 and 2*

KS1

Skills and techniques	Visualiser activities for KS1, including cross-curricular ideas
Learn to read	Share class texts using a single book.
Learn to identify features of text	Use zoom and scroll features to help children follow the text and comment on features.
Listen to a story	When reading a story to the children, use the visualiser to show them the pictures – turn a standard book into a big book.
Support small-group reading aloud activities	As each pupil reads aloud from their individual book, the others in the group follow the words on the screen with the guidance of an adult.
Ask questions	Share a picture book to encourage asking questions and creating answers.
Learn to write	Demonstrate correct letter formation.
Model close-up techniques that would be difficult to show to the whole class	Demonstrate using a ruler accurately. Model an art technique. Show how to sew simple stitches. Show how to build shapes with maths equipment. Display brush-work skills.
Note differences	Compare leaf shapes. Compare how a snail and a woodlouse move. Compare fabric samples and the differences in structure between woven, knitted and felted materials.
Identify and count coins	Count money/coins together as a class.
Observe details and parts of objects	Show shells, feathers, flowers, historical and religious artefacts, items to be compared in DT projects. NB: Children should also handle such items whenever possible.

Lower KS2

Skills and techniques	Visualiser activities for LKS2, including cross-curricular ideas
Make comparisons	Compare book images with live materials.
Demonstrate a close-up technique that would otherwise be difficult to show to the whole class	Model ways to create a circuit. Dissect a flower. Use a saw. Use a data logger. Create and annotate a timeline. Use a dictionary. Demonstrate sewing techniques so they can be seen in detail. Use multi-link blocks, Dienes cubes, Cuisenaire rods, coins and other apparatus to show counting, problem-solving and activities involving symmetry.
Compare and contrast	Magnify rocks, soil, seeds, leaves, cloth and other materials.

Lower KS2 continued

Skills and techniques	Visualiser activities for LKS2, including cross-curricular ideas
Develop observation and classification skills	Examine live animals that are difficult to pass around the class (e.g. mealworms and other minibeasts). Do not keep them on the machine for more than 15 seconds or they may become overheated. Point the visualiser camera at the class fish tank, ant's nest or other small animals brought into class.
Write fluently	Model writing on paper under the visualiser. Annotate texts to compare poems and writing genres. Share texts, expanding knowledge of different writing styles, punctuation, grammar, sentence construction etc.
Record, compute and calculate	Model setting out work in a maths book. Go over worksheet activities in literacy or maths. This saves the teacher copying a sheet onto a dry wipe board or scanning it to use on the IWB, as the sheet can be written on when it is under the visualiser.
Make deductions from documents and artefacts	Examine historical, geographical and religious artefacts.
Communicate in a range of ways	Use camera facility for stop-motion animation to record stories using plasticine or small plastic figures. Use as a video camera, turning the camera to record class events, e.g. an experiment in science, a debate in PHSE or a conversation in MFL.
Record data	Record activity on a bird feeder close to the class. Show musical notation to introduce new music/songs/composers and learn notes.
Develop evaluation skills	Peer-assess individual and group progress comparing against success criteria.

Upper KS2

Skills and techniques	Visualiser activities for UKS2, including cross-curricular ideas
Look in detail at plants and animals	Zoom in on dead animals, e.g. flies, butterflies, bees. Magnify microscope slides.
Demonstrate a close-up technique that would otherwise be difficult to show to the whole class	Demonstrate how to use a dictionary. Use a protractor to measure angles accurately. Show how to read a thermometer. The liquid is more easily seen rising and falling at the touch of a hot/cold hand using a visualiser. Dissect owl pellets. Model accurate use of tools, including protractors, measuring cylinders, brushwork in art, needlework, safe use of kitchen tools, bench-hooks and saws. Model how to tackle maths problems.
Communicate using web-conferencing and the Internet	For video-conferencing, turn the camera to face the pupils as your webcam and link to Skype.
Identify dangerous substances	For drugs education, project the labels on cigarette packets. Use prepared resources to show what illegal drugs might look like, e.g. a wrap of white powder (use salt).
Examine artefacts and make deductions about them	Share religious items such as icons, prayer beads, pictures of stained glass windows. Wherever possible, artefacts should still be passed round and touched.
Read maps, measure distances, use grid references and see how to align a compass	Use a range of maps and aerial photos to demonstrate key techniques. After watching a demonstrating of correct compass use, it is essential that pupils practise using one by themselves.
Record data	Create stop-frame animations by taking a series of snapshot images to create a time-lapse film. Use to capture flowers opening/food decaying.
Examine a sequence of growth	Plant a seed every two days. Wash the roots and examine a sequence of germinated seeds under the microscope or visualiser.

13 Graphics software in the primary classroom

Introduction

Images are an important part of visual literacy. We are surrounded by images of digital origin, from the logos on our toothpaste to the images and cartoons on TV and the photos in the papers we read. Children need to learn how to read these images and communicate using their own visual illustrations, which can be more powerful than a page of words. As Loveless and Thacker point out,

> Although the use of ICT certainly opens up interesting possibilities in learning to look at images, it is in the creation of visual images to communicate and express ideas that these technologies make a significant contribution to developing children's visual literacy.
>
> (Loveless and Thacker 2005, p. 122)

There are six main types of graphics program that pupils should have the opportunity to work with in school:

1 paint programs
2 draw programs
3 photo-editing software
4 computer-aided design (CAD) programs
5 desktop-publishing programs
6 graphical organisers.

Images from each of these programs can often be pasted into the other programs, if the file formats are compatible, and then manipulated using the facilities in the new program. Images can be created, saved, retrieved and reworked, with several versions kept until the desired effect is achieved. Paint programs are not intended to replace the experience of using real paintbrushes, and it is easier to draw many effects with a pencil than a computer mouse (which has been liked to drawing with a brick), but computer programs offer effects that may not be obtainable by conventional means, and pupils should compare the advantages and limitations of each technique to see which design solution is most appropriate in every case. Pupils' ideas, rather than their artistic techniques, can become the focus for their work (Long 2001). Some graphics programs can edit animation or digital video. To get the most from each type of program, it helps to understand how each type of file stores and saves data.

Paint programs

The program Dazzle is a good example of a paint program. These programs are pixel-based programs that work in one layer. Tools such as brushes, sprays, lines and shapes can be drawn over each other in a range of colours. Parts of the work can be selected, erased, rotated or copied and pasted again on to the whole image. Most programs have an undo facility, which allows the user to go back one or several steps. The work is saved as a bitmap file, which can be very big, as data are saved for every pixel on the screen, even those that may appear blank. Bitmap files are good for images that require a lot of detail. Scanned images, digital photos and most detailed digital art use this format. Digital photos can be pasted into these programs and then cropped and enhanced using the paint tools. Images created in paint programs may become fuzzy when enlarged or compressed (zoom in on an image, and the individual pixels can be seen).

Draw programs

Draw programs work in many layers. Each line and shape on the screen has its own layer, which can be brought forward or back. Images can be moved, joined, stretched and shrunk. The images are saved as vectors, which are maths formulae that describe the properties and location of each part. Vector files are smaller than bitmap files. They are good for designs that have large areas of similar colour and simple shapes. Digital photos can be pasted into some draw programs, often those that are part of writing programs such as Word. Here, they can be cropped, resized and joined to other shapes in a single layer, and have text wrapped round or beside them in many ways. Individual components can be resized, grouped and ungrouped without distortion.

Some graphics programs now combine elements of both types of file. Most WP packages allow the user to make and manipulate simple diagrams and may provide some

Figure 13.1 A bitmap image from a paint program needs a lot of computer memory

Figure 13.2 These houses were created using AutoShapes in Word. They are saved as small vector files

ready-made images, such as clip art and charts. Vectors are saved as GIF (graphics interchange format) files. As these files are very heavy on memory, it is unwise to save too many versions of each file. Corral Draw is an example of this type of program.

Photo-editing software

Many of these programs, such as Photoshop or Paint Shop Pro, tend to be quite advanced and, although too complex in their entirety for most primary-school pupils, have some special effects that can be used by the majority of KS2 pupils. Trial versions can usually be downloaded free from the Internet. There are some free programs, such as Google's Picasa, that can be downloaded to make simple edits to digital pictures, such as removing red eyes, cropping, altering the brightness and creating web albums. The results can be copied and pasted into many paint and draw programs to create special effects or diagrams to label. Microsoft Picture manager is a simple one that comes with some versions of Microsoft Office.

Computer-aided design programs

These use object-orientated graphics and are useful when planning a design layout for a new room, garden or even play area. Several are free on the Internet if you look on sites such as IKEA or other furnishing retailers. Lego has one that can be used for virtual Lego building.

They are useful for planning real or imaginary dens, bedrooms and homes. Google SketchUp is a powerful yet easy-to-learn, free 3D software tool that combines a simple, yet robust, toolset with an intelligent drawing system that streamlines and simplifies 3D design. BlockCAD is a freeware program for building virtual models with Lego-like bricks.

2Simple software has online CAD software suitable for KS1 projects, and nets from the designs can be printed and made up by pupils who are enrolled on the site.

Desktop publishing

This is software that combines WP and graphics tools and enables layouts to be planned and edited. Materials from other graphics and WP programs can be pasted into the program and edited in the required layout to suit the reader. This is particularly useful for creating brochures, posters and magazines. Wizards (templates that come with the program and tell you what to do) can be used to create cards, posters, newspapers and many other formats. Publisher and Textease are examples of this type of program.

Graphical organisers

There are now graphical programs that help to organise information visually and show relationships between different areas. The resulting graphics can be printed as mind/concept maps. Creating one can help learners to organise their ideas and see relationships between different areas of learning. They are useful for teachers to assess learning and perhaps misconceptions. Kidspiration is a program commonly used for this work in primary schools. 2Connect from 2Simple is a concept-mapping and -planning tool that will help children from KS1 and older to organise their thoughts individually or collaboratively on a network. This program has templates and supports sound, and the work can be exported to other programs.

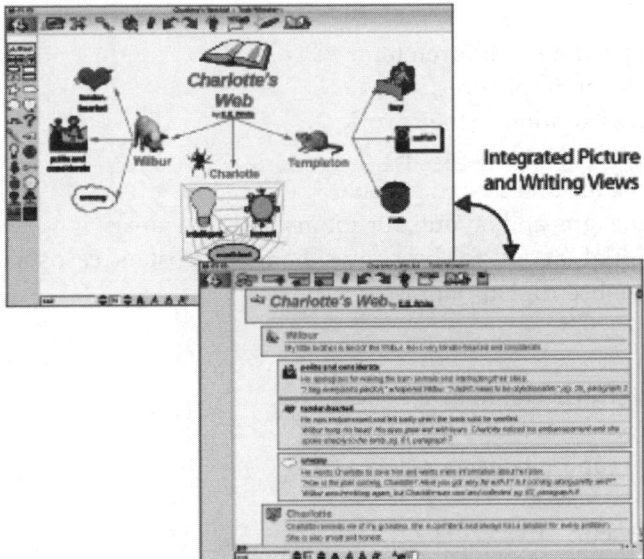

Integrated Picture and Writing Views

Figure 13.3 Screen shot from Kidspiration showing how pupils can expand their ideas from a concept map to a written form

National Curriculum requirements

As part of the 'essentials for learning and life' (ICT capability), children learn how to:

- **Find and select information:** When using graphics programs, children can select sophisticated tools to manipulate lines, shapes and colours to create particular effects. Digital images and photos can be selected and inserted into their work in many contexts and can be modified and adapted for use in a wide range of ways.
- **Create, manipulate and process information:** With graphics programs, quite complex effects can be obtained with simple tools. This enables children to develop their creative design skills. Pupils can predict, explore the effects of a wide range of tools and reverse the results if they do not like them.
- **Collaborate, communicate and share information:** Graphics programs enable children to share creative ideas, sometimes at long distance, and to collaborate on designs. Different versions of the same design can be worked on at separate machines, compared and copied to the same location for discussion and use. Their results can be shared digitally through e-mail, wikis and websites.
- **Refine and improve their work:** When using graphics programs, children can review and compare versions of their work. They can experiment extensively at no cost, without mess, and can produce complex designs with perfectly drawn shapes in a multitude of clear colours. They can take risks and explore ideas because they can save different versions of their work and easily undo actions that do not create the effects they want.

How graphics programs can help children

Graphics programs can help children to:
- personalise work with pictures;
- improve the presentation of their work;
- create their own labelled diagrams;
- develop creative art and design skills;
- model plans, designs and layouts for rooms and play areas;
- create professional layouts for brochures, banners, posters, cards and invitations;
- edit and personalise digital photos.

How graphics programs can help teachers

Graphics programs can help teachers to:
- create interactive screens;
- make their own clip art;
- personalise worksheets, templates, labels and records;
- explore their own creativity and share this with pupils to set an example.

Table 13.1 *Progression in Graphics Skills from KS1 to KS2*

KS1	
Skills and techniques	*Graphic activities for KS1, including cross-curricular ideas*
Draw shapes and lines (draw program)	Use to illustrate maths work on shapes. Add text notes about the properties of the shapes.
Resize, rotate and fill shapes (draw program)	Experiment with shapes of different sizes to create landscapes, crowd scenes, with duplicated trees, animals, faces or buildings (see Figure 13.4).
Create repeating patterns (draw program)	Copy given patterns and create new ones; use as borders for stationery.
Explore potential of brush, line, spray and stamp tools (paint program)	Create designs for cards, bookmarks or wrapping paper (use the latter to cover small items such as boxes/books).
Create picture (paint program)	Use to illustrate stories, poems or work in any subject.
Take digital photos and copy into own work	Record work in any subject area and use to illustrate work. Take pictures of friends to show their personalities/interests.

Figure 13.4

Lower KS2

Skills and techniques	Graphics activities for LKS2, including cross-curricular ideas
Investigate pattern and symmetry using shapes (draw/paint programs)	Use flip and rotate tools to explore aspects of symmetry. Some graphical programs have symmetry tools to aid this work.
Link shapes (draw program)	Combine shapes to create simple graphics. Use to illustrate work. Link shapes to create own cartoon character. Use to help explain learning in any subject area (see Figure 13.5).
Add clip art to work (draw program)	Insert copyright-free clip art to illustrate work where detailed illustration is required or where there is not enough time to create own art. Use clip art, including maps, to create posters about a current issue, e.g. pollution.
Create mind maps using text boxes, arrows and clip art (draw program)	Use mind maps to show learning at the start of a topic and then add subsequent learning to assess learning by the end of the project.
Make simple diagrams to label (draw/paint program)	Create simple diagrams to label instead of using commercial clip art, e.g. parts of a plant in science, a shapes chart in maths, a family tree for history (see Figure 13.6).
Create charts using chart wizard (draw program)	Use computer software to create bar/pie charts in any subject area.
Select an area to copy and paste (paint program)	Make repeating patterns for fabric design by selecting parts of a paint drawing and repeating and rotating them to create a design.
Use paint tools to create particular effects (paint program)	Use Mondrian, Kandinsky or Pollock pictures as inspiration for own artwork.
Compose/crop digital photos	Compose/crop pictures to improve composition, remove irrelevant or distracting elements or to show particular details.
Use CAD to create a room design	Connect to a commercial design tool and redesign a bedroom/den.

Figure 13.5

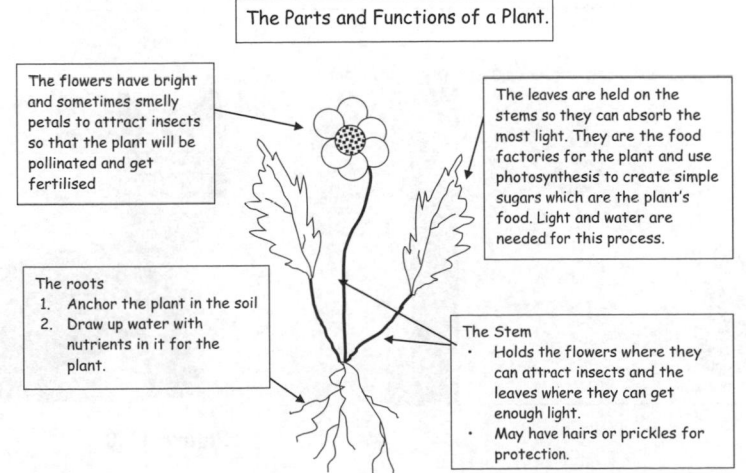

Figure 13.6

Upper KS2

Skills and techniques	Graphics activities for UKS2, including cross-curricular ideas
Make more complex diagrams/own clip art to label (draw/paint program)	Create diagrams to label instead of using commercial clip art, e.g. a religious building for RE, a water-cycle diagram for geography, the layout for circuit training/'potted' sports in PE. Create layouts for board games to revise learning in any subject area. Draw designs for DT work using draw software to resize and locate design components. Create concept maps to show learning in any subject.
Create animated pictures (draw program)	Use clip art/own pictures and copy into PowerPoint. Use the custom animation to add an effect and create a motion path for the shape. Each page of a story can be animated to make an interactive story for a younger child (see Figure 13.7).
Use special effects in advanced graphics program (paint/draw program)	Experiment to see the effects that can be created and decide on most appropriate use to create a mood in a picture. Use to illustrate a poem or story.
Alter brightness of a digital photo to improve it	Look critically at digital photos and use appropriate tools to improve them.
Paste digital photo into a program where the background can be rubbed out (paint/draw/photo program)	For example, photos of planes taken at a WWII museum can have the backgrounds erased to create a picture of a plane that can then be copied into a paint document as a piece of clip art to create a new battle scene background. Photos of children can be given new bodies to show what animal they would like to be (see Figure 13.8). Modify photos of themselves so they appear in historical costume and then write a historical story to go with the images.
Add a digital photo to a shape to frame it	Insert digital photos into shapes created with draw tools. Use in DTP publications.
Compress digital photos and attach to an e-mail	Compress, attach and send digital photos in e-mails.
Use a CAD program	Redesign a bedroom/create a new play area using an online CAD planning tool, e.g. from Ikea (www.ikea.com/ms/en_GB/rooms_ideas/splashplanners.html) or Google Sketchup (http://sketchup.google.com/product/gsu.html). Redesign the classroom on http://classroom.4teachers.org/.
Create a collage of digital photos	Create a collage of photos to convey the atmosphere of a location or the character of a person the pupils know.
Use CAD to create a model	Connect to a Lego site to design without losing small items on the floor! In a draw program, create a floor plan of a classroom/or bedroom and add furniture to meet specific requirements.
Design nets for products	Use a draw program to create a net for a template that can be printed onto card.

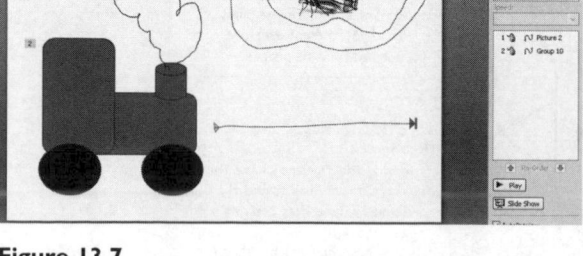

Figure 13.7   **Figure 13.8**

14 Simulation software in the primary classroom

Introduction

Using simulation software allows children to experience activities that would be impossible, inconvenient or dangerous in real life. In science, for instance, simulations that involve very hot items or activities where equipment is normally not available are particularly valuable. Subjects as diverse as history, maths, art and technology make use of simulations. In maths and science, simulations can contribute to a useful start or final plenary session. Pupils should be helped to evaluate simulations by comparing them with real situations and considering their usefulness, as well as moral issues, such as those involved in some types of gaming.

Other simulations can be used to model astronomical events, such as the orbit of the Moon around the Earth. Figure 14.1 shows a screen shot from the National Schools' Observatory (www.schoolsobservatory.org.uk/astro/esm/moonphs.shtml).

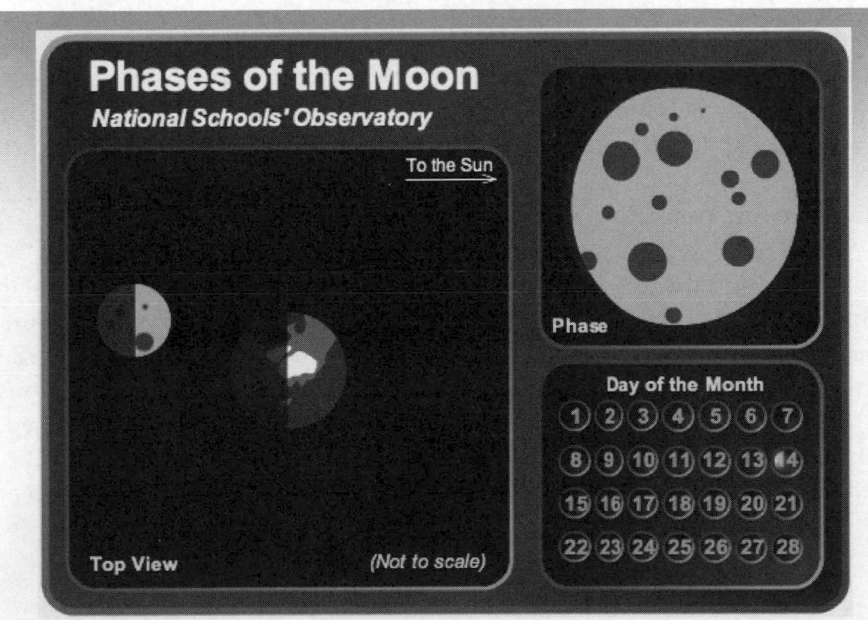

Figure 14.1 Demonstration of phases of the Moon

National Curriculum requirements

As part of the 'essentials for learning and life' (ICT capability), children learn how to:

- **Find and select information:** Pupils can select the variables they will alter in a simulated test.
- **Create, manipulate and process information**: Data can be manipulated to test ideas.
- **Collaborate, communicate and share information**: Children can collaborate to tests ideas with a simulation and then compare the simulation data with their own test data.
- **Refine and improve their work:** Using a simulation with carefully controlled variables should help pupils to refine their understanding of a topic and improve their own practical work.

Simulations can be used to stimulate writing and talking. The BBC website is a rich source of simulations, games and activities. The following site is a good starting point: www.bbc.co.uk/schools/ks2bitesize, and there is a wide selection of strategy, action, construction and shooter games on http://primarygamesarena.com/gametype.php?id=0.

To develop speaking and listening skills, immersive simulations such as SimCity or Millennium Village Simulation, where the user is assigned to a family in a village and expected to guide the family through fifty years, can be a powerful stimulus. These simulations can be carried out in groups, independent of the whole class.

How simulation software can help children

Simulation software can help children to:

- learn through 'hands-on' activities, so that they become participants, not just listeners; tests can be repeated as many times as needed, without access to specialised equipment;
- feel involved, as their input is welcome and makes a difference to the world on screen;
- take on responsible roles, find ways to succeed and develop problem- solving strategies;

Simulation software can help teachers teach in the following ways:

- Simulations put the teacher into a new role as a facilitator, who has the same information as the children they are helping. This helps teachers who want to have classrooms where peer-to-peer talk is valued, and the teacher is no longer seen as the main source of information for defined periods. There are many simulations on this site, www.mymgl.com/teachers/subjects/ict/unit3d.htm, that can be used to help children test their ideas.
- Simulations can show situations too remote or dangerous to be explored in any other way.

Table 14.1 *Progression in using simulation software from KS1 to KS2a and KS2b*

KS1

Skills and techniques	Simulation activities for KS1, including cross-curricular ideas
Enter data into a computer simulation	Suggest numbers that will complete a maths or science task on-screen.
Use a simulation to test ideas	Use a simple simulation to dress a toy, on-screen, for different types of weather.
Use a simulation to test skills	Use a Wii for exercise and talk about the ways this is as good as a real game and the ways in which it is different.

Lower KS2

Skills and techniques	Simulation activities for LKS2, including cross-curricular ideas
Compare simulations with real-life situations	Try a coffee-making simulation and compare the pros and cons of doing this with making lots of real, hot coffee (http://ngfl.northumberland.gov.uk/ict/qca/ks2/unit3D/colins%20coffee/colins%20coffee.html).
Use a simulation to test design ideas	Use a simulation to practise design skills in a historical context. Design a room in a Tudor, Victorian or modern house (www.geffrye-museum.org.uk/kidszone/room/). On this site, you can design buildings such as castles: www.citycreator.com/.
Test variables to their limits	Try out every variable to its limit in a problem in a science context.

Upper KS2

Skills and techniques	Simulation activities for UKS2, including cross-curricular ideas
Experiment with different ideas to create a successful project	Use this rollercoaster builder simulation to test ideas: http://puzzling.caret.cam.ac.uk/game.php?game=roller.
Learn how input devices can control a process	Use a simulation to control traffic lights and crossings by correctly ordering the steps in the input device. Or use this cat and dog simulation to test alarms: www.ngfl-cymru.org.uk/vtc/explore_control_sims/eng/Introduction/default.htm.
Plan and work collaboratively	Help support a virtual family through difficulties in an African village. Discuss the problems involved and then compare this with real living and problem-solving (http://mvsim.wikischolars.columbia.edu/Player+Quick+Start+Guide).

15 Control technology, Pixies and Roamers in the primary classroom

Introduction

Control technology in its simplest form is switching on a light or adjusting the volume of a radio. In schools, we develop this into creating instructions stored in a computer to operate electrical devices, using a series of commands called a program. The simplest devices use versions of Logo to program a floor or tabletop device such as a Roamer. Other versions of Logo are used to guide a virtual object around a screen. All versions of Logo allow the children to tell the device to move a number of body lengths forward or back, or to turn to the right or left. Use of Logo is a way to develop children's cooperative skills, as groups of children are usually given them to work with. In addition, children learn left from right and amounts of turn, either measured in quarter turns or degrees.

More able children can use a control unit plugged into a USB port to switch on and off bulbs, motors, buzzers and bells. These instructions can be stored in the computer, and a sequence of lights and motors can be used. Sensors can also be connected to the control units. These sensors can detect the environment and can be used to trigger actions by the control box. The instructions are in the form of 'IF/THEN' commands and can be very simple. Control technology can be introduced by asking children to programme the movement of a friend, e.g. 'move three steps forward, turn right and move two steps forward'. This simple sequence can be developed for Lower KS2. At Upper KS2, children should be encouraged to analyse a sequence of events, such as making a cup of tea, and list all the actions in sequence. The person being instructed should follow each instruction literally but safely!

National Curriculum requirements

As part of the 'essentials for learning and life' (ICT capability), children learn how to:

- **Find and select information:** Children need to choose the right controls to make things happen.
- **Create, manipulate and process information:** Children should devise their own sequences of instructions to control devices.
- **Collaborate, communicate and share information:** Children should develop their own design ideas, creating and improving systems for control. They should use a range of equipment, including an ICT control program.
- **Refine and improve their work:** Children should analyse ways in which the sequences they program can be improved.

How control technology can help children to learn

Through using control technology, children can learn:

- how to give sophisticated commands, leading to programs that might have ten or more commands;
- logic and organisation.

How control technology can help teachers

Control technology can help teachers to:

- teach using motivating, action-packed situations;
- facilitate problem-solving, leading to a great deal of independent learning.

Table 15.1 *Progression in using control technology from KS1 to Lower KS2*

KS1	
Skills and techniques	*Control activities for KS1, including cross-curricular ideas*
Program a simple floor turtle or Roamer	Sequence a floor robot. At first, allow play; then program two or three steps into floor or screen robots.
Investigate cause and effect	Children switch on and off simple, battery-powered electrical items.
Use model-making kits such as Flowgo by Dataharvest	Use a simple simulation to load boats in a harbour.

Lower KS2	
Skills and techniques	*Control activities for LKS2, including cross-curricular ideas*
Program a floor turtle or other robot	Set challenges for children to meet in making the robot follow a complex program of instructions.
Make and control electrical devices	Make circuits where more than two electrical devices are controlled by switches.
Use kits that incorporate control activities	Make models that incorporate control programs, e.g. the 'e-learn and go' from www.dataharvest.co.uk.

Upper KS2	
Skills and techniques	*Control activities for UKS2, including cross-curricular ideas*
Program screen turtle using a series of commands	Use nested commands that cause the robot to repeat movements with small variations.
Develop commands as a sequence using a control box	Use the control box to turn devices on and off.
Incorporate inputs into program	Use inputs into the control box to allow a sequence of events to start, e.g. a model car approaching a model traffic light changes the lights to green.
Develop awareness of devices with sequences of control	Analyse the control needed to record using a DVD or make a washing-machine work.

16 Digital audio equipment in the primary classroom

Introduction to using digital sound files

The downloading of music files or radio programmes, as well as the creation of sound files and podcasts, is routine in many homes and in some schools. Children have access to MP3 players and iPods; they listen to audio guides at places of interest and record digital messages on their phones and computers. Listen on demand and creating personal collections of digital music are becoming commonplace for young people, and there are many ways to develop these skills in an educational context.

Sound can be recorded digitally on many computers through microphones built into the computer. These are suitable for short messages or voice-overs, where quality does not have to be high, and the user can sit close to the computer in a quiet environment. For better-quality recording, a digital audio recorder and/or an external microphone are needed. Sound files can be saved in several formats, the most common being MP3 and WAV files, which can be used by many types of software, such as PowerPoint and other multimedia presentation programs. MP3 files compress the data, thus creating smaller files, which can be useful when transferring the files from one location to another, or uploading them to the school website or virtual learning environment (VLE). Before the files can be used, they usually need editing. Audacity is a free program that can be downloaded from the Internet (http://audacity.sourceforge.net/). It has no sound files of its own but can be used to record, edit and add special effects to audio recordings created by pupils, and it can also convert between file types. Audacity is useful for both speech and musical projects, e.g. podcasts as well as adding soundscapes to multimedia presentations. There are also commercial packages for editing sound files such as Podium.

Digital audio recorders (digital voice recorders)

These are compact devices that have replaced mini tape recorders as a more versatile device for recording digital sound. MP3 players are a type of digital audio player. When buying a digital audio recorder, you need to consider whether you prefer an external microphone, for improved sound quality, or an internal one, for more slimline handling. If devices have removable memory cards, then the devices can more easily be shared among pupils, with each group having its own card. Digital recorders can be useful tools for anyone learning English or an MFL. Such devices can be used to practise pronunciation or to make recordings of words and phrases to develop vocabulary.

Podcasting

Podcasts

A podcast is an aural digital recording. To create a podcast, you need a microphone, a PC and audio editing software. The microphone can be an external one linked to a recording device or an internal one on the device.

Podcasts can be saved to CDs or data sticks. One podcast can comprise several sound files that have been edited and linked. For more advanced podcasting, the use of dedicated podcasting software and a microphone can dramatically improve the quality of the broadcast. There are many educational podcasts to listen to on: www.primaryschool. com.au/learningtechresults.php?strand=Podcasting&grade=General.

Podcasting has the potential to improve personalised learning in schools. Differentiated podcasts can be created by teachers for the use of specific groups of children, such as those with English as an additional language (EAL) or other SEN, such as the gifted and talented, or those who need extra help with learning a language. Podcasts can be created by pupils for themselves or their peers, to record learning in any area of the curriculum. The resulting podcasts can be accessed in a wide range of contexts, both in school and at home, if the material is stored on the school's website or intranet with home access. For children who have trouble with written methods of communication, recording a story or an account of an event could give them a voice in a motivating context.

Further information about podcasts, as well as many examples, can be found at: http://recap.ltd.uk/podcasting/index.php (a UK directory of podcasts, with over 300 carefully selected podcast channels for educational use – ideal for teaching and learning activities with children, young people and educational professionals).

Digital audio recorders

Digital audio recorders include MP3 recorders and mobile phones. The resulting sound file is saved as an MP3 audio file or .wav file and can be uploaded to a website or school intranet. From there, it can be downloaded and then listened to on a portable MP3 player, another computer or other mobile devices.

Digital music composition

There is a range of musical composition software, some of it freely available on the Internet, for children to practise composition by combining sound files. Some of these provide pre-recorded musical sections for pupils to link together. Others allow for a more creative and personal approach, where pupils can select notes and chords on a simulated keyboard. For Apple users, the software iLife includes GarageBand, for performing, recording and creating music and podcasts. For PC users, Dance E-Jay, Music Maker and RM Music Explorer provide sound samples that can be remixed to create musical compositions. The 2Simple Music Toolkit is a musical composition program suitable for KS1 and KS2.

If software programs such as PowerPoint, Movie Maker or iMovie have sound files inserted, and they are to be used away from the computer on which they were created, the sound files need to be copied with the presentation, as they are not actually embedded into it, but just linked. On a PC, this is done by choosing 'Package for CD' from the File menu, so that all the files needed are linked and copied together. Along with the technicalities about how to create sound files, pupils should be taught the ethical way to

---

National Curriculum requirements

As part of the 'essentials for learning and life' (ICT capability), children learn how to:

- **Find and select information:** When using digital sound files, children need to find and select the sounds they need and compose the texts required for a soundscape or podcast. They should consider the needs of their audience and the moods they wish to create.
- **Create, manipulate and process information:** Using digital sound files, children can explore and manipulate digital sounds, try out compositions and prepare podcasts or sound files to insert into multimedia presentations.
- **Collaborate, communicate and share information:** Digital sound files created by pupils can be shared, e-mailed or added to e-zines and collaborative work. They can communicate ideas and work collaboratively to produce podcasts and musical compositions for particular audiences.
- **Refine and improve their work:** When using musical software or podcasting, children should listen to their work and improve it in the light of suggestions from their peers and supporting adults.

---

use the tools, such as not recording other people without their permission and respecting copyright laws when putting together a multimedia presentation.

How digital sound files can help children

Digital sound files can help children to:

- develop speaking and listening skills;
- develop ICT skills in a new direction;
- access lessons they have missed, if the teacher has made a podcast of part of the session;
- engage with learning, as they easily engage with MP3 technology;
- create multimedia presentations and radio-type broadcasts;
- share their work with a wider audience;
- create their own audiobook library;
- engage with learning if they have EAL or SEN and need extra support;
- be supported with homework tasks, if podcasts are placed on the school's VLE;
- record aural notes for writing activities rather than written notes. This could be especially useful on field trips, whether recording ideas for a poem about the sea while on a beach or notes for a brochure relating to a castle while exploring it. They can be transcribed later when needed.

How digital sound files can help teachers

Digital sound files can help teachers to:

- create podcasts that pupils can use to revise learning;
- share lessons with absent children or show parents what is being taught;

- display/celebrate school achievements;
- record pupils' speaking and listening skills;
- keep a digital audio portfolio of class/pupil work;
- vary the teaching and learning approach in any subject;
- create additional learning materials, to extend the gifted and talented or to support those with specific learning needs;
- develop additional materials, to support independent learning or revision or homework;
- record instructions/stories to be heard alongside written text for EAL pupils. This could be useful for children who might struggle with reading the instructions, but not with the actually activities or tasks themselves.

Table 16.1 *Progression in developing digital sound activities**

KS1

Skills and techniques	Sound activities for KS1, including cross-curricular ideas
Learn that speech can be recorded and played back	Pupils record and listen to themselves speaking/singing.
Learn to record and play back	Record and play back speech and songs from their peers. Record sounds around school and then identify them back in class.
Use a recording to identify ways to improve a performance	Listen to themselves reading a story and discuss ways to improve reading, e.g. use punctuation/more expression. Record and play back musical performances with percussion instruments.
Explore the potential of musical composition software	Experiment to see how given phrases and beats can be combined for particular effects.

Lower KS2

Skills and techniques	Sound activities for LKS2, including cross-curricular ideas
Use a recording to identify ways to improve a performance	Use digital recordings to improve performance in reading and reciting. Use digital recording to develop correct pronunciation in an MFL.
Record interviews with people pupils know	Interview relatives about family history (the interviews could be archived for future use). Interview adults in the school about their jobs. Use in PHSE lessons.
Record reading for a particular audience	Record a story for younger children/poems for people in a retirement home. Devise and record instructions/directions for a particular audience. Record a commentary on an event, e.g. a competition/sports day.
Record, edit and combine several sound files	Create a radio programme, with contributions from several sources. Record a music show. Create an audiobook of poems, either written by the children or by their favourite poets.
Create a soundscape by recording and editing sounds	Record a variety of sounds and edit for use in a multimedia presentation.
Use musical composition software to create original compositions	Create musical compositions for a particular purpose, e.g. an advertisement jingle, the background to a poem or to accompany a song they have written. Design their own ring tone.

Upper KS2

Skills and techniques	Sound activities for UKS2, including cross-curricular ideas
Record interviews with people they do not know	Under supervision, record interviews with members of the public, as part of a fact-finding mission about public opinions, e.g. about the development of a local facility.
Use audio recording to develop speaking and listening skills in creating explanations	Record explanations of processes in science or operations in maths (could be useful for revision).
Create an audio tour of a local facility	On a field trip, record information for a tour of a local museum or historical site. Edit the files on a computer to produce a professional audio tour.
Use a sound recording to document a meeting	Use an MP3 player to record a school council meeting. Use the recording to produce the minutes.
Use digital recording to develop MFL skills	Listen to MFL recordings to help develop understanding of MFL speech. Record and replay pupils' speech to improve pronunciation.
Locate and download a podcast	Use the BBC site to identify and download a podcast that would be useful in class work.
Create a podcast	Record and edit sound and music to create a podcast about topics covered in any session, e.g. guides to local facilities, a programme about the Tudors, a guide to the school for new children or an audio magazine.
Use musical composition software to create and edit compositions	Create musical compositions using either an electronic keyboard connected to a computer or musical composition software.

*A tape-recorder could also be used for some of these activities

17 Hand-held devices in the primary classroom

Introduction

A hand-held computer is a mobile device that might also be known as a hand-held. It is a pocket-sized computing device that has a display screen, with touch input or a miniature keyboard. Hand-held ICT devices include smart phones, laptop computers, cameras, video recorders, audio recorders, games consoles and GPS devices. Some have built-in keys so that they can be used to identify plants and animals (e.g. Wildkey). They can be used to fix a location very precisely. Hand-held devices allow children to record what they see/hear, using cameras, video recorders or audio recorders, or to produce written descriptions using a hand-held word processor. In addition, all these pieces of information can be e-mailed from a smart phone to people in the classroom or even on other continents.

How hand-held devices can help children to learn

Hand-held devices can help children to learn to:

- identify specimens and record activities while out of doors; the simple and robust design of many hand-helds means that even very wet weather will not affect them, in contrast to paper and books, which become impossible to use in heavy rain;
- improve logical, mathematical and memory skills using a brain-training program.

National Curriculum requirements

As part of the 'essentials for learning and life' (ICT capability), children learn how to:

- **Find and select information:** Hand-helds can help identify wildlife, locate positions and record visual, numerical and textual data chosen by the child. They can also give Internet access on field trips.
- **Create, manipulate and process information:** Screens and keyboards on these devices allow the speedy creation and processing of graphics and text.
- **Collaborate, communicate and share information:** Mobile-phone technology aids communication and collaboration as ideas are shared.
- **Refine and improve their work:** Some games consoles encourage the user to improve scores in what is termed brain training.

How hand-held devices can help teachers teach

Hand-held devices can help teachers teach by focusing on helping children to interpret their surroundings. Wildkey, for instance, helps pupils to identify plant and animal specimens. This frees the teacher to concentrate on showing the patterns in the area being studied.

Progression in using hand-held devices, from early to middle and later stages

There are so many different types of hand-held digital device that it would not be practical to list a progression of skills for each of them. Pupils should use them, when appropriate, to record ideas and data on field trips and to identify specimens with their keys if they are available. Even young children are keen to try brain training and to develop a range of skills using hand-helds. Pupils should be taught to text and take photos in a responsible manner.

18 Multimedia authoring programs in the primary classroom

Introduction

Multimedia is the integration of different media forms into one program. Our children are consumers of multimedia images and presentations through films, TV programmes and advertisements and many of the games they play. Enabling them to create their own multimedia presentations helps them become multiliterate and engage with their learning. Multimedia authoring is a powerful learning medium that requires creativity and cooperation, as students combine a number of media into a final cohesive project.

A multimedia-authoring program allows pupils to blend text, graphics, animation, audio and video to create presentations of their work and ideas. Not all these features have to be used in any one presentation, but the option to do so widens the range of communication methods available to the children. Multimedia presentations attract learners who find visual media engaging and appeal to active learners who enjoy creating and innovating. Most multimedia applications that children can use involve linking a set of screens together through hyperlink buttons. This type of work is ideal for group presentations, as teams of children can share ideas as they collaborate on sets of screens that are later combined into a single presentation. The presentation can be made interactive, so that the viewer has a choice of routes through the presentation. This is a motivating and exciting way to learn to communicate. Suitable programs for this are PowerPoint, Hyperstudio and Headstart.

An Australian project is currently looking at ways to develop multimedia authoring in schools because, 'The world in which students inhabit is increasingly digital, multimedia and online. A multimedia writing pedagogy is urgently needed to prepare students to be effective authors and participants in such a world' (Chandler *et al.* 2009).

A simple multimedia-authoring program for children who are starting to write is 2Create a Story from 2Simple. This program allows children to draw on the screen, write text to accompany the picture and record themselves reading the text or commenting on the work. They can also add sound effects and then have the screen animate the drawing in a range of different ways. Several screen pages can be put together to create a complete text.

Multimedia projects in programs such as Textease Presenter or PowerPoint can also be saved as web pages. Saving as a web page is an option to choose when saving, and the computer converts the page automatically to make it suitable for the Internet or just the school intranet.

National Curriculum requirements

As part of the 'essentials for learning and life' (ICT capability), children learn how to:

- **Find and select information:** When creating multimedia presentations, children have to select the most appropriate type of medium to engage the reader.
- **Create, manipulate and process information:** The creation of a multimedia presentation requires children to select the most appropriate medium type, possibly transposing text into dialogue or vice versa. They must decide when and what type of graphic or chart is most appropriate to get the ideas across and combine the information in a visually appealing way. The addition of speech or musical sound files should be considered to help the user to access the presentation.
- **Collaborate, communicate and share information:** A multimedia presentation is an excellent project to develop pupils' collaboration and communication skills, both during the compilation of the project and when considering the needs of the intended audience.
- **Refine and improve their work:** At all stages, children may need help to identify which parts of their work are being presented most effectively and which will require further development. A project devised for one audience might be adapted and refined for another one with differing needs.

How multimedia programs can help children

Multimedia programs can help children to:

- choose the most appropriate medium for a particular subject/audience;
- work collaboratively;
- present information in a professional, creative and attractive way, which motivates them;
- engage in a design process to solve a need for a particular audience;
- use a range of IT skills, such as WP, digital manipulation, research and editing skills;
- develop critical evaluation skills.

How multimedia programs can help teachers

Multimedia programs can help teachers to:

- engage pupils of all interests, abilities and learning styles;
- link to Internet sites with relevant material;
- demonstrate new techniques with an IWB or introduce projects that require several screens of presentation;
- combine the work of several children or groups into a single presentation, to be shown to parents or peers.

Table 18.1 *Progression in multimedia program activities*

KS1	
Skills and techniques	*Multimedia activities for KS1, including cross-curricular ideas (At this stage of learning, most pupils will require help from their teachers to complete these projects)*
Combine text and digital paint picture	Use KS1 multimedia program, e.g. 2Simple or Textease, to combine text and screen drawings on a page.
Combine text, graphics and sound in a linear presentation	Combine text, drawings/digital photos and sound to write a short story over several screens.
Combine text, sound and digital photos in a linear presentation for a specific purpose	Combine text and digital photos on several screens to report on a school project, e.g. in science or DT.
Work as a group to combine text, graphics and sound	Combine text and digital photos to report on a trip/topic work in school. Each group of pupils is to create three screens on a different aspect of the trip/topic to be combined by the teacher into one presentation. Images could include digital paint/draw pictures, digital photos and scanned images of paint/collage work. An audio commentary by the children could be added, with help from their teacher.

Lower KS2	
Skills and techniques	*Multimedia activities for KS2, including cross-curricular ideas*
Use hyperlinks to go to another page/screen	Use hyperlinks to create questions and answers for jokes or in a simple quiz.
Plan and work in groups to prepare a presentation with links to and from each slide	Use hyperlinks to add additional information to each page. These might link to a glossary at the end of the presentation, or a sideways link to a screen with more detail about one particular subject. The sub-screens link back to the main series of slides each time.
Create a multimedia presentation for a particular audience	Create a multimedia presentation to teach a younger class about a subject, e.g. properties of shapes. This could include quiz pages.
Create a multimedia presentation that uses sound throughout	Create a talking book. Write and illustrate a story over several screens. Add text to each page, as well as a voice-over and sound effects when particular icons are clicked.
Create an individual multimedia presentation	Create a personal multimedia project on a hobby/interest.

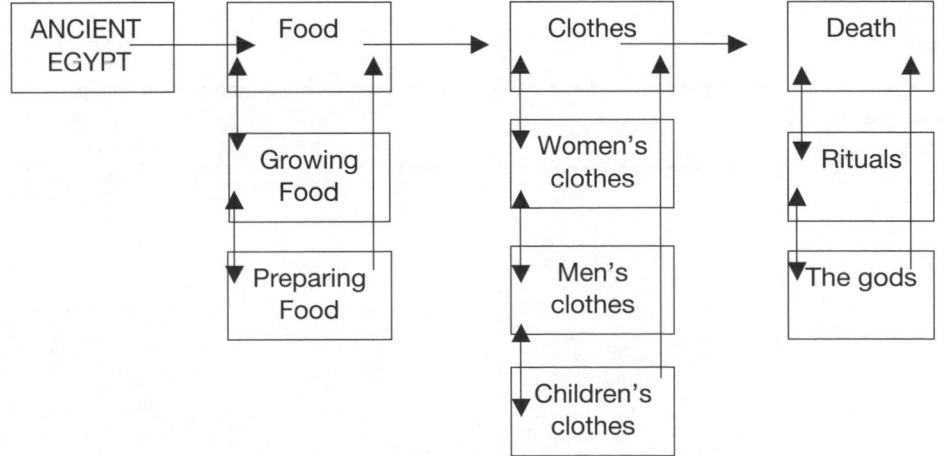

Figure 18.1

Upper KS2

Skills and techniques	Multimedia activities for UKS2, including cross-curricular ideas
Plan and create a hyperlinked presentation that uses multiple stacks of slides, hyperlinked in a simple organisation	Prepare a presentation for a specific audience, e.g. information about a residential trip to show to parents. Each year group could report on the trip they made to explain the benefits to parents of the next class to go. This could be done with small groups of pupils working on each stack of screens, which they then link to the main title screen. As this is a more complex way to link the slides, it is best to create a paper-based map at the planning stage to check each link as it is made. If working in PowerPoint, the slideshow should be turned to kiosk mode in the 'Set up show' menu, to avoid the user accidentally clicking at random on a page, as the default setting then sends the reader to the next page. This would be a useful technique to compile a class anthology of poems, either written by the children or chosen by them from those that can be found online.
Create a multimedia presentation that uses a range of charts and graphics to explore an argument	Use text and a range of graphics to create a multimedia presentation about the pros and cons of a proposed development.
Create an e-portfolio	Create an individual portfolio of work on a school topic, showing how key questions were identified and researched.
Create a personal reflective e-portfolio	Create individual portfolios of a year's work, with reflective comments and targets.
Add a range of sound files to a presentation	Create a multimedia presentation that uses a number of voice and sound effects, e.g. interviews with people who have experience of a war or who feel strongly about a particular issue.
Create a presentation to use as part of an oral presentation	Compile a set of slides to accompany an oral presentation, e.g. about an enterprise or design activity. The slides should be suitable for showing on a big screen and complement the speech given.
Compile a series of screens to show the stages in a process	For example, animate a series of screens to show a volcanic eruption. To do this, use the paint tools to create a series of images, one on each screen, of the different stages of the lava rising up inside the volcano and erupting from the top. Tell the program to show these in quick succession, so the lava appears to rise and erupt. Add buttons, one to start the eruption sequence and one to return to the first screen in the sequence. This could be adapted to show the changing course of a river, or the stages of frog/butterfly development.
Plan and create a hyperlinked presentation that uses multiple stacks of slides, hyperlinked in a complex organisation	Create a multi-option adventure story, where the reader can choose different courses of action for the characters. Each stack could result in a different set of events. This can be as simple or as complex as the children require.
Create pages for a web-based presentation	Design pages for the school website and link them into the current web plan.

Part 3

Really useful ideas for using ICT across the curriculum

The activities suggested here are intended to complement, not replace, other non-ICT-based learning experiences in each subject. The ideas given are examples of what many teachers are already doing and do not form an exhaustive list of activities that must be undertaken. Ideas proposed for KS1 may also be appropriate in KS2, and vice versa. Practical, firsthand experience and investigation are essential at every stage of learning, but ICT can be used to support, extend and reinforce learning, or substitute for experience if practical investigation is not possible for reasons of safety or practicality. From these starting points, teachers should use their own judgement and creativity and find their own ways of using ICT to suit their class, the topic studied and the equipment available.

Words in **bold** can be found in the glossary.

(A4L) indicates activities that might be used to assess learning. Some can be prepared as screen activities where items have to be sorted, highlighted or annotated in some way, which will enable the teacher to see if the pupil has understood a concept or mastered a particular skill. Screens can be easily adapted to suit the needs of different groups. If only one standalone laptop or computer is available, a whole class can still be assessed over a week, with pupils taking no more than 5–10 minutes out from other activities. Children see these assessments as enjoyable games and are keen to take their turn.

19 English

Language is the main root of communication, and the digital age has a wealth of ways to aid expression, develop reflection and assist the exploration and sharing of ideas and information through language. Web 1 technology gave us the World Wide Web, with access to international communication. Web 2.0 technologies give learners personal opportunities for creative communication through **multimodal texts**, **multimedia presentations**, **blogs**, **wikis**, **podcasts** and other forms of ICT, many of which can be used to help them explore the power of language to communicate their ideas. Pupils can use websites, **simulations** and **WP packages** to see how languages work and change over time and to consider their structures and conventions, both in paper-based and screen-based texts. They need to become critical media users and to understand and appreciate literacies from different cultures and times. The use of ICT can aid independence in learning by developing the skills of drafting, checking and presenting work in different forms.

Digital technologies offer opportunities to explore and widen knowledge, to listen, read, write, discuss and debate. The varied and often visual modes of presentation appeal to different learning styles, which enables pupils of all abilities to engage with texts and respond in ways appropriate for their needs. No longer do writers have to think about spelling, grammar, layout, content and audience simultaneously. A writer can create content first and then process it digitally, to correct and suit the intended audience. Many editing techniques, such as instantly changing layouts, fonts and headings, can only be done in a WP package. Oracy skills are still at the heart of all communication, and pupils now have a greater opportunity than ever before to develop their speaking skills and broadcast their ideas and opinions. Skills such as critical thinking and creative expression developed in literacy sessions are needed in all subjects, and thematic work can provide the context for developing literacy skills, while IT can help to organise ideas. Many activities suggested below should be first demonstrated on an **IWB**, with the pupils doing as much as possible of the interacting. This can be followed by reinforcement through individual or small-group work, possibly with the use of **templates**, to structure or help assess learning.

Table 19.1 *English KS1: Knowledge, skills and understanding*

Speaking and listening

Speaking	Order **digital photos** of an activity and use as prompts for an oral recount.
	List simple headings on a **template** about what they want to say, reorder, number, print and use as notes, e.g. to talk about a hobby/interest or to summarise learning in a particular area.
	Use a tape-recorder to review their oracy skills in group discussions and identify ways to improve.
Listening	Listen to a **talking book** or story from www.bbc.co.uk/cbeebies/stories/theme/world/ and ask questions about it.
	Use **listening stations** to share a story before discussing and analysing it.
	Listen to tapes, **CDs**, radio or web-based media and identify the variation in the speech for different circumstances and listeners.
	Listen to a **tape/digital recording** of an expert's visit, e.g. a fireman/vet, to the school and use to plan questions to be answered by the class teacher.
Group discussion and interaction	Use a range of ICT artefacts, such as **digital camera**/mobile phone/**fax**/computer/**microphone**, in role-play situations. Comment on use of register and tone in different role-plays.
	In pairs or groups, retell a story from different characters' points of view: e.g. Little Red Riding Hood, the grandmother, the wolf and the woodsman. If each version is typed on to a few PowerPoint screens, they can be hyperlinked by the teacher to the title screen, so that children can choose to read the story from a number of different viewpoints (see p. 202 for how to do this).
Drama	Write play scripts and film scripts using a **word processor**. Use the tab key to indent speech. Add stage directions in *italics*.
	Use **video** or tape recorders or **digital audio devices** to record puppets enacting narratives.
Standard English	Plan formal talk to class/year group, perhaps as part of a school assembly. Write speech on a **word processor** and edit to reflect standard English.
	Write short play script/advertisement in colloquial English. Edit on a **word processor** to suit the intended audience. Rewrite as formal text and compare features.
Language variation	Comment on the ways TV presenters use non-verbal communication.
Breadth of study	Pupils should have access to a range of audio-communication technologies, including interactive books and walkie-talkies or mobile phones. They should have the opportunity to listen to purely aural texts, e.g. short radio broadcasts/taped poems and stories, as well as **digital recordings** of their own voices to help them to reflect on personal fluency.

Reading

Reading strategies	Read text on an **IWB** segment and blend phonemes to decode meaning. A teacher could highlight/split the phonemes on screen to help identify the words. Small-group practice can then follow. (Promethean and SMARTboard websites have prepared sessions for this.)
	Use a **WP** program with speech facility, e.g. Textease, to identify syllables in a **word bank** of words. Sort the words on screen according to the numbers of syllables they contain. A template could be used to assess pupil progress. (A4L)
Reading for information	Use **hyperlinks** in a **CD-ROM** to find words in a glossary. Use icons, headings, index and contents to navigate around a digital text.
	Use find facility with keywords in a non-fiction, screen-based text.
	Use highlight/underline/screen-pen on an **IWB** text to identify particular words and patterns of rhythm, rhyme and sound in a poem or story.
Literature	Use highlight/underline/screen pen on an **IWB** text to identify the characteristic features of different texts.
Language structure and variation	Use the **IWB** to compare examples of different genre. Use highlighters and notation to mark differences.
Breadth of study	The IWB makes it easy for pupils to share a range of digital texts, including those on CDs, websites and WP programs and other software. They will need to be taught the conventions of screen-based texts, such as hyperlinks, and be helped to use digital dictionaries, encyclopaedias and other reference materials.

Writing

Composition	Use bullets to make lists of things they like/dislike/are good at /want to be good at. Use the highlighter tool on a **word processor** to identify headings and keywords in a text or website. Copy these to a **word processor** to see summary of text. Combine text from a **word bank**, **digital photos**/computer-generated pictures from a **paint/draw program** and sound files into a **multimedia presentation**. This is easily done in programs such as **PowerPoint, Textease, Black Cat** and **2Create a Superstory**. Use e-mail to work with a partner in another class/school to create a shared text. The text can be swapped back and forth between the two writers as it is developed, paragraph by paragraph or sentence by sentence.
Planning and drafting	Use **WP** to type text and edit to practise grammar and syntax. An **IWB** can be used to model the process with large groups. Ensure no sentences start in the same way, unless for a special effect. Reorder a **template** of scrambled sentences to change meaning. Use the highlighter tool to identify particular features of their own texts. (A4L) Use word banks to write sentences about themselves and their work. Newspaper/science recording **templates** could be used for less-confident writers. Add class news to a school website/**intranet**/shared **blog** or **wiki**.
Punctuation	Help a teacher to punctuate text on **IWB**. Use a screen template to punctuate text. (A4L)
Spelling	Use a computer spellchecker. Use a spelling test generator for practising spelling.
Handwriting and presentation	Form large letters on an **IWB** with a program that emphasises movement and correct direction of formation. Practise typing skills, perhaps with a program designed to help with this, such as www.bbc.co.uk/schools/typing/. This could be done as an ongoing homework task. See Figure 19.1.
Standard English	Use a grammar checker on the computer at the end of a writing task.
Language structure	Use an **IWB** to drag words and sentences into the best and most effective order.
Breadth of study	Pupils should have access to a range of fictional and factual digital texts, on an **IWB**, a **CD-ROM**, TV, interactive books or texts on mobile phones. They can use different **WP** formats to compose newspaper articles, recipes, instructions, stories, letters, diaries and reports, using **WP** facilities such as headings, subheadings, bullets, numbering and word banks. Even the youngest can be helped to prepare labels and captions for work across the curriculum. They can be helped to compose mobile-phone messages using correct spelling and grammar. More able pupils could take texts written in one format and adapt them to another format, considering the changes of layout and vocabulary that are needed. Teacher-made **templates** can be a useful starting point for such work. Pupils should experiment with different layouts of the same text and compare printouts of different drafts to check revisions.

Figure 19.1 Taken from www.bbc.co.uk/schools/typing/

Table 19.2 *English KS2: Knowledge, skills and understanding*

Speaking and listening

Speaking	Make notes for an oral presentation using a **word processor**, using a variety of font sizes, bullets, numbering and other WP devices to help organise and simplify complex ideas. Identify powerful words/phrases that will add interest for the audience. Record on tape or **audio file** an oral presentation on a topic that interests them. Answer the phone and take messages during lunch-times and break-times. Listen to recordings of their speech and identify ways to make it clearer.
Listening	Use a **tape recording/digital recording** of an expert's visit to the school, e.g. school nurse/shopkeeper, and use to plan questions to be sent in an **e-mail** to the expert.
Group discussion and interaction	Use recordings of class discussion to see how to develop ideas and modify them. Write short play script/advertisement in colloquial English. Edit on a **word processor** to suit the intended audience. Rewrite as formal text and compare features. Play online **simulation** games, such as those on the BBC site, that require discussion and negotiation (www.bbc.co.uk/schools/teachers/keystage_2/games). See Figure 19.2.
Drama	Use **video** to help review and reflect on group drama, role play and discussion. Make a **video** of a drama with people or puppets, organising and adjusting the dialogue to the needs of the audience.
Standard English	Use a grammar checker on the computer at the end of a writing task. Create a formal **podcast** to report on work done in school for parents/governors. Create a less formal **podcast** as a radio broadcast to engage young listeners.
Language variation	Use a **webcam**/phone or **skype** to communicate, e.g. with pupils in a school in a different area. Identify how speech in film clips from TV or radio programmes varies from one person or area to another and suggest reasons for this. Look at a range of paper-based and screen-based advertisements and identify the ways language is used to attract and engage an audience. Compare play scripts and narrative text to see the differences between spoken and written language. Change a narrative dialogue to a play script using a **word processor** to alter the text.
Breadth of study	See suggestions for KS1. Also use **video-conferencing** facilities to discuss issues with people from other schools. Establish ground rules for taking turns. Develop clear diction and microphone technique. Use **video** to record role play of drama developing conciliation techniques.

Figure 19.2 Thorkel and the trading voyage

Reading

Reading strategies	Analyse texts on **IWB** using highlight tool/screen pen to identify features. Listen to a **talking book**. Compare its features with paper-based books. What are the advantages and disadvantages of each, and which do the children prefer and why? A talking book may give them the option of hearing the story read to them, seeing the relevant text highlighted as it is read, hearing it in another language, or at different speeds. What other options might they like? Which options are distracting?
Understanding texts	Work with teacher on the **IWB** to analyse text in a two-column table. Put text in the first column and identify non-literal meanings in the second column. Annotate a given text on screen, with textboxes to show meanings beyond the literal. (A4L) Use some of the ideas on the Ictopus site (www.ictopus.org.uk/index.php?sc=2&sub=1&pg=3) to help explore character and motivation. Use two highlighter colours on screen to identify viewpoints of character and author in a narrative. Add text boxes to add their own views at relevant points.
Reading for information	Research information to do with class topics on the **Internet/CD-ROMs** using focused questions and keywords. See what screen- and paper-based texts have in common. Use contents, index, glossary and icons on **CD-ROMs** to locate information. Use keywords and prepared research questions to find information from the **Internet**. Conduct advanced searches that use phrases in quotation marks to locate information.
Literature	Annotate the text of a poem through the use of text boxes, arrows, highlighting and underlining to show how writers use select words and a variety of language forms. Take a poem on screen and alter it word by word or line by line, to create a new poem with a similar structure to the original. See Figure 19.3.
Non-fiction and non-literary texts	Use the find facility in a **WP** program to locate information in a digital text. Use contents, index, glossary and icons on **CD-ROMs** to locate information. Use keywords to find out about pupils' favourite authors on the Internet.
Language structure and variation	Compare different versions of the same event/topic online to check accuracy and detect bias; e.g. compare Wikipedia text with other online and paper-based texts, bearing in mind that anyone with a computer can alter text in Wikipedia. Highlight sections that are opinion rather than fact. Discuss the advantages of each text type. Compare screen-based texts with paper-based magazines and stories to see how they differ from paper-based texts. Do the texts use any electronic devices, e.g. pop-up dialogue boxes or animations, which add other layers of meaning? Are they more/less subtle than paper-based texts? Consider headings, **hyperlinks** and layout. Which are easier to navigate? Annotate texts on-screen to show specialist (e.g. historical or scientific) terms. Highlight organisational features such as headings, bullets and text alignment. Compare the layouts of text written in different forms and for different purposes.
Breadth of study	Watch video clips from YouTube, adverts and short extracts from TV programmes, as well as **multimodal texts** on **CD-ROMs**, and analyse how the words, images and sounds have been combined to create a particular effect. Create **digital films**, **multimodal texts** and **podcasts** for a particular audience and purpose. Watch **digital film** clips, e.g. advertisements or clips from YouTube, and identify ways that meaning is conveyed, e.g. speaking to camera, voice-over, flashes of text and repetition.

The owl and the pussycat went to sea In a beautiful pea green boat. They took some honey and plenty of money Wrapped up in a five pound note. The owl looked up to the stars above And sang to a small guitar What a lovely pussy! O pussy my love What a beautiful pussy you are	The cat and the crocodile went to town In a battered bright red sports car. They took plenty of cash and cut quite a dash Though the car wouldn't go very far. The cat looked round at the shops so smart And danced as the crocodile sang, 'How we love to shop and spend till we drop,' And they did, as the cash tills rang.

Figure 19.3 The Owl and the Pussycat

Composition	Use the find-and-replace facility to replace dull words with more powerful ones.
	Reduce a piece of screen text to key points using the delete key. (A4L)
	Create **multimedia** stories, presentations, **podcasts** and articles.
	Write play scripts and create **podcasts**, animations or videos from them.
	Use **WP** facilities to organise layouts for printed and screen-based texts, e.g. a village brochure and a village website.
	Type up a factual report of an event, e.g. a visit by musicians to the school, or a proposal for change, e.g. the building of a local leisure centre. Save the text. Alter the account to add personal views on what happened/might happen and save as a second version. Swap texts and distinguish the fact and opinion used in each account.
	Combine research from the **Internet** with data from interviews and pupils' own personal opinion to present an argument about a local issue, such as developing a new supermarket/play area.
Planning and drafting	Use concept maps, flow charts, diagrams, graphs, graphics and texts to simplify complex ideas for the reader. These could be used as part of a brochure, magazine, **multimedia presentation**, website, oral presentation or report.
	List ideas, words and phrases for a story/poem/argument/persuasive report in a **WP** document. Edit to reorder and develop ideas. Use align, font and spellcheck tools to present work appropriately.
	Learn how to text friends without giving offence.
	Contribute to a class blog or wiki. (A4L)
	Use **WP** to change a piece of poetry to prose, or a story to a play script.
	Shape poems on a **word processor** to suit the content, e.g. see Figure 19.4.
	Use speech bubbles to create comic-book text.
	Use align and font facilities to make posters and invitations.
Punctuation	Use paragraphs, bullets, screen layout and headings to organise sections in a **hyperlinked** presentation, e.g. a class poetry anthology, or in a story with multiple-choice events and endings.
	Practise punctuation skills on a screen **template** that has no punctuation or organisation. (A4L)
	Try challenges from the BBC 'Skillswise' site on grammar, spelling, reading and writing (www.bbc.co.uk/skillswise/words/grammar/).
	Use **IWB** text with class teacher to identify and alter punctuation in order to clarify structure and meaning in a text.
Spelling	Use a spellchecker or spelling software package, e.g. Wordshark, to correct work.
	Sort words on-screen according to their spelling patterns (see Figure 19.5). (A4L)
	Match pairs of rhyming words on-screen. (A4L)
	Use a program such as Starspell from Fisher Marriott, which has many activities to aid spelling.
	Use find facility to search a text for words with common spelling patterns.
	Use online thesaurus/dictionary to find the meanings and origins of words.
Handwriting and presentation	Use text **templates** to write newspaper articles, letters, instructions for spells and recipes and reports.
	Create caligrams to show word meaning, e.g. LOUDER.
	Practise typing skills, perhaps with a BBC program.
	Break a poem into lines in different ways using **WP** and comment on the effect.
	Make a digital collection of poems from favourite authors. Add notes to each to explain choice and preferences.
	Use animating software such as **Kar2ouche** to create animated films and stories.
	Create a Big Book for younger readers on www.mape.org.uk/activities/BigBookMaker/.
	Evaluate the layout of several websites/**CD-ROMs** and then create pupils' own **hyperlinked** presentation on a class topic/interest of their own.
	Write an interactive story using **hyperlinks**. This might include stories from multiple viewpoints or with multiple consequences.
Standard English	Use editing facilities, spellcheck and grammar check to improve work in any context.
	Use the find facility in a **WP** program to make a collection of words with particular strings.

Language structure	Compare the layouts of paper-based and screen-based texts, including **CD-ROMs**, **e-zines** and other web pages and see what they have in common and how they differ. Discuss how the layout and format can affect meaning. Experiment with pupils' own formats and layouts to create screen-based texts, e.g. a class magazine that uses a range of formats and layouts. Transform a text from one format to another through copy and paste and editing facilities. Work with teacher on an **IWB** to analyse text in a two-column table. Put text in the first column and identify non-literal meanings in the second column. Annotate a given text on-screen, with textboxes to show meanings beyond the literal.
Breadth of study	Pupils should have access to a range of digital texts as well as creating their own. They can use **e-mail**, **blogs** or **webcams** to communicate with pupils in another school, e.g. through an international link such as the Comenius project. This might involve carrying out joint projects, such as a yearbook that describes the celebrations in each country or a **CD-ROM** guide to localities in each country. Pupils can create a **multimodal** text, which shows a technique or idea through the use of *image*, explains it through *speech* and describes it through *writing*, and **multimedia** presentations, which involve *text*, *pictures*, a short *film* and *voice-over* to report on a school activity, e.g. an enterprise project or science/history topic. They could create radio broadcasts/**podcasts** of stories and play scripts, with music and sound effects. Look at the structure, organisation and presentation of a short film. See how it has been constructed and use lessons learned to create a **digital film** of their own, e.g. for a newsflash, forecast, advert or short story. Create a class **e-zine** or class/school/club website. Try for free hosting and templates and awards.

A
TREE
of speckled
birds, sings a brittle
song of dusk
to
the
dark
wind

Figure 19.4

care   here   hear   bear   hair   pear   where

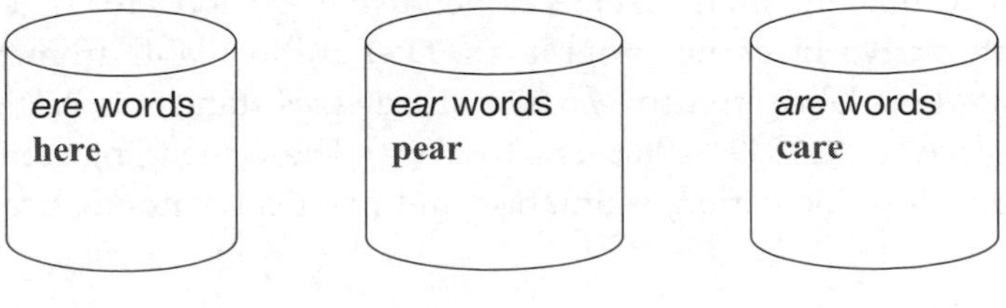

ere words here

ear words pear

are words care

Figure 19.5

20 Mathematics

Maths starts with practical exploration of ideas and numbers, an exploration that can be supported by the use of ICT facilities to record and calculate accurately. Turtles, calculators and spreadsheets can be used to solve problems, model different scenarios, make sense of data and inform decisions. ICT equipment can help deal with huge numbers, beyond the normal reach of the pupil, and make mathematical comparisons understandable. Satellite navigation systems and GPS facilities, now in common use in pupils' home life, can help them to measure, represent shape and space, as well as understand distances and positions. Brain trainers, which are fun to use, can challenge people of all ages to develop spatial awareness, logical thinking and rapid-calculation strategies. Programs with random number generators may aid understanding of risk and luck, while the myriad of games available online or on CD-ROM are excellent for developing the notion of maths as an enjoyable activity, as well as fostering calculation and strategy skills.

Once pupils understand the processes required, a calculator or spreadsheet can reduce the time taken for a task, while increasing accuracy and improving the presentation beyond the skills of the user. To make progress, pupils need to explore ideas and strategies and apply logic and reasoning; the use of a spreadsheet, a calculator or game designed for the purpose can make this process more enjoyable and carry out calculations on behalf of the thinker. Computer-generated charts can help learners see patterns and spend more time on analysis and less on hand-drawn, less-accurate charts. Clear visual presentation can help pupils to identify patterns, equivalences and relationships. Pupils can spend more time on interpretation and less on correction. ICT presentation facilities can help children to communicate their ideas and findings to a wide audience, through e-mail and websites.

Skills learned in maths should be applied in subjects right across the curriculum, from budgeting in DT or calculating travel arrangements in geography to working out timeline scales in history or scores in PE. Skills such as mapping, employed in geography, can be developed in maths sessions, while solving problems in science investigations will use a wide range of skills that are often best developed using ICT tools for speed and accuracy.

Excellent **interactive teaching programs (ITPs)** are available from the government standards website (available at: http://nationalstrategies.standards.dcsf.gov.uk/search/primary/results/nav%3A49909%20facets%3A27904). These engaging games and activities can be used to develop calculation, estimation and practical mathematical skills.

Table 20.1 *Mathematics KS1: Knowledge, skills and understanding*

Number	
Using and applying numbers	Count numbers of objects on-screen, using a series of prepared screen templates. Drag numbers to label set. (A4L) Use simple data-handling software, e.g. temperature sensors to record the temperature of cooking liquids/melting ice.
Problem-solving	Use maths strategy games in small groups on an **IWB**.
Communication	Use Venn diagram and Carroll diagram on an **IWB** to sort numbers according to their properties. (A4L) Use clip art to make number posters. (A4L)
Reasoning	Use a **branching database** program to group and sort numbers according to their properties. Use on-screen Venn and Carroll diagrams to sort numbers according to their properties. (A4L)
Numbers and the number system	Use number lines and number squares with an **IWB** to insert or colour numbers in the correct order. The **Counting on and back ITP** and the **Difference ITP** will be useful here.
Counting	Add numbers to number line/snake/ladder template, with increasing complexity, depending on ability. (A4L) See Figure 20.1.
Number patterns and sequences	Use calculators to explore number patterns. Colour 100 squares on-screen using, for instance, the four times table, to explore number patterns (quicker and easier to correct than doing this on paper). The **Number grid ITP** generates a 100-square grid for many activities.
The number system	Use random-number-generating dice on IWBs to play board games. The **Moving digits ITP** can be used to explore the effect of multiplying and dividing by 10 and 100.
Calculations	Use interactive games on **IWB**.
Number operations and the relationships between them	Complete number sentences on screen to enable the patterns to be seen more clearly. (A4L) Use the **Number facts ITP** to model addition by combining and counting, and subtraction by partitioning and taking away.
Mental methods	Share strategies on **IWB** to develop skills and make the mental calculations visible and therefore memorable. Use a calculator to see how many ways the number 10 can be made. Use the **Place value ITP** to partition and recombine three-digit numbers. Match pairs of numbers on screen that will add up to a multiple of 10, e.g. $70 + 30 = \ldots$; $60 + \ldots = 100$; $57 + 33 = \ldots$; $57 - 17 = \ldots$. Dragging numbers on-screen or linking them with a line enables those with poor manual dexterity to concentrate on the mental calculation. (A4L)
Solving numerical problems	Drag price tickets on-screen to order according to value. (A4L) Use screen game to match coins to cost of a pictures item. (A4L)
Processing, representing and interpreting data	Use data-handling software, e.g. database, to sort data and answer questions. Use the **Data-handling ITP** to explore handling data and create bar or pie charts.

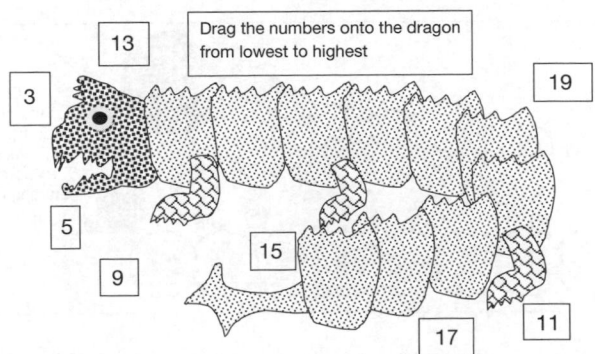

Figure 20.1

Shape, space and measures

Using and applying shape, space and measures	Use a graphing program to compare the heights of children or their toy bears. Link with a line on-screen template to match pictures of items to their mass. Complete on-screen timeline or timetable or calendar to show what happens at different times of the day, week or year. Drag lengths in centimetres to match those in metres, e.g. 175 cm = 1.75 m. Use simulation software with scales to measure liquid and mass, e.g. the **Measuring scales ITP** allows the child or teacher to add different masses of 1, 2, 5, 10, 50, 100 and 500 units to a scale pan. The scale intervals can be changed to challenge children to interpret different scales.
Problem-solving	Play shopping games on IWB using large coins to pay for items and get change.
Communicating	Use spreadsheet and graphing programs to store data and create charts to help analyse them.
Reasoning	Instruct a **Roamer**, **floor turtle** or **Pixie** to move around a route.
Understanding patterns and properties of shapes	Use a Venn diagram to sort shapes according to their properties, e.g. sort a prepared template of polygons, ovals and circles, according to the number of sides they have. This on-screen activity should take place *after* experience with real objects. It has the advantage of working with completely 2D shapes, as even the thinnest plastic shape is in fact a solid 3D shape. (A4L) Use a graphics program to create tessellating and symmetrical patterns on-screen. Use the **Area ITP** to explore numbers, shapes and space and problem-solving.
Understanding properties of position and movement	Use an on-screen turtle program to draw shapes and complete routes devised by pupils.
Understanding measures	Use Area ITP using volume and mass activities.
Breadth of study	**ITPs**, **spreadsheets** and graphing programs, **branching databases**, calculators and **turtles** can all be used to make learning about maths and exploring mathematical concepts relevant and enjoyable for pupils.

Table 20.2 *Mathematics KS2: Knowledge, skills and understanding*

Number

Using and applying numbers	Use digital temperature **sensors** to find the temperature of different places/liquids and a calculator to work out the difference between them. Use **spreadsheets** to make function machines to add or find the difference between two numbers. These can be decorated in an art session to look like complex machines. Pupils can change the formula to create different types of sum. Figure 20.2 shows the formula: =IF(C5+E5=G5, "well done", "try again") in the 'Try again' cell. Use a **spreadsheet** to record team scores, averages and positions in a league table.
Problem-solving	Use **spreadsheets** to plan holiday budgets, work out exchange rates and plan travel times and distances. Use **spreadsheets** to work out pocket-money savings or plan party or celebration budgets.

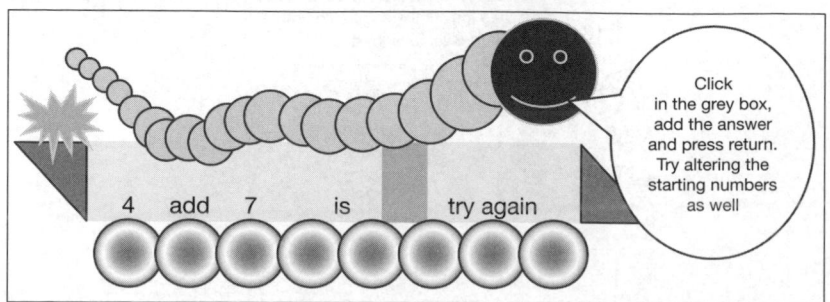

Figure 20.2

Communicating	Use the **Line graph ITP** to enter data into a table and then create a line graph to represent the data. Existing data sets can be amended to show the impact on the graph. The data table can be hidden, so that questions can be asked about the graph – for example, what a horizontal section on the graph means.
Reasoning	Use a **binary database** to sort numbers according to their properties. Create and use Carroll diagrams; e.g. see Figure 20.3.
Numbers and the number systems	Use the **Internet** to find out about numbers in different contemporary cultures, e.g. Arabic, Chinese and Indian numerals.
Counting	Use an on-screen table to record equivalent amounts of money in pounds and pence. Use prepared **templates** for children to develop their navigational skills, e.g. on a snakes and ladders game in Black Cat's Logo.
Number patterns and sequences	Use **spreadsheet** formulae to generate multiples and other number patterns. Begin a pattern on a **spreadsheet** that doubles the previous answer. Create a program to calculate/check their knowledge of 2, 3, 4, 5 and 10 times tables using a **spreadsheet**. (A4L)
Integers	Explore the **Place value ITP**, which displays place-value cards that can be used to construct and partition three-digit whole numbers. (A4L)
Fractions, percentages and ratio	Use the **Fractions IPT** to compare fractions on fraction strips. The strips can be labelled as fractions, decimals (to three decimal places) or percentages. Use a template in a **paint** program to colour fractions of shapes on-screen. This is better than the traditional paper/crayon-based activity, as it is quicker and easier to correct mistakes. (A4L) Use the **Ratio and proportion ITP** to compare amounts of liquid (see Figure 20.4).
Decimals	Order negative/fraction/decimal numbers on-screen by dragging to a number line. (A4L) Find out about fractions and decimals with the **Fractions ITP**. Use the **Decimal number line ITP**.
Calculations	Use calculators to check estimates. Use a calculator to see how many sums can be made with the answer 20. Pupils devise own calculation games, where the answers are checked with a calculator. More advanced pupils can do this with decimals. Use the **Number Dials ITP** to practise multiplying and dividing by one- and two-digit whole numbers and decimals.
Number operations and the relationships between them	Use the **Multiplication Facts ITP** to support the exploration of multiplication and division. Work with **Multigrid ITP** to set up a multiplication grid to demonstrate the grid method of multiplication for whole and decimal numbers.
Mental methods	Use an **IWB** to share and demonstrate mental-calculation strategies.
Written methods	Use IWB resources to see the equivalence of fractions and decimals. Use an on-screen grid to create fraction equivalence grids and convert them to show decimals.
Calculator methods	Use a calculator or spreadsheet to work out large sums, e.g. how much TV do pupils watch in a year? Does this end up as hours, days or months of their lives? Use an **IWB** clock to compare analogue and digital time.
Solving numerical problems	Create a **table/spreadsheet** to aid conversion between metric units.

	Even Number	Odd Numbers
Multiples of 3		
Multiples of 5		

Figure 20.3

Shape, space and measures

Using and applying shape, space and measures	Use a screen with a grid to create symmetrical pictures. One pupil could draw half a house/face for another pupil to complete. Mistakes are more easily corrected than with paper and pencil. Use screen grid to scale diagrams up and down in size. A screen drawing is easier to correct than a paper-based one. Use **Measuring scales ITP** and the **Measuring cylinder ITP** for simulation measuring experience (see Figure 20.5). The **Thermometer ITP** can be used to develop children's understanding of vertical scales and negative numbers in the context of temperature. Use the **Internet** to find out about the development of metric and other number systems.
Problem-solving	Use a **spreadsheet** to work out the perimeter of rectangles. Pupils should work out the formula they need (a + b + c + d / (a + b) x 2 / 2a + 2b). They can check this with a number of examples. Will this work for all quadrilaterals? How can they adapt the formula for other shapes? See area and perimeter activities at: www.bgfl.org/bgfl/custom/resources_ftp/client_ftp/ks2/maths/perimeter_and_area/index.html
Communicating	Use screen **turtles** to create a maze. Each child has to navigate through the maze designed by their partner. The partner gives directions using maths language to reinforce directions and angle vocabulary.
Reasoning	Use a **spreadsheet** or simple **database** to collect data about the height, weight and wingspan of different birds. Sort and graph data to check for anomalies. Use a simple **database** to record the number and types of animals in local habitats. Interrogate the **database** to look for patterns, e.g. are all the flying animals found in trees/are some animals found in only one habitat?
Understanding properties of shapes	Use **graphics** tools to draw 2D shapes and identify their properties. Drag shapes on a screen template to make new polygons. Count sides and label. (A4L) Use a **decision-tree** program to identify plane shapes. Use a **graphics** program to draw symmetrical and repeating geometric patterns. Use a large on-screen protractor to measure angles on an **IWB**. Use the **Coordinates ITP** to identify the coordinates of points on different grids. You can mark points and draw lines and shapes. You have a choice of one, two or four quadrants to work in to introduce both positive and negative coordinates. Use the **Polygon ITP** to explore the properties of regular and irregular polygons. Use the **CalcAngle ITP** to place shapes around a point and investigate their angles. Use **Autoshapes** to explore the tessellating properties of plane shapes. Find different routes for a **turtle** through a maze/from bottom left to top right of a screen.
Understanding properties of position and movement	Use a large protractor on **IWB** to measure angles. Teach a screen **turtle** to draw regular polygons (e.g. Forward 50 right 60 will draw a regular hexagon if the instructions are repeated six times).
Understanding measures	Record measurements from practical work in **tables** that can be ordered, rounded or graphed for ease of use. Try the measuring activity at: www.bgfl.org/bgfl/custom/resources_ftp/client_ftp/ks2/maths/measures/index.htm which has challenges for different units of measurement. Measure the same objects/distances in different ways. Display results in a **table**. Record brief explanation about the need for standard measuring/the benefits of metric measurement. Use the **Tell time ITP**, which displays on-screen analogue and digital clocks, to identify time before and after given intervals and to undertake calculations that involve time. Create simple, screen-based challenges with text and clip art to assess understanding of measures (see Figure 20.6).
Breadth of study	Record times and distances for PE activities. Pairs of children should check each other's results. Use a **digital camera** to record practical work in this area with 3D shapes.

Handling data

Problem-solving	Use a calculator to see how many numbers can be created with all four operations and four numbers that are the same, e.g. 4, 4, 4, 4 or 6, 6, 6, 6; e.g. 4 + 4 ÷ 4 x 4. Pupils should explore the order in which the operations are performed to see what difference this can make.
Communicating	Use a **digital camera** and Internet information to compile information. Create posters or presentations to report learning to others. Older children can use a presentation program, e.g. **Hyperstudio** or **PowerPoint**, to create **hyperlinked** texts to teach younger children about a topic they have studied, e.g. the properties of shapes or fractions facts.
Reasoning	Give pupils a decimal challenge with a start number and a target number. Players use a calculator and take turns to choose a number to multiply the start number by to get as close to the target number as possible.
Processing, representing and interpreting data	Use **spreadsheet** functions to compare different kinds of average and give reasons for why those were chosen. Show how to round numbers on a **spreadsheet** by changing the number of decimal points. Use frequency diagram on-screen to record results of traffic census. Convert to bar charts.
Breadth of study	Pupils should learn to decide when the use of ICT is appropriate and be able to explain the advantages of its use. They can search the **Internet** to find out about the origins and use of maths in different cultures and use presentation programs to record their learning.

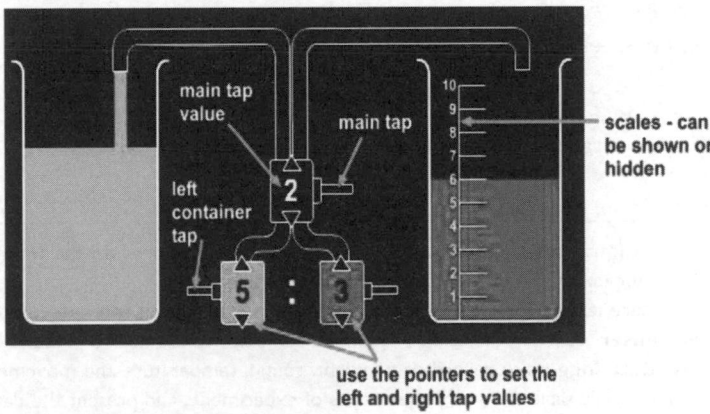

Figure 20.4

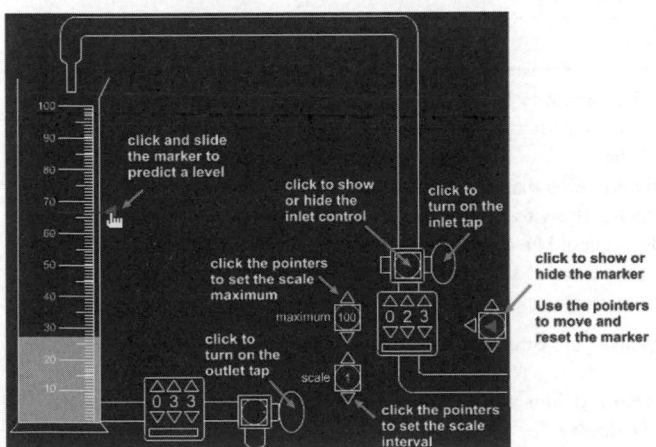

Figure 20.5

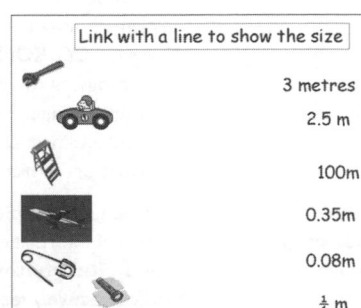

Figure 20.6

21 Science

Science is essentially a practical and investigative subject, but the use of ICT can make planning, recording and analysing such investigations quicker, simpler and more accurate. Planning and recording **templates** with appropriately differentiated prompts can help with organising ideas and drawing conclusions from results.

To make progress, children should develop ICT skills that help them to obtain information from a range of primary sources, e.g. data-logging, and secondary sources, e.g. the Internet, and use spreadsheets and simulations to help predict possible outcomes of experiments that would be hard to access in reality. They should select suitable ICT tools to control risks, record data, create tables and charts and organise and present information in posters, leaflets, podcasts and multimedia presentations.

Table 21.1 *Science KS1: Knowledge, skills and understanding*

Scientific enquiry	
Ideas and evidence in science	Use a **digital camera** to record the results of investigations into the ways materials can be changed, e.g. the melting of chocolate, candles or ice. Compare leaves, flowers, shells and materials using a **digital microscope** or **visualiser**. Take photos using a **visualiser** or **scanner** to add to presentations. Use **data loggers** to record data in light, sound, temperature and movement tests. Use a simple table to record the results of experiments and present the data to someone else. In **Word**, the data can be graphed straight from a table without using a spreadsheet. A child-friendly **template** would be useful for this to make entering the data and drawing a graph quite easy.
Investigative skills	
Planning	Use **templates** in a **WP** program to help plan investigations, record data and make charts to analyse. Templates should include sections for asking questions, planning, predicting and explaining how the test is fair. Navigate **CD-ROMs** and websites that provide reference material for science and technology. Show the children how to use the icons/contents/index and keywords/glossary facilities. A paper-based quiz could help them to explore the features, as well as learn relevant science. Discuss the pros and cons of a CD text over a book or magazine of information. Which are most enjoyable/quickest/most up to date/easiest to use?
Obtaining and presenting evidence	Use text, tables, **pictograms** and other charts to make it easier to describe and compare pieces of information. Use **digital photos** and **sound files**/taped accounts of investigations to present pupils' work effectively for public display. Use a **WP** program or simple **multimedia presentation**, combining text, charts and photos, e.g. in **PowerPoint** or **Pawprints**, to present results to a particular audience.

Considering evidence and evaluating	Create a **scattergram** to see the relationship between the height and age of people in the school, or between foot size and hand span. Use a **template** with differentiated questions to help evaluate findings. Doing this in a **WP** program can make it easier to edit and develop ideas. Use **WP** to list and reorder, if necessary, key points of an oral presentation.

Life processes and living things

Life processes	Use sorting circles on a screen/whiteboard to group things into those that are living and those that have never been alive. (A4L) **Digital cameras** and **spreadsheets** could be used to record investigation processes and results. Use a **WP package** to make a list of instructions for the care of different living things and the local environment. Order according to importance.
Humans and other animals	Use a **CD-ROM** or **Internet site** to make comparisons about the main external parts of the bodies of humans and other animals. Explore ways of looking after living things: for plants, this is best done with real seeds and plants. A simple **simulation** program could be used to explore what might happen to plants and animals in different situations. Use a simple **database** or **spreadsheet** to create a class database about the similarities and differences between class members. In a **WP** program, make labelled diagrams using photos, clip art/pupils' drawings from a **paint program**. Choose a healthy meal from an **interactive screen template** made from clip-art food. (A4L)
Green plants	Label parts of plants using clip art or pictures drawn or photographed by the children and scanned into the computer. Add further details in text boxes that can be adjusted and edited to fit information. Use a **spreadsheet** to sort plants according to the type of flower or leaf.
Variation and classification	Use a **branching database** to sort, group and identify familiar plants, animals and materials. Use a **spreadsheet** to sort animals according to the number of legs they have. Use sorting circles on a screen/**IWB** to group pictures of animals, including humans, into those that can swim/fly or walk/hop. If these are prepared as **templates**, they can be used many times. Challenge pupils to find their own ways to sort the animals. These are the first steps towards understanding classification. (A4L) Combine words and pictures when sorting and grouping familiar living things according to observable features and properties. A **word bank** with clip art would be useful for this. For poor readers, use a program such as **Clicker** or **Textease**, which can read the words aloud to the pupils on selection. Use data to compile a class **database** about birds/minibeasts/plants.
Living things in their environment	**Digital cameras**, **digital film** and digital maps can be used to collect, review and present evidence when investigating the local environment. Films about recycling could be used to reinforce messages about the correct disposal of waste. Use a **CD-ROM** or specific Internet sites to find out about the way the production of some materials can affect our world, e.g. the use of wood, oil or water and the production of food. There are many links to children's sites on http://oils.gpa.unep.org/kids/kids.htm. **Ollie's Island Educator** explores chains of sustainable production and consumption across several major industries (www.olliesworld.com/club/club.htm). Look at **Google Earth** pictures and maps of the local area to help identify different habitats.

Materials and their properties

Grouping materials	Use **word bank** and clip art to write about materials and objects, recording properties such as roughness, hardness, shininess, ability to float, transparency and if they are magnetic or non-magnetic. Record what they learn on a table **template** prepared by the teacher. See Figure 21.1. Use a **CD-ROM** or website to find out where everyday materials come from, how and why they are used, and how they can be recycled. Use sorting circles on a screen/**IWB** to group materials for texture, hardness, flexibility and other properties. NB: first-hand experience should precede screen-based revision. (A4L)

Changing materials	Use a **digital microscope**, **visualiser** and **data-logging** to investigate the properties of materials and what happens when they are changed/recycled (e.g. paper recycled as papier mâché). Record test results from heating/cooling in simple **bar charts**.

Physical processes

Electricity	Exploring electrical circuits is best done practically, with real components. A simple **simulation** program could be used to reinforce the learning (www.learningcircuits.co.uk/flashmain.htm and ideas on www.learnanytime.co.uk/Science/Electrical%20Circuits.htm). Use a **CD-ROM** to find out how electricity is used in homes, school and industry. Use a **simulation** program/website to find out how electricity is used in the home and what can be done to reduce its use, e.g. by switching off computers and TVs, instead of leaving them on stand-by.
Forces and motion	Mechanisms are best explored in a practical context. Simple reports with charts could be produced with a **WP package** and **digital photos** to communicate their findings. Graph test results with a **data-handling package** or a table in **Word**. A **simulation program** could be used to reinforce or extend learning on pushes and pulls.
Light and sound	Use a **digital camera** to record shadows and make a visual quiz to identify each. Use **data-logging** to record light, temperature and sound in investigations, e.g. which is the darkest/coolest/noisiest place in the school? Use a **tape recorder** or **digital audio recorder** to record sound sources.
Breadth of study	Skills learned in other subjects can contribute to understanding in science. Pupils' ICT skills should be developed to help them use a range of ICT-based sources of information and data. They should make the most of ICT opportunities to help them organise and explain information. **Simulations** on websites and **CD-ROMs** can be used to reinforce teaching on health and safety issues.

Where do my clothes come from?		
From plants	**From animals**	**From the ground**
cotton	wool	nylon
rubber shoes	silk	lycra
rayon	leather shoes	fleece (made from recycled plastic bottles and oil)
		acrylic

Figure 21.1

Table 21.2 *Science KS2: Knowledge, skills and understanding*

Scientific enquiry

Ideas and evidence in science	This site has many good leads to help explore ideas in science: www.learnanytime.co.uk/Science/Science.htm. Use **simulations** to understand a range of scientific processes. Use the **Internet** to find out about advances in science, e.g. Jenner's vaccination work. Use **IWB** to collect a range of explanations from the pupils for test results. Encourage pupils to make creative links between cause and effect.

Investigative skills

Planning	Use a **WP template** to plan and record ideas in an investigation. Planning templates should encourage predictions, detailed observation, accurate measuring and explanations. List what needs to be done in a science experiment. Cut and paste the activities into the most useful order. (A4L)

| Obtaining and presenting evidence | Use **hand-held devices** and **palmtops** to collect data on field trips.
Use **data-logging** sound, light and temperature sensors to detect and compare sounds.
Use a **data logger** with a movement sensor to find out if the class goldfish go to sleep at night or keep swimming, or at what time birds start to visit a feeder and when they rest for the night.
Use the Internet/**CD-ROM** to find out about the physical characteristics of a locality and a contrasting locality, and habitats within them.
Use **e-mail** and **digital photographs** to communicate with pupils in another school about scientific investigations, e.g. comparing habitats.
Use a **digital camera** to record the stages in an investigation.
Pupils should be taught how to share information in a variety of forms, including diagrams, drawings, tables, charts, line graphs and photos, to communicate data in an appropriate and systematic manner, e.g. use **Powerpoint** to make multimedia presentations that consider users' needs. Import **digital photos** of investigations and charts. Require key scientific vocabulary to be used to ensure rigour. |
| Considering evidence and evaluating | Use **spreadsheets** or **databases** to graph the results of science tests to save time for analysing evidence and drawing conclusions, rather than colouring hand-drawn graphs.
Record investigation data on **templates** and use them to help explain conclusions. These could incorporate a section that helps pupils to evaluate their scientific skills and identify ways they could improve these processes in future work, e.g. see Figure 21.2.
Use **Internet** research to find out about significant innovations and inventions from the past and record in a timeline or a presentation.
Take **digital photos**, video clips and sound recordings and add key terminology using **Windows Movie Maker** to make a film about a project. This might be about significant inventions in the past and/or about pupils' own experiments. |

What I did best	
What I learned	
Evaluation	If I did this work again I could improve it by ...

Figure 21.2

Life processes and living things

Life processes	Watch video clips from YouTube or a **CD-ROM** to see things that cannot be directly observed, such as animals skeletons/the life cycle of a butterfly (www.youtube.com/watch?v=IRiwXMeKoGk); inside a beehive (www.youtube.com/results?search_query=inside+a+beehive&search_type=&aq=f); how an apple rots (www.youtube.com/watch?v=IRiwXMeKoGk). Use **digital photos**, clip art, **scanned** images or pupils' own computer drawings to make labelled diagrams, e.g. of parts of an animal/the human body, to aid explanations about life processes.
Humans and other animals	Use a food **database/spreadsheet** to store information about the nutritional content of a range of foods, e.g. cereals/yoghurts. If each child enters data for one product, then any child can graph all records for one food family, such as fat, sugar or salt. The results showing which are highest/lowest in salt, fat and sugar can be dramatic and provide a starting point to compare the nutritional value of a range of foods, drinks and snacks. Use a **WP** program to create posters and leaflets about keeping healthy. Use a **video** or **CD-ROM** to see things that cannot directly be observed, e.g. circulation of the blood. Use **data-logging** to record a pulse before and after exercise. Make labelled diagrams using clip art/photos, with text boxes and arrows to show what has been learned about different body systems, e.g. skeletons and muscles.
Green plants programme	Scan/photograph a whole plant, including the roots, for labelling in a **WP**. Use a **digital microscope/visualiser** to see the magnified structure of the flowering parts of a plant.

Record plant growth through photography, using **freeze-frame animation/time-lapse photography**, if possible, to record this. If not, look at videos on YouTube that show this. Search the Internet on selected sites to find out how plants grow and are used around the world. Teachers could devise an **Internet quiz** to help focus this exploration.

Use a **paint program** to draw the parts of a flower. Copy to a **WP** program for labelling and explanations, using inserted text boxes.

Variation and classification	Use **databases** to store information about local habitats, such as the light, dampness, temperature and type of shelter they provide. Interrogate the database to see trends or relationships in the data collected. Use a **branching database** to make keys to identify the minibeasts/plants pupils find. Create a **decision-tree** program to identify a range of trees, animals or birds. Use the filter on **spreadsheet** programs to sort and group animals or plants.
Living things in their environment	Use the Internet to research water sources/endangered species and sites of special scientific interest (SSSI) in a range of localities. Use **palmtops** with **GPS** and keys to identify the plants and animals in different habitats and compare the features of different localities. Create concept maps using text boxes/specialist software, e.g. **Kidspiration**, to show the relationships between plans and animals and their habitats. Use **clip art**, **text boxes** and arrows to record food chains and food webs. See Figure 21.3. (A4L) Log on to **webcams** to see how different uses of technology affect land use. Use **simulation** software to show the changes in the populations of micro-organisms in different conditions. Simulations enable children to visualise micro-organisms that are too small to see or that may be harmful. Research the **Internet** for diseases caused by micro-organisms. This will need careful preparation, to ensure the pupils read only relevant material.

Materials and their properties

Grouping and classifying materials	Use a **simulation** program to compare the elasticity of materials/other practical investigations. Use this after practical work to reinforce ideas tested. After practical work, create a Venn diagram or Carroll diagram on-screen to compare the properties of a range of materials, such as rocks and minerals, e.g. thermal insulation/electrical conductivity/texture and permeability. Take pictures with **digital cameras** to record the different materials used in the high street, a park or the school. Use to devise a materials trail for another class.
Changing materials	Use **data-logging** to record the changes in temperature when materials are heated or cooled. This could be part of a project about insulation and making the best cover for a hot-water bottle. Watch videos about changing materials, e.g. those on www.abpischools.org.uk/res/coResourceImport/modules/solids-liquids-gases/fullscreenflash094c.cfm?flash=en-flash/launcher_movie.swf&title=Solids,+Liquids+and+Gases&version=6. Create a set of **hyperlinked** pages to explain scientific terms, such as evaporation and condensation, in a document that uses these words. Use **tables** to compare changes that are reversible and irreversible. Use **graphics** tools to create mind maps and diagrams to explore and record the relationships between reversible changes.
Separating mixtures of materials	Make clip art to illustrate science experiments, either by grouping Autoshapes or by grouping ready-made clips from Black Cat or Textease, e.g. Figure 21.4. Use a **spreadsheet** to record which materials create solutions or suspensions. Record the speed at which different sugars dissolve in water at different temperatures, and analyse data using a **spreadsheet** and graphing program.

Figure 21.3

Physical processes

Electricity	Use **graphics** tools/Autoshapes to create circuit diagrams. Use **simulations** to explore the effect of changing components in a circuit. Use electrical devices that show how much energy is being consumed when different electrical devices are turned on/off.
Forces and motion	Explore the effects of different forces in **simulations** to reinforce learning from practical investigations, e.g. from the Learn Anytime site (www.learnanytime.co.uk/Science). Plan a **multimedia** slideshow for another class to explain the effects of different forces. Add **digital photos** of investigations and **videos** of parachutes falling in pupils' tests. Record results of investigation measuring forces using **spreadsheets** and graphing software.
Light and sound	Use **light sensors** to see which materials are most opaque/transparent, and which locations/habitats are darkest. Use **graphics** tools to record diagrams about sight and seeing. Use **control technology** to explore what happens when instructions in a lighting sequence are altered. Use **sound sensors** or a **tape recorder/digital audio** equipment to compare noise levels for different activities or places round the school. If only a tape recorder is available, the noise level can be monitored by seeing the volume at which the sound has to be played back to make it audible. Use a **tape recorder/digital sound files** to make a sound quiz. Use a **digital recording** of a sound from a triangle or drum to make a standardised sound test. Turn the volume up until the sound can be heard. Which type of sound carries furthest? Who can hear the highest-/lowest-pitched sounds? Use a **digital camera** to record the changes in a shadow of a stick/human sundial during a day. Record learning as a strip cartoon account of a science experiment. Give keywords to be explained to ensure rigour.
The earth and beyond	Use a video, **CD-ROM** or **simulation** to study models of the Earth in space and its relationship to the Sun and Moon and the solar system. Use the **Internet** to find out how the length of day and night/the seasons affects plant growth/animal behaviour, such as migration, in different parts of the world. Create a mind map of what pupils learn, with **hyperlinks** to relevant websites/pages of information. Use **WP** and **graphics** to create health and safety posters and leaflets.
Breadth of study	A wide range of ICT tools can be used to teach the knowledge, skills and understanding that can be explored both in school and further afield. Pupils should discuss their understanding and use of technologies that are familiar to them, such as tape recorders, digital cameras, the digital sensing of temperature in cookers, rooms and cars, as well as movement sensors in burglar alarms and speed cameras and the light sensors used by street lamps. **Webcams**, the Internet and **e-mail** can be used to obtain information from places pupils are unable to visit themselves. ICT can be used to create accurate records and presentations in less time than a hand-drafted version. **Simulations** should not replace all first-hand experience, but they can be useful to explore hazardous situations that would not be safe to explore in practice.

Figure 21.4

22 Modern foreign languages

Table 22.1 *Modern foreign language study*

Area of learning	Languages – speaking and listening
Identify and respond to key sounds, rhymes and rhythm in the new language	Match pairs of rhyming words on-screen. (A4L) Use a **WP** with a speech facility to hear words pronounced.
Experiment with and practise making the sounds of the new language	Give directions to a floor robot/Roamer in a **MFL** to make it go to specific places in the room/on a floor map. Record a weather forecast in a **MFL** using **digital video**.
Begin to assign meaning to words and sounds that are unfamiliar	Learn songs in another language on www.mamalisa.com/. Hear MP3 recordings of the songs and download the music to sing along to.
Recognise and respond to familiar words, word categories and short sentences that they hear	Use the find facility in a **WP** program to make a collection of words with particular strings.
Engage in conversations and ask and answer questions	Construct a **branching database** to ask and answer questions about animals/people/objects in a **MFL**.
Understand simple conventions of different languages	Try some of the many **MFL** activities from the Ictopus site (www.ictopus.org.uk/index.php?sc=0).
Recognise and understand familiar words, phrases and simple sentences	Act out simple role play/drama in an **MFL**. Take **digital photos** of key points and add to a **multimedia presentation**. Add speech bubbles in the appropriate language to show what is being said.
Read and interpret a range of simple texts	Read **e-books** and stories online. Find poems on the **Internet** in **MFL** they enjoy and add simple illustrations in **paint program**. Copy both into a **WP/presentation** document.
Select and use familiar words and phrases to convey meaning in written text	Create an **e-book** by drawing images in a **paint document** and copying them into a PowerPoint or other WP program to add text.
Understand that different languages are spoken in different parts of the UK and the world	Read and sing some of the songs in the multilingual songbook (www.laukart.de/ctm/index.php?id=239). On this site, they can read and hear the same song in several languages. Use an online dictionary to look up the meanings of words and to translate words into another language (www.yourdictionary.com/languages.html).
Recognise that languages have words and features in common as well as differences	See where some of our English words have come from on www.krysstal.com/borrow.html#a. Use a 2-column **table** to write short English sentences in column 1 and a translation in column 2. Use screen highlighters to show the adjectives/verbs/nouns and compare where each occurs in a sentence. Which features are common/different? (A4L)
Explore similarities and differences in everyday life, traditions and celebrations in different cultures and countries	Use the **Internet** to find out about lives in other countries through focused questions and keywords. Communicate through **e-mail/blog** with pupils in another country, sharing information about different lifestyles, traditions and celebrations.

23 History

Digital technologies enable pupils to gather a wide range of information about the history of the world around them, from historical maps and surveys to written accounts and records, and to organise and present it in appropriate forms. Chronology and a sense of time are essential to an understanding of the past, and spreadsheets can create timelines to help with this. Digital maps from the past and present can be annotated by pupils with text boxes and photos of particular features. Tables help to organise data, so that learners can compare differences between ways of life at different times. Pupils can research documents on the Internet and CD-ROMs to see ways in which the past has been represented in different times, and the knowledge gained can be used to develop historical interpretation and enquiry skills. They will need to look at contemporary records with criticality, to look for bias and inaccuracy. Public records such as census returns can be viewed online, and pupils can make virtual visits to museums, galleries and buildings of historical interest through the exploration of websites and CD-ROMs.

Table 23.1 *History KS1: Knowledge, skills and understanding*

Chronological understanding	Use a timeline about the invention of toys.
	Children should place objects in chronological order. Can they find the year when a toy was invented?
	The **Textease** Timeline comes with a timeline of toys.
	The BBC website has useful listening activities to help with identifying toys (www.bbc.co.uk/schools/primaryhistory/victorian_britain/).
	See Figure 23.1.
	Can the children guess the toy from hearing the description? Pupils could write their own descriptions and add them to a **Textease** page with a speech facility, or use a tape recorder for the rest of the class to guess which toy they are describing.
	Write stories about the past using words from a word bank, such as *long ago*, *before*, *a long time ago*, *in the past*, *many years ago*. Give other words appropriate to the story, such as names of people and places.
Knowledge and understanding of events, people and changes in the past	Use a **table** to compare features of a particular time in the past with the present. See Figure 23.2.
	Discussions about the differences, rather than the table creation are the important part of the learning. A third column could be added to record explanations.
	Use **tables** to record events and their consequences.
	See Figure 23.3.
	Use a **table** to make a simple time chart about lives of people they know.
	See Figure 23.4.
	Use a speech bubble **template** to explain a story from the past. Pupils add text to show what people may have said or thought about an event at the time.
	See Figure 23.5.

Use a screen **template** with pictures of clothes both old and new, for children to drag toys to circles labelled 'Clothes from the past' and 'Clothes today'. Explanations for their choices need to be discussed, so that it is the process rather than the finished sets that are valued. This could also be done with food, toys and different modes of transport.

Historical interpretation

Use a **digital camera** to take photos in identical locations to those on old photos. Compare differences and explain the changes.

Compare old and new maps on a **visualiser**.

Compare old and new paintings and photos on the **IWB**.

Use virtual museum visits on the **Internet** to examine artefacts; then pupils could create their own museum of real and created artefacts, with **word-processed** labels to explain them to visitors.

Watch short film clips/TV programmes about life in the past on the **IWB** and talk about ways they may or may not be realistic.

Share fictional e-books about the past on the **IWB**. Compare illustrations with contemporary pictures from the time.

Historical enquiry

Use the organisational features of a **CD-ROM** to find out about the past (contents, hyperlinks, glossary, help box, captions, illustrations, maps, index).

Use a **word processor** for drafting and redrafting questionnaires sent to parents and grandparents about life and times when they were growing up. Identify what has changed and if it is for the better.

Compare old and new artefacts on a **visualiser** to see the details without damaging the items. (If possible, handle them as well.)

Organisation and communication

Use **word bank** of historical terms to write a factual account about the period studied. Assemble and organise ideas on-screen. Use the edit facilities to sequence events and add appropriate details after feedback from a teacher.

Use the **IWB**, with teacher as scribe, to write stories, poems, plays and factual accounts of the past.

Record their accounts of their learning about the past using a tape recorder or **digital audio recorder**. Discuss ways to develop these ideas.

Use arrow-shaped text boxes to explain an order of events, e.g. see Figure 23.6.

Use **digital video** and plastic figures or plasticine models to retell a story from the past in an stop-motion animated film.

Breadth of study

At this key stage, pupils can obtain some of their information from e-books and **CD-ROMs**, as well as Internet sites selected and accessed by their teacher, which will help them to compare maps, pictures and artefacts from the past with those of the present day. The information is just the start of the process, while the subsequent discussion, organisation and communication of their learning are the processes that develop understanding.

The use of ICT tools to create films, audio recordings and presentations, as well as to share information in a range of ways that are easily adapted from one form to another, will help develop skills from many curriculum areas.

Figure 23.1

	In Grandma's day	*Today*
Holidays	Usually by car	Often by plane
Food	Usually home cooked	Sometimes ready meals
Clothes	Often made at home	Usually shop bought
Home entertainment	radio/wireless/board games	TV/playstation/board games

Figure 23.2

Date	Event	Result
1840	Queen Victoria married Prince Albert	They were very happy and had many children
1861	Prince Albert died	The Queen was sad for many years and wore black for the rest of her life.

Figure 23.3

1925	Great Grandma was born
1950	Grandma was born
1974	Mum was born
2000	I was born
2003	My brother was born
2005	I started school
2010	I went to Spain on holiday.

Figure 23.4

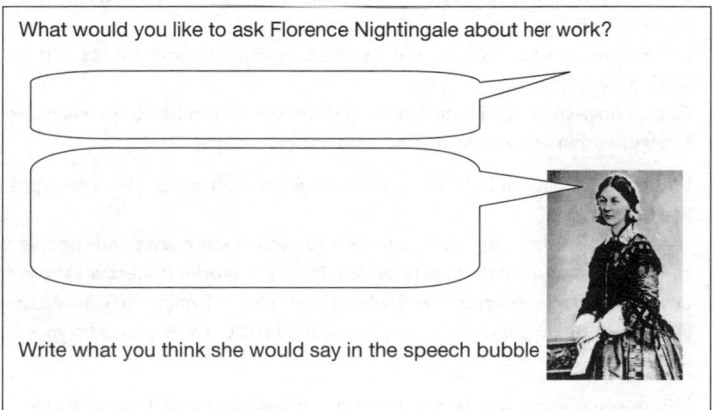

Figure 23.5

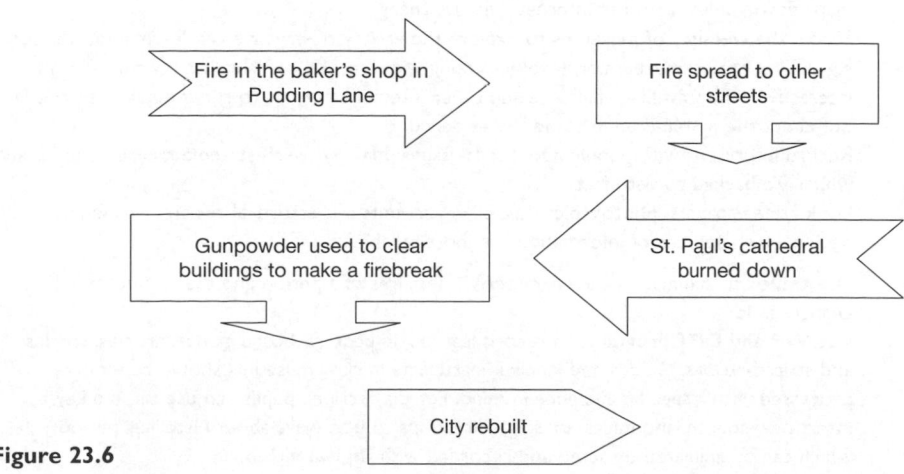

Figure 23.6

Table 23.2 *History KS2: Knowledge, skills and understanding*

Chronological understanding	List events and their dates and reorder chronologically (this is most easily done in a **WP table**).
	Use online timelines to develop an understanding of chronology.
	Create timelines using **spreadsheets**. This can be done both horizontally and vertically and made more interesting by the addition of photos, pictures and text boxes with comments and explanations.
	Navigate a history trail using documents selected by the teacher from sites such as www.besthistorysites.net/WWII.shtml. This would help pupils to answer focused questions about the chronology of different events in a particular period. Information collected can be copied into a presentation or other electronic record of their learning.
Knowledge and understanding of events, people and changes in the past	Explore sites such as the BBC children's history site on www.bbc.co.uk/schools/primaryhistory/ using an **IWB**. Look at films, photos and simulations to see how different societies have been organised and governed through the ages.
	Use a **database** to record facts about inventions. Sort the records to see them chronologically, or according to country of origin or progress in a particular category, e.g. in communication or transport.
	Use a **spreadsheet** to collate and help analyse data, e.g. about land use or population changes.
	Use a **database** to record facts about inventions. Sort the records to see them chronologically or according to country of origin or by inventor or by category such as communication/transport.
	Use the **Internet** for up-to-date information about a significant individual who has influenced the locality or the wider world. Use the information to create a **digital presentation** or **podcast** about them.
	Compare old photos of localities/people in different occupations with recent ones. **Scan** in both and use arrows and textboxes to indicate changes and explain them.
	Use a **branching database** to help identify the ages in which different local buildings were constructed.
	Use **tables** to help organise and analyse information about events in the past. See Figure 23.7.
	Create flow charts and mind maps to show the relationships between events, situations and changes within and across periods and societies studied.
Historical interpretation	Use tables or speech bubbles to show how different people have interpreted the past. See Figure 23.8.
	Use tape recorders/**digital recording** to record interviews with people who have moved to the locality from other parts of Britain or the world. Reflect on the fact that we are all descended from immigrants and where each of our families may have come from and why. Investigate the origins of place names in the locality (www.domesdaybook.co.uk/places.html).
Historical enquiry	Use drawing tools, text boxes and digital images to make a **mind map** of ways we can learn about the past.
	Compare maps from different eras using a **visualiser** with a split screen or an **IWB** with maps downloaded from the Internet. Discuss changes.
	Search the websites of museums to explore the variety of ways we can learn about the past, e.g. at www.britishmuseum.org/explore/young_explorers1.aspx. This has a virtual dig, an interactive time-travelling challenge and other interactive games to show pupils ways we find out about the past and understand the evidence.
	Record interviews with people about local issues. Identify which statements are opinions and which are backed up with facts.
	Look at newspapers, photos, pictures, diary accounts and statistical reports online and decide which sources of information are most reliable.
Organisation and communication	Use **tables** to summarise the characteristic features of a period and the significant changes in it.
	Use **WP** and **DPT** programs to record learning in posters, board games, articles, stories and strip cartoons. Guides and labels for artefacts in class museums should be word-processed with a specific audience in mind. For play scripts, pupils can use the tab key to insert new speech, and italics for stage directions to plan plays about historical periods, which can be animated or acted and recorded with **digital video**.

Use **PowerPoint** to make **multimedia presentations** that record learning in key periods. Import digital photos of visits and visitors and create timelines of the periods studied. Ensure key historical vocabulary is used to ensure rigour.
Use text boxes and arrows to draw family trees and timelines.

Breadth of study	Almost every type of digital technology can be used to help KS2 pupils' history work at KS2 which should include: • a local historical study; • three British history studies; • a European study; and • a world history study.
Local history study	Use digitised maps to identify and colour code features important to local study. Use speech bubbles/callouts to show two points of view about an incident in the past, or to show the questions children might ask an adult about the past, and the adult's responses. Put questions and answers in different styles of text. See Figure 23.9. Use a **word processor** for drafting and redrafting questionnaires sent to parents and grandparents about life and times when they were growing up. Use prepared questions and keywords to find information about the locality on the **Internet**. Find data that explain the changes, e.g. changes in population and the spread of housing/industry.
British history	Search the **Internet** using specific questions and keywords to keep focused. Copy, paste and edit in a **WP** document. Use a **spreadsheet** to work out the ways they might have spent their sixty-six clothing coupons if they had lived during WWII. Compare with current expenditure on clothes, if appropriate. Use a **spreadsheet** to record information on the changing use of buildings according to Kelly's directory (www.historicaldirectories.org/hd/index.asp), or changing occupations (from the census forms on www.ons.gov.uk/census/index.html), and relate these to changes in economic, technological and scientific development in Britain and the wider world. Watch an animated version of the Bayeux tapestry on YouTube to bring the story to life (www.youtube.com/watch?annotation_id=annotation_559561&v=LtGoBZ4D4_E&feature=iv).
Romans, Anglo-Saxons and Vikings in Britain	Use history sites on the **Internet** to find out about the different settlers who have come to the UK from Saxon times to the present day, e.g. www.coventry.ac.uk/ec/~nhunt/180sor/leathem/AngloSaxonEngland.html. There is an interpretation challenge about Saxon settlements on www.primaryhistory.org/lessons/saxon-settlers,20,RSC.html. This settlement game introduces children to the factors involved and the chronology of the time.
Victorian Britain or Britain since 1930	Use history sites on the **Internet** to find out about the different settlers who have come to the UK from Saxon times to the present day, e.g. www.bbc.co.uk/history/british/modern/windrush_01.shtml. Find out about the first black professional footballer, Arthur Wharton.
A European history study	Word-process biographies of famous people, inserting copies of relevant portraits, maps and photos.
A world history study	Create mind maps to show the relationships between events in British history and world history. Annotate digital maps with arrows and text boxes to show the movement of people and changing boundaries. Take a flight **simulation** through an ancient Egyptian temple or look at life in Ancient Greece.

Date	Event	Reason	Result	Consequence
1901	Coal mine closed.	Coal no longer economical to produce.	Many people unemployed. Land left spoiled and wasted.	New business started up using free land and local labour.

Figure 23.7

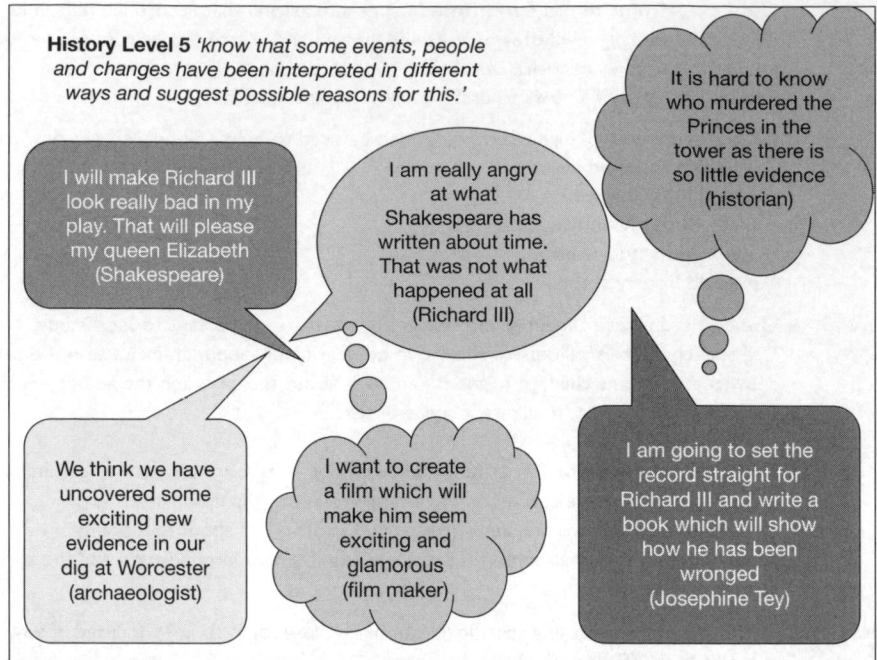

Figure 23.8

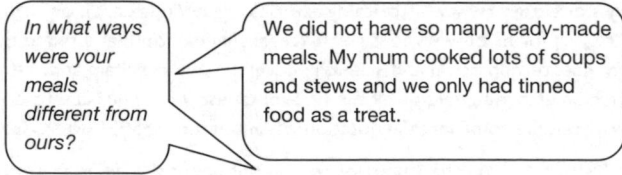

Figure 23.9

24 Geography

Digital technologies provide pupils with up-to-date information about the geography and social structure of their locality and the world around them; they enable pupils to collect, organise and analyse accurate data and present them in a variety of forms. Digital maps can be annotated with text boxes and arrows, and photos of particular features can be added. Tables help sort data so that children can see what we have in common with other communities in the world, and the differences. Online maps such as Multimap can be viewed at a range of scales, and the photographic overlays help pupils compare the diagrammatic form of a map with a visual picture.

ICT can help pupils carry out investigations with more accuracy and detail and in less time than some traditional methods. Digital photography is an immediate and accurate way to record in the field, and computer charts and tables help organise data for comparison and interpretation more effectively than hand-drawn charts. The possibilities offered by digital technologies include podcasting, multimedia presentations and web-based formats that can be published to a wide audience. E-mail, podcasting and video-conferencing are ways for pupils to develop and extend local and global links through effective communication tools. Fieldwork skills can be widened through data-logging and geographic information systems (GIS). Issues such as sustainability can be accessed through the Internet, provided searches are well organised and limited to particular keywords or websites, checked out by the teacher. Amazing simulations of flight through areas such as the Grand Canyon, on Google Earth, help bring learning to life for the desk-bound pupil.

Table 24.1 *Geography KS1: Knowledge, skills and understanding*

Geographical enquiry	After a local walk, on which old and new buildings are compared, draw buildings from simple shapes on screen. This can be done in many programs using infill textures such as stone/slate/brick. Pupils should write about the changes in building materials and describe those used to make different buildings today.
	See Figure 24.1.
	Use **word banks** to write questions suitable for geographical enquiry.
	Use **WP** facilities to record ideas, edit and present learning as posters, reports, articles and labels for craft work.
	Use speech bubbles in a **WP** program to make a class poster about pupils' views on local issues.
	Record pupils' questions about the area in the first column of a **table**, with answers to the questions in the second column. This may take several sessions to complete as a class project, but would be a good way to summarise personal learning.
Geographical skills	Use differentiated **WP** templates with given geographical vocabulary (e.g. hill, river, north, south, near, far) to record learning for geographical projects.
	Search Multimap or Google Earth to find the school using the postcode to see where the

locality is in relation to the rest of the UK. Look at aerial photographs and identify local roads, amenities and physical features with the help of the overlay tool. Plan routes round the locality using the map.

Help pupils to draw a simplified floor map of their locality, or one with which they are familiar (e.g. the island of Struay from the Katie Morag series). Mark places they know, or those mentioned in the Struay stories, on the map. Show the class how to program a **Roamer** or **floor turtle** to visit places on the map. The Roamer could be dressed as a postman, and pupils could work in groups to devise a sequence of instructions to send it on missions from one location to another. Teach them a standard recording method, e.g. 'F', an arrow, for 'forwards', and then write the number of turtle units. Explain that a right angle is a measure of a quarter turn, and that they need to use half and quarter turns in both clockwise and anti-clockwise directions.

Carry out a survey on how children travel to school. Enter the information into a **data-handling package** and display it as a pictogram or other chart to help understand the data. Discuss the reasons for their choice and why other options are not chosen. A chart to show how they go on holiday might look very different. Talk about ways people would have travelled in the past.

Use lines and text-boxes in a **WP** program to label features on digital photos of a local street/park.

Use a **graphics** program to learn to draw pictorial maps of real or invented locations and label geographical features, e.g. hill, river, road, bay, sea, lake. Clip art could be used to add relevant physical features.

See Figure 24.2.

Search **CD-ROMs** for pictures and information about places studied.

Annotate a digital plan of the school to identify different habitats or areas to improve. (The advantage of doing this digitally is that mistakes are easily corrected.)

Annotate a **scanned** local map to show routes to school and local facilities. This could be a whole-class **IWB** activity.

Knowledge and understanding of places	Use a **WP program** to design a survey to find the places that pupils or Barnaby Bear have visited, both in the UK and abroad. Enter the information into a **database or spreadsheet**. Search the database to answer questions and draw conclusions from the evidence. Make charts to show the most popular destinations. Use Multimap or Google Earth to find these places and see which ones are furthest away.
	Discuss the best ways to get to each: road/rail/boat/air.
	Use **Internet/CD-ROM** to find out about the lives of people in other areas/countries.
	Use an audio recording device for pupils to record their views and descriptions of the landscapes, jobs and weather in different localities.
	Use **tables** to compare the features of different localities.
	See Figure 24.3.
	Record data from litter surveys on graphs using **spreadsheet** graph templates set up by the teacher to see which parts of the locality are most affected.
	Look at waste packaging of foods, or clothing labels to see where each has come from. Chart this to see which countries have the most connections with the class.
	Discuss what will happen to each object when it is no longer used. Sort objects on a screen **template** made by the teacher to show how different types of waste can be recycled.
	E-mail or **fax** the local refuse disposal depot to find out what happens to local waste.
Knowledge and understanding of patterns and processes	Take photos with a **digital camera** of local facilities and/or danger spots around the area. Talk about ways these could be made safer.
	Compare **digital maps** and **digital photos**, e.g. on Multimap, to help understand where facilities are located, e.g. a pedestrian crossing.
	Record seasonal weather changes on a **spreadsheet** or **WP table**. These data could be built up over a year to give a useful overview of local weather. Paper-based records might become scruffy or lost in this time.
Knowledge and understanding of environmental change and sustainable development	Find areas in the locality that are subject to vandalism or littering or are in need of development. Use tape recorders to record residents' views. Use **DTP** to make posters about improving the areas. **E-mail** a local councillor or Streetpride group to find out what can be done to develop the area.
	Word-process a survey about ways to develop the playground/improve untidy or noisy areas around the school. Use a **database** or **spreadsheet** to collate the results. Sort and graph data to help answer questions using data as evidence. Take digital photos/video as evidence when explaining pupils' views to the school council or governors about improvements.

Use a graphing program to record data from traffic surveys for analysis.

Identify an area in the locality that is in need of care. In groups, use **WP** software to write a report to send to the local council, describing the problems and asking if there are any plans to improve it. A writing frame such as a **Clicker** Grid or a **Textease word bank** could be used to structure the report and help with vocabulary.

Breadth of study   In KS1, pupils can use ICT to collect data, process and analyse them and present information in various ways to suit their audience. **Digital cameras** are very useful for collecting information from the locality. Visits to sites of interest can be recorded with **digital videos**, and visitors to the school can be recorded with digital audio recordings. A **CD-ROM** might be used to find out about a contrasting locality.

Fieldwork skills involving mapping and data-handling can be made easier through digital facilities, so that time is spent on discussion and analysis rather than the drawing of charts and maps.

Old buildings are often made of stone with slate roofs. Some new buildings near our school are made of concrete with big glass windows. I live in a flat.

Figure 24.1

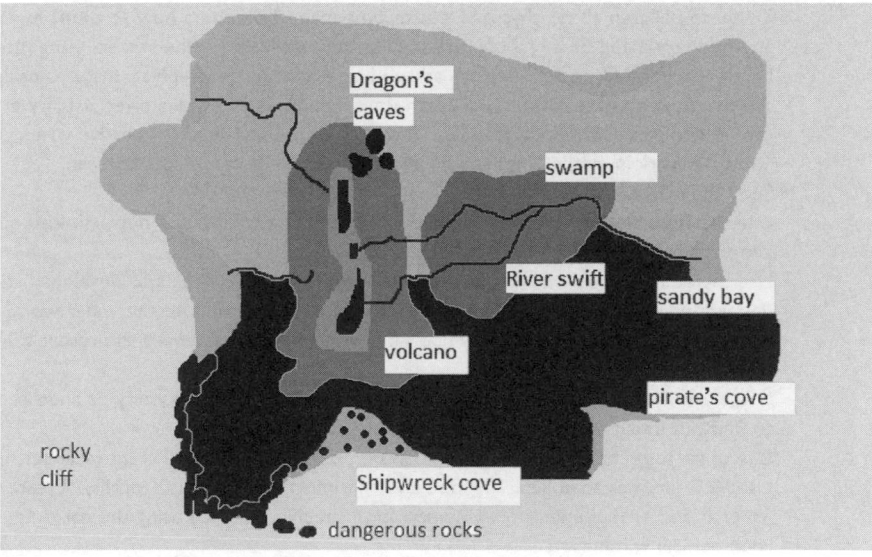

Figure 24.2

Feature	Town	Seaside
Landscape		
Shops		
Other buildings		
Weather		
Litter		
Jobs		

Figure 24.3

Table 24.2 *Geography KS2: Knowledge, skills and understanding*

Geographical enquiry	Use **Multimap/Google Earth** to find out about coastal erosion, rainforest depletion and the effects of tourism around the world. Use **desktop publishing** to produce articles and posters that suggest ways to alleviate these problems. Use **palmtops** with keys and **GPS** to identify plants and animals in a locality. Access the weather forecast (on http://news.bbc.co.uk/weather/forecast) and compare predictions with actual weather records made by themselves. Devise routes between different locations using route-planning software (AA or RAC routefinders).
Geographical skills	Use Google Earth to see where they live and how far it is from places they have been or read about, or where their food and clothes come from. Use a local street map that has been downloaded or **scanned** in for pupils to insert labels in text boxes about local features and facilities using correct geographical vocabulary. Add notes about routes and distances to local attractions. Use a **database** to store information about the local area. Interrogate the database to look for local information about leisure facilities within 5, 10 and 20 miles. Use a **spreadsheet** to graph data from fieldwork surveys to help with analysis of the data. Take **digital photos** of local geographical features and facilities to help develop an understanding of the locality. Use digital maps at different scales. Zoom in and out of an Internet map such as Multimap and use the aerial camera view to compare map and photographic views of an area. Find the school using the postcode. Look at aerial photographs and identify urban and rural areas with the help of the map overlay tool. See how the physical landscape influences the urban landscape. Search the **Internet** for up-to-date information and images about India/a contrasting country. Pupils should work out a search strategy and keywords to identify and explain the similarities and differences between their locality and a village/town in India. Sort this work in a **table**. Find out about recycling in India and how it compares with recycling in Britain. Investigate litter in different areas of the school grounds. Use a **spreadsheet** to produce graphs to present pupils' findings. To teach children about physical features on a map, show them how to **paint** a map of an imaginary island or a real country such as India or Haiti on the screen, using the brush and flood-fill tools. They can add and label specific geographical features using the paintbrush and text tools, e.g beach, cave, headland, mountain, river, estuary etc. These can be compared with local features. The work could be linked to creative writing and compass work in maths. Keys can be added to explain geographical features. See Figure 24.4. Use the **Internet** for the information and PowerPoint to create a **hyperlinked** quiz on a geographical theme, such as rivers or a specific locality. Use regional, national or international television weather forecasts to develop children's understanding of where they live in the UK and its relationship to the wider world. Develop their understanding of weather symbols by using the **IWB** software to present a TV-style weather forecast. Use **e-mail** or **texting** to communicate with pupils in another locality or another country to find out about conditions in a contrasting geographical area. Use **data-logging** to collect information on noise pollution in different localities. Use **WP** facilities to collect, organise and edit information about a locality. Create a paper-based or multimedia presentation for a specific audience using the correct geographical vocabulary.
Knowledge and understanding of places	Use the **animation film** and lesson notes on this BBC site (www.bbc.co.uk/schools/citizenx/teachers/rights/using_animation_1.shtml) to help pupils understand about the rights and needs of asylum seekers. There are films and lesson plans here on conflict, community action, local democracy, crime, the global community and about being a local/national and global citizen. Observe the weather around the UK and world via **webcams**. This site has many to choose from: www.btinternet.com/~paul.gilliver/weathercam.htm. Monitor and record the weather on a spreadsheet from a chosen place. Compare the weather in different locations. Record the amount of rainfall over a course of a month. Enter the information on a **spreadsheet**. Use a formula to work out how much rain falls in an average week. Collect data on the weather over a period of time. Compare with data from the same

week in another part of the world (www.worldweather.org or www.holiday-weather.com). Create a film about the local area, made of still photos, downloaded maps and movies put together in **Windows Movie Maker**.

Use **tables** to compare two areas under headings that will help to highlight both physical and human geographical features.

See Figure 24.5.

Create an electronic information leaflet of pages that are hyperlinked, e.g. in **Hyperstudio** or **PowerPoint**, to describe the locality and explain facilities and items of local interest. This can be browsed by readers, who choose their route through the document.

Find out what it is like to live in poverty, struggling every day to stay healthy, keep out of debt and get educated.

Access charity websites to see what is being done around the UK and the world to help people to develop their communities.

Knowledge and understanding of patterns and processes	Create a mind-map using a **graphics** tools and text which shows the relationships between physical, built, economic and social environments. Correspond by **e-mail** with a school in another country. Send attachments that provide information about your local area, e.g. photos taken with the digital camera, scanned-in maps, sketches and other images, graphs and charts representing data collected in surveys, a guide to the area produced using **WP**, **DTP** or **multimedia** presentation software. Children could ask questions of the pupils at the other school about their area and send a questionnaire as an attachment. Watch the animations on the BBC 'rivers and coasts' web pages about erosion, the creation of a V-shaped valley, how a river meanders and flood planes are formed (www.bbc.co.uk/schools/riversandcoasts/coasts/whatis_coast/index.shtml). Use the activities on the Ordnance Survey site (http://mapzone.ordnancesurvey.co.uk/mapzone/) to learn more about maps and mapping. This site has a **GIS** section with role-play missions to help children understand working with digital map data. Pupils can attempt to control floodwater, site wind turbines, track ambulances, control crime and manage a farm. The scenarios show how **GIS** is used in the modern world. Create **multimedia** presentations that explain how physical and human processes cause change in an environment, e.g. on the theme of litter and recycling.
Knowledge and understanding of environmental change and sustainable development	Design a graphical model of what the high street could look like without traffic. Create objects to represent buildings, street furniture etc. Pupils could produce plans for the development of a new shopping centre or leisure facility, such as a country park or bowling alley. They could collect and graph the views of a range of interested local parties, including children, parents, local businesses and local counsellors, about how this might affect employment or house prices in the area. This would provide material for a debate, as well as articles written with **desktop-publishing** facilities. Use puppets and play scripts created on a computer to explore local/national/global issues. This can also be done online from the site **Virtual Puppeteers** (www.vpups.com/), which is a virtual puppet theatre. Use it to create characters and sets, then act out and record your plays. The stories can then be posted on the Internet for worldwide viewing. Use **spreadsheets/a database** to collect data about local issues, e.g. litter and recycling. Interrogate it to answer questions about the types of litter/recycling in the locality. Use the information to inform a response to improve the situation. Use the BBC water calculator (http://news.bbc.co.uk/1/hi/in_depth/629/629/5086298.stm) to see how much water is used in pupils' homes and then look at ways of using it more efficiently. See Figure 24.6. Use text boxes and speech bubbles to help explain different points of view about a controversial development project or a new law proposed by the class. Write a news report about a local issue, e.g. a new housing estate, closing a corner shop, traffic congestion or the loss of local hedgerows. Publish it using **WP** or **DTP** software. Create posters about the issue to display around the school, to which other children can respond. Carry out a survey to find out what is recycled in pupils' homes. Enter the data into a **data-handling package**, draw graphs to make the results easier to analyse and draw conclusions. Once all data have been collated, use the results to produce a report on the impact of recycling. Use the **IWB** to help brainstorm ideas about issues such as drought or creating a new nature reserve.

Breadth of study   **E-mail**, **podcasting** and **video-conferencing** are ways for pupils to develop and extend local and global links that require effective communication tools. Fieldwork skills can be developed through the use of data-logging and GIS. See Mapzone for information about this. ICT provides tools that can be used to collect and process information about contrasting localities or environmental themes, so that pupils have more time to spend asking questions, debating issues and working at solutions to local and national problems. Up-to-date information about the locality, weather, as well as issues such as sustainability and coastal erosion, can be accessed through the Internet, provided searches are well organised and limited to particular keywords or websites checked out by the teacher. **Webcams** can show what weather, tides or people are doing in real time in other parts of the globe. (NB: as it is real time, some webcams will be very dark, if it is night-time in that location.)

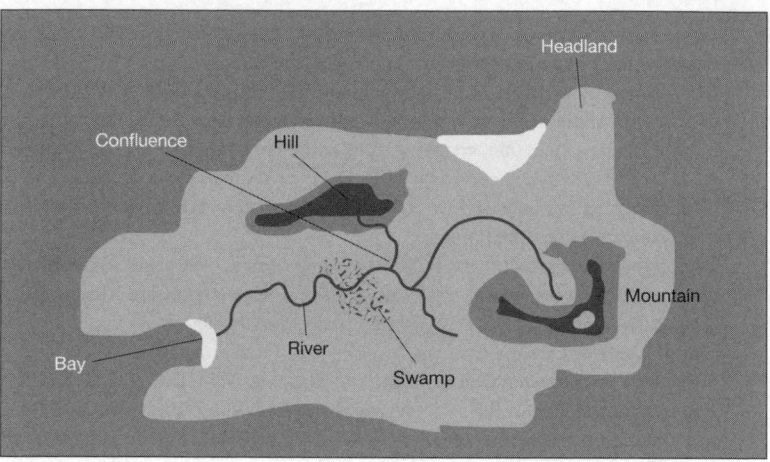

Figure 24.4

	Sheffield	Whitby
Population		
Physical features		
Local facilities		
Occupations		
Transport links		
Plants		
Animals		

Figure 24.5

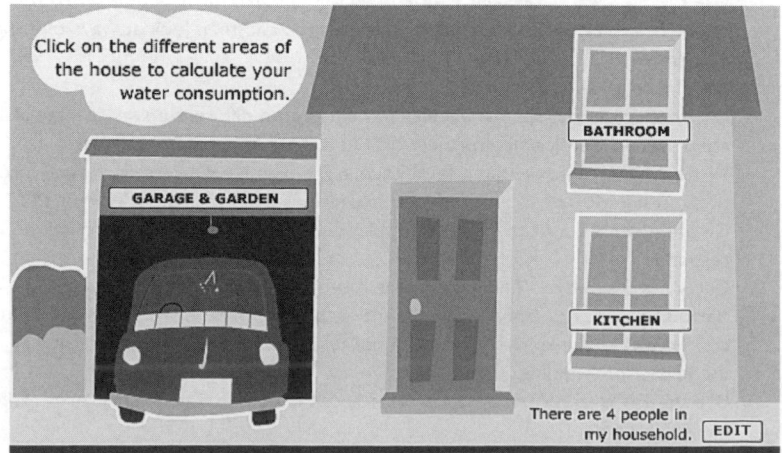

Figure 24.6

25 Design and technology

In design and technology (DT), children should be helped to explore their own and others' ideas about the scientific and technological world we live in. They need to learn to solve problems and work on projects that can bring about beneficial change, such as finding ways to reduce school waste at lunchtime, solve storage problems around the school and improve local habitats, including those in the school grounds. While investigating and evaluating processes and products, ICT can be used to collect data, anlayse them and present conclusions to different audiences. Planning and recording templates with appropriately differentiated prompts can help with organising ideas. Graphics programs can be used to improve the appearance of products designed by the class through the use of word-processed labels or printed patterns and decorations.

At both key stages, pupils should investigate functional products and consider user needs when designing and making their own products. The use of digital film, spreadsheets and simple design packages will be essential for this. Some use of **CAD** packages may widen the children's understanding of industrial processes. Pupils' design ideas should explore the use of mechanisms, structures, systems and control. The latter may involve simulations or electrically controlled models.

Table 25.1 *Design and technology KS1: Knowledge, skills and understanding*

Developing, planning and communicating ideas	Use a computer **template** (see Appendix 2) to plan and evaluate a product pupils make.
	See Figures 25.1 and 25.2.
	Use a simple graphing/pictogram program to see which features are most popular when generating ideas for a new product, e.g. which ingredients to use when creating a healthy salad or snack.
	Copy and paste small art clips to make a 'snack chart' pictogram. Discuss why it is necessary to choose from a limited list. Make sure that the choice available suits the ethnic diversity of the class.
	List, redraft and reorder instructions for making recipes/craft projects.
	Help pupils to identify the order in which they should perform a set of instructions to work a video, record an item on a tape recorder or programme a photocopier.
Working with tools, equipment, materials and components to make quality products	Use **paint software** to produce a pattern or logo for finishing a product.
	Develop IT skills using a **graphics** program by combining shapes and clip-art pictures to design labels for artefacts in an exhibition or badges to show each child's interests.
	Larger versions can be printed and laminated as prizes for good work.

Evaluating processes and products	Use **spreadsheets** or **databases** to graph the results of tests to save time for analysing evidence rather than colouring hand-drawn graphs, e.g. compare the types of food found in a school lunch and a packed lunch.
	All design **templates** should include a section on the design criteria by which the success of the finished product can be judged. (This could be done on a separate evaluation sheet.) See Figure 25.3.
Knowledge and understanding of materials and components	Use a **visualiser** to compare the structures of different materials when deciding which would be most suitable for making a coat for a toy.
	Use a **digital camera** to record the stages in an investigation. Add text and graphics to create an instruction leaflet for the project. This could be added to an **e-zine** or other web page for wider sharing.
	Use **data-logging** to collect information about light, sound or temperature, in order to collect data to inform product design, e.g. which materials would make the best scarf, blind or earmuffs.
	Use **light sensors** to measure the amount of light given off by different torches or lamps to see which would be the best to read by in bed.
	Use **sound sensors** to detect and compare sounds made under different conditions, e.g. when looking at ways to make earmuffs to absorb sound.
	Use **light/temperature sensors** to see which materials would make the best blind for a room or the warmest blanket for Barnaby Bear.
	Use **Internet** sites such as www.mystery-productions.info/hyper/Hypermedia_2003/ Muirhead/website/index.htm to see how different components, such as cams, gears and levers, work when designing a toy. This is a good site for exploring the use of cams, gears and levers.
Breadth of study	Pupils should talk about their experience and use of familiar digital technologies, such as using a video recorder, a digital camera and digital timers. Trips to a supermarket or garden centre would familiarise them with digitised bar-coding of items and traffic lights that respond to pedestrian requests. **Simulations** can be used to reinforce ideas about testing materials and making healthy-eating choices, though these should not replace practical activities. Their own computerised toys can be a useful starting point for many practical investigations.

Figure 25.1

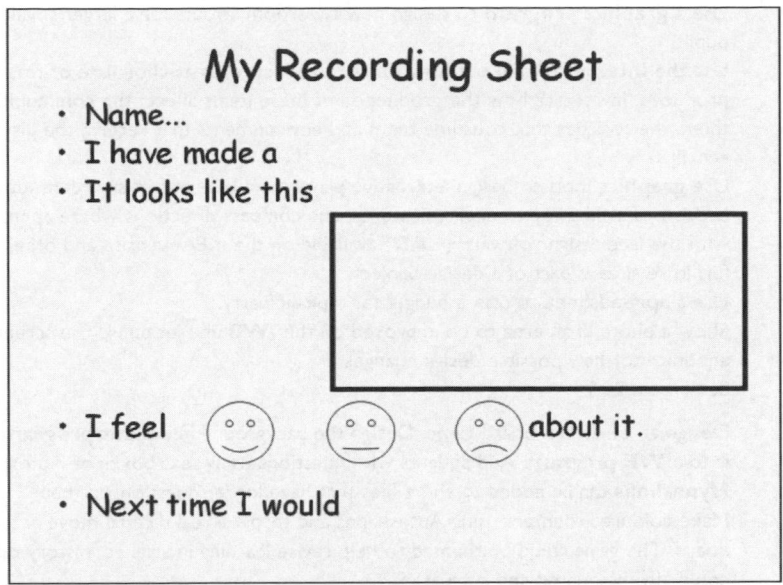

Figure 25.2

Design criteria	Evaluation (Circle answer)
Vehicle must travel in a straight line	yes / no
Must travel a long way off a ramp	< 5 metres > 5 metres > 10 metres
Appearance must be smart	marks out of 5 1 2 3 4 5

Figure 25.3

Table 25.2 *Design and technology KS2: Knowledge, skills and understanding*

Developing, planning and communicating ideas	Use **WP** to design questionnaires to find out about user needs.

Store data and create charts in **spreadsheets** to help compare the results of consumer research before designing a new product, e.g. a game for wet playtimes or a new type of snack.

Search the **Internet** to find out about a range of current designs, e.g. bird feeders, before designing their own product. If exploring different design alternatives for a home for a pet hamster, use information from suitable Internet sites or take photos of hamster housing that some children have at home, before using a **drawing package** to develop their own designs. Practical tests will need to be carried out to assess which materials, components and joining techniques would be most suitable, and the results of these can be recorded in tables and charts or as a presentation.

Use a design **template** on a computer to help develop ideas for products. The template might have sections for user needs, design criteria, order of work, materials and tools needed, as well as space for plans and elevations. This works especially well with a small group of pupils who can be given feedback and helped to improve the design before printing it.

See Figure 25.4.

List and order a plan of work, redrafting it on the **word processor** in the light of suggestions from a teacher.

Use a **graphics program** to design packaging for a new cereal, a party bag or a play tent.

Use a **paint** or **draw program** to design games, e.g. a maze through which pupils challenge a friend to draw a line or move a small shape on screen. This can be done through drawing regular or irregular shapes past which the target shape has to travel without touching another object. Ask friends to evaluate the effectiveness of each design.

Use **paint** or **draw** programs to design spot-the-difference pictures for a class magazine. Once the main picture is complete, save and then add extra details to it before saving under a different file name.

Use a **graphics program** to design new classroom layouts for a larger/smaller number of pupils.

Use the **Internet** to find out how familiar products such as chocolate or magazines are produced. Investigate how the production of these items affects the communities that create them, the societies that consume them and environments that receive the discarded remains.

Use **graphics** tools to design alternative playground layouts/parks/gardens/ideal homes and bedrooms. Add a key to explain features, and compass directions where appropriate. Work with the free design software (**CAD**) available on the IKEA website and other fitted-furniture sites as part of a design project.

Use a **spreadsheet** to plan a budget for a picnic/party.

Show a photo of an area to be improved on the **IWB** and let pupils use screen pens to annotate to show possible design changes.

See Figure 25.5.

Working with tools, equipment, materials and components to make quality products	Design an on-screen board game. Design the background in a **paint program** and copy it to a **WP program**. Add squares with questions using text boxes or Autoshapes. **Hyperlinks** can be added to short files that have longer questions in them. Make coloured counters using Autoshapes and throw a real dice to move around the board. The game could be themed to help revise learning in science, history or RE. It could also be printed and laminated.
	Use a **graphics** program to create patterns, designs, labels and logos to improve the quality of a product.
	Work with the free design software (**CAD**) available on the IKEA and Lego sites as part of a design project.
Evaluating processes and products	Record results of tests to improve products in a table or bar chart to help identify areas to improve.
	Investigation-planning-sheet **templates** could include differentiated prompts to evaluate approaches and outcomes. See Figure 25.6.
Knowledge and understanding of materials and components	Use a **data logger** to see which material would give the best protection when designing a pair of sunglasses for a toy. NB: Children should never use home-made sunglasses for looking at the sun nor for real protection from the sun. They could measure which pair of real sunglasses lets the most light through.
	Use a **scanner** or **visualiser** to take photos of fabric samples. Use these as part of written and presentation work to explain a choice of materials for a project.
	Use a **visualiser** to compare the structure of different materials when deciding which material will make the best phone sock.
	Watch videos to find out how people in other cultures make their homes/shelters/fabrics/foods and experiment to see which techniques can be applied to projects in school.
	Refine instructions for **screen turtles** to make them move in different ways.
	Guide a remote-controlled vehicle/**Roamer** through a maze.
	Use **control technology** to explore what happens when instructions in a lighting sequence are altered.
	Look at **simulations** to see how several simple machines work (www.learnanytime.co.uk/Design%20Technology/Mechanisms.htm and www.learnanytime.co.uk/Design%20Technology/D%20&%20T.htm).
	Use Internet sites such as the Next Generation Learning site to see how different components, such as cams, gears and levers, work when designing a toy (www.nextgenerationlearning.org.uk/At-Home/parent-resource-finder/Moving-Toy-Mechanisms-/).
Breadth of study	Pupils could write to local authorities (**word-processed letter** or **e-mail**) to find out about local waste disposal and recycling initiatives and how they affect the local environment. They could contact local businesses (**word-processed letter** or **e-mail**) to invite them to visit the school and explain to the class how science and technology are used and applied in everyday life. Trips to local businesses such as supermarkets or country parks could be recorded on video/with digital cameras and palmtops for further scrutiny in school, and 'thank you' letters can be **word-processed** and sent after the visit.
	Use the Internet and relevant programs, if available, to see how **CAD** can maximise the use of materials. Discuss with pupils their experience of technology outside school, such as the way washing-machine cycles, satellite navigations systems and interactive computer games, can affect their lives.

Our Biscuit Design by...The Crispy Crunchers

NAMES *Abi, Daniel, Sue, Pete*

- We want to make *some savoury biscuits for our packed lunches because we are bored with the sandwiches we get each week. To be successful they must be crunchy but not too crumbly, have some healthy ingredients (not too much fat and salt,) taste delicious and be easy to make so our Mum's won't have to make them all the time. they should look good as well.*

We will do this by ;-

using a basic *savoury pastry recipe & adding*

*oats (because they are good for our guts),

*paprika (to make them spicy)

*cheese to make them savoury)

*mixed herbs because Abi says they are nice.

We think they will look like this

cheese   oats

mixed herbs

Figure 25.4

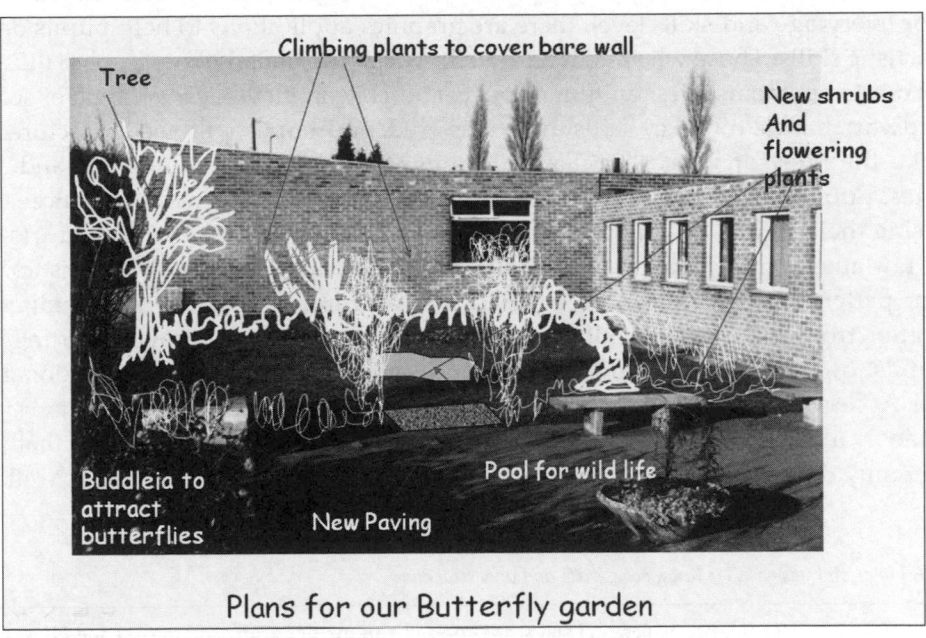

Climbing plants to cover bare wall

Tree

New shrubs
And
flowering
plants

Buddleia to
attract
butterflies

New Paving

Pool for wild life

Plans for our Butterfly garden

Figure 25.5

Evaluation of test	I could have improved the design of this test by …
Evaluation of outcome	I have learned that … To make this test more reliable I could …

Figure 25.6

26 Art and design

Digital technology involves many forms of hardware and software that can be used by pupils to explore creative ideas, as well as to research the artistic work of different cultures, both today and in the past. Digital photography and graphics software enable pupils to create their own works of art. The Internet and CD-ROMs not only allow virtual exploration of art galleries and collections around the world, but also access to many stimuli as starting points for their own designs. Through digital film, pupils can record their work in dance and drama to help evaluation and further development, and they can produce films that are art forms in themselves, as they explore stories, evoke moods and communicate ideas.

For every age and skills level, there are graphics applications to help pupils develop their artistic skills. Those who find it hard to draw can use digital photography; those who prefer not to act themselves can film puppets and clay animations. Each type of software or hardware has its own key skills to be mastered, and pupils will need structured help to make the most of what is available. Through multimedia presentations and school websites, pupils can choose to share their artistic creations with a wide audience.

Using their digital skills, pupils can develop skills from other subjects in an arts-based context. Mathematical patterns and tessellations can be used to provide a basis for fabric design; patterns in nature can be inserted into a graphics program for manipulation. Inspiration from historical and cultural searches on the Internet will provide starting points for pupils' own design work and can aid development of their personal emotional ideas as well. Access to information about cultural events and wider social issues of interest could be made available to classes through recorded TV and radio programmes, so that pupils can not only discuss the issues concerned, but also give an artistic response as well.

Table 26.1 *Art and design KS1: Knowledge, skills and understanding*

Exploring and developing ideas	Use the brush, flood-fill and shape tools in a **paint program** and the 2D and 3D shape tools in a draw program; compare with using real paint and drawing tools and box modelling. What are the advantages of each? Explain your ideas to someone else.
	Finger-paint on an **IWB** and compare with finger-painting with wet paint.
	Scan fabric samples, leaves, flowers, hands or other interesting textures and use as part of a digital art project. Compare results with drawing/painting these artefacts.
Investigating and making art, craft and design	Use **paint and draw programs** to create simple shapes and use the tile or the cut-and-paste facility to create a repeat pattern for fabric or gift wrap.
	Use a **paint program** to show how a piece of music makes pupils feel. Discuss whether this is best done on a computer or with real paint.
	Combine shapes in a **graphics program** to make pupils' own clip art (e.g. face/house).
	Create pictures with a digital camera. Learn to improve composition. Add details to the pictures in a **paint program**.

Evaluating and developing work	Use **floor turtles/screen turtles** to make shape patterns, e.g. spirals, concentric squares, battlements and star shapes. Working in pairs, one child can make a pattern recording the steps taken and then read the instructions to another child, to see if they complete the same pattern. Teach the class how to use a **Logo** program to use simple shapes to create rotating patterns. Compare the ease of on-screen rotating patterns with the techniques used to make them by hand. Which do the children prefer? Select the artwork done by non-digital means that pupils like the best or have enjoyed doing the most. **Scan** this into an electronic portfolio for sending to the next class. Electronic art could be added as well.
Knowledge and understanding	Use **CD-ROMs** to explore the work of other artists in art and sculpture. Study artwork by abstract painters such as Miró, Mondrian and Kandinski. Show pupils some of the features of a **paint/draw program** and challenge them to develop their own compositions in this style. View the work of artists such as Andy Goldsworthy online. Use his ideas as a starting point to develop their own land art images, which can be recorded with a **digital camera**.
Breadth of study	The use of **paint** and **draw programs**, **digital cameras** and **scanners** can greatly increase the breadth of experience for children at this age. In particular, the **camera** and **scanner** enable them to make compositions far beyond the capability of their manual dexterity. **CD-ROMs** and the Internet allow them to view a wider and more up-to-date visual gallery than could easily be accessed by other means. Their experience should include computer art, kinetic art, animations and videos.

Table 26.2 *Art and design KS2: Knowledge, skills and understanding*

Exploring and developing ideas	Use pupils' own hobbies and interests, e.g. sport/animals, to create digital collages of images associated with the subject. Use a **painting program** to create a photo montage using the select and crop options. Take **digital photos** of children or scan in pictures from home that can be digitally altered or incorporated into digital art projects. Use symmetry tools available in some **graphics applications** to design a new type of insect. Make sure it has the main insect features of three body parts, six legs, compound eyes, antennae and perhaps wings. See Figure 26.1.
Investigating and making art, craft and design	Use **paint** and **draw programs** to explore shape, colour and pattern. Take **digital photos** of themselves/the world around them and manipulate them in a **paint program** to express pupils' ideas. See Figure 26.2. Use a **paint program** to create a simple shape and use the tile or cut-and-paste facility to create a design for a scarf or tee shirt. Use symmetry tools available in some **graphics applications** to design Islamic-style patterns for a prayer mat. Make sure it is purely decorated with patterns and no images of living things. Create patterned border designs for writing paper in a **graphics program**. Use the more advanced features of **paint** or **draw software**, e.g. **Photoshop**, to create designs for fashion items such as clothes and art posters. Design a piece of kinetic art! Draw a basic background to a picture in a **PowerPoint** document. Then create objects, such as fish or butterflies or birds, to come in, move round or leave the picture. Use the animation tools to design their paths, speed and when they start to move. Pupils could design animations to fit the stories they write. Create a **digital video** about factual or imaginative situations and stories. This could be done by sculpting modelling clay in a **stop-frame animation** movie. Create patterned border designs for writing paper in a **graphics program**. Use digital images as a starting point for creative textile work. Pupils could develop ideas on the computer and use printer transfer paper to apply it to fabric. Take **digital photos** of themselves that express their character/ideas. Develop the images using digital software, e.g. to enhance particular features/show what might be inside their heads!

Figure 26.1

Use **scanned** images such as ferns/flowers/lace to create designs for artefacts such as gift bags or CD covers.

Create simple **animations** on video equipment, such as **Digi-blue** cameras and software. (Any camera with video and **stop-frame** animation facilities can be used for this.)

Evaluating and developing work	Create electronic galleries of pupils' work by **scanning** pictures of paintings, photographing their clay and other 3D work and adding poems and stories to a program such as **PowerPoint** or **Hyperstudio**. Descriptions, comments and interpretations of their and others' work can be added by each pupil to make a personal portfolio. They could write about what they think and feel about their work in individual electronic portfolios. Use a camera to keep a digital record of sculptures and (parts of) buildings in the locality that pupils find attractive or interesting. Pupils can add pictures of personal items, either bought or found, that have particular artistic appeal. They should explain the appeal of each. Visit art galleries online and compile (subject to copyright) a digital collection of art and sculptures, along with their own comments on each item. Develop pupils' own class art gallery on the school website or using **PowerPoint** in order to express their ideas about professional artists' work.
Knowledge and understanding	Use **paint** and **draw programs** to explore colour, pattern and texture, line and tone, shape, form and space, combining these elements for different purposes. See Figure 26.3. Use the **Internet** to find out about the roles and purposes of artists, craftspeople and designers working in different times and cultures. Research an artist's work, or the history of an art movement, craft or culture. Pupils could use the Internet to visit online galleries and explore paintings close up. Watch film clips, e.g. from **YouTube**, to see how different materials and processes are used in art. Watch a history of art through women's portraits on **YouTube** (www.youtube.com/watch?v=nUDIoN-_Hxs&feature=related). This film morphs the faces of women over the centuries through a myriad of styles and famous paintings. Other films on the site look at different aspects and would need careful selection by the teacher.
Breadth of study	The use of ICT allows children access to arts all over the world, as well as back in time. Through websites and **CD-ROMs**, they can see how the arts are created and enjoyed today and find out how they have developed through the ages and across continents. Pupils' creations and performances can be exhibited for a range of audiences, and they can be in regular contact with artists beyond the classroom. **Graphics programs** should be used to explore *line*, *shape*, *form*, *colour*, *texture* and *pattern*.

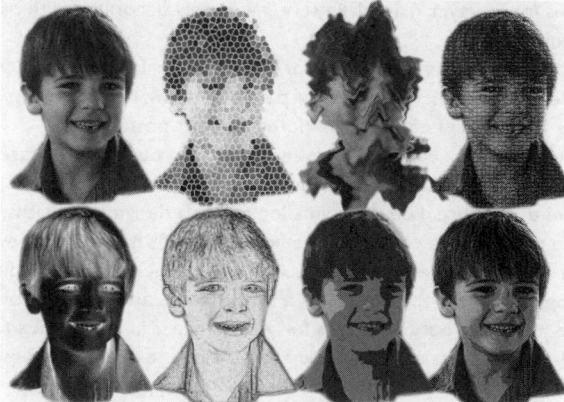

Figure 26.2

Figure 26.3

27 Music

Digital keyboards, whether in hardware or virtual software forms, offer even pupils in KS1 the opportunity to compose using musical samples that can be arranged to develop musical ideas and create simple compositions. For older pupils, inbuilt rhythms and the facility to create music using synthesised sounds similar to the instruments in an orchestra give unlimited creative opportunities, even for those who have never learned to play the original instrument directly. Recording and playing back performances created by other means can aid reflection and improvement. The NC recommends that pupils should use ICT to capture, change and combine sounds. Pupils should be encouraged to apply this knowledge and understanding for particular purposes, and create musical scores, soundtracks and soundscapes to accompany multimedia presentations and plays and as responses to artwork they have seen and current news events.

Although viewing a live performance is always preferable to a recording, where this is not possible, digital recordings of dance, drama and musical concerts should be made available to children of all ages. Teachers can play music to pupils while they work in any subject. Such background music can familiarise them with a wide range of musical cultures, styles and traditions, aid concentration and promote a calm atmosphere in a class.

Table 27.1 *Music KS1: Knowledge, skills and understanding*

Controlling sounds through singing and playing: performing skills	Choose a story/poem with which children are familiar. Ask pupils to suggest ways to enliven it by adding sounds in appropriate places. This might include body percussion and voices and could also include **digital sound files** of breaking glass, a lion roaring or other sounds not easily and safely reproduced in class. The performance could be recorded on tape and played to another class or taken home to their families in turns.
	Use tape recorders or programs such as Kindergarten Karaoke to develop ensemble singing skills. Kindergarten Karaoke can be accessed on the BBC's Parents' music room (www.bbc.co.uk/music/parents/yourchild/index.shtml).
	Use the many songs, with lyrics and sound files, on Sing Up (www.singup.info/songbank/). More resources are made accessible to those who register on the site.
	Join in with, copy or respond to songs/sounds downloaded from the **Internet**.
Creating and developing musical ideas: composing skills	Observe musical patterns or simple scores on the **IWB** and follow the teacher's instructions about when to join in or to improvise. Learn about the instruments of the orchestra, either before or after a visit from a local peripatetic music group. Use the activities from BBC Guide to the orchestra (www.bbc.co.uk/orchestras/guide/) on an **IWB**.
	Work with a virtual music studio, e.g. Dance eJay from Tag Learning, which provides a variety of short musical samples that users can organise to create their own pieces of dance music. Each sound is represented as a coloured box with its name on it. The length of the

box represents the length of the sound. Sounds of a similar quality have the same colour and are placed together as a sound group. Selected sounds can be dragged on to a screen, with a variable number of tracks chosen by the user. The resulting compositions can be saved. Create simple musical compositions in several layers with the 'Super duper music looper' software on www.sonycreativesoftware.com/products/sdml/sdml.asp.

Responding and reviewing: appraising skills	Listen to **digital recordings** of music from other cultures and discuss key features and how they make them feel. Use a **digital sound recorder** or **MP3** player to create **soundscapes** to go with pictures studied in art, local habitats, events in history or locations pupils have studied. Listen to **digital sound files** and sort them into those that warn and those that entertain. Help them to find other categories, such as those they like/dislike, those that are musical/unmusical. Use tape recorder/digital audio files to record their performances with percussion instruments and use to evaluate and improve performance.
Knowledge and understanding	Use **digital music software** to compose music for adverts and jingles, for presentations and films, lullabies or a dance. Compose a short theme for a mobile phone call. Use **graphic software** to create illustrations for pieces of music, so as to appreciate the music in more depth.
Breadth of study	At this age, children's work exploring sounds can be enhanced through the use of digital recordings to evaluate and improve. Their experience of listening to music should be widened whenever possible by playing them music from cultures with which they are not familiar. This can be done, not only at the start of the day and during wet playtimes, but also while they work in other subjects. Research has shown that, with the right type of music, this can aid concentration and improve classroom harmony.

Table 27.2 *Music KS2: Knowledge, skills and understanding*

Controlling sounds through singing and playing: performing skills	Use a tape recorder/**digital audio recorder** to record pupils' performance so as to identify ways to improve it. Use downloaded musical backgrounds to which they add song, speech, percussion or improvisation. Use the activities on the BBC website Music Sense. Children might benefit from whole-class revision of musical terms and could then work in pairs to revise and explore musical layering in the 'timbre and dynamics' section.
Creating and developing musical ideas: composing skills	Use interactive **music software** to start composing simple tunes. For free online examples, try Pattern Builder (www.hbschool.com/activity/pattern/pattern.html), Compose World (www.rm.com/Primary/Products/Story.asp?cref=pS211343) and 2Simple (www.2simple.com/music/). Use letters or graphics to devise their own notation when composing simple pieces of music. Doing this on a computer makes it easier to copy and paste repeating sequences. Listen to a wide range of musical genres to accompany work in other subject areas. With experience, they will be able to choose suitable music to accompany different activities. If the music is kept on an iPod/computer, it can be quickly selected and played through whiteboard speakers. Get to know pieces of classical music on Making Tracks (www.bbc.co.uk/orchestras/play/peergynt.shtml). Use presentations and activities on sites (such as www.primaryresources.co.uk/music/music.htm) where there are useful presentations to introduce children to music such as the *Danse macabre* and the *Carnival of the Animals*, as well as an introduction to instruments of the orchestra. Pupils could use these for inspiration to create their own presentations for other pieces of music/their own musical instruments. Use **music software** such as that published by **2Simple** to compose pupils' own work. Add voices and choral parts where appropriate. Use **Sibelius** software (www.sibelius.com/products/index.html) to teach children how to compose. This works well on an **IWB** for class and group work. See Figure 27.1.

Responding and reviewing: appraising skills	Explore, analyse and compare changing sounds with the **Audacity** software from Sourceforge (http://audacity.sourceforge.net/). **Audacity** is free software for recording and editing sounds.
	Use **digital audio** recordings to inform ways to improve a performance.
	Create **podcasts** of school choral or musical compositions that can be added to **multimedia presentations** or web-based publications. Find out more about podcasting from Teaching Ideas (www.teachingideas.co.uk/ict/podcasting.htm).
	Use the listening game on the BBC's Parents' Music Room (www.bbc.co.uk/music/parents/yourchild/index.shtml). Use this on an **IWB** so the children can take turns to identify the sounds they hear and explain their ideas. Later they could create their own listening game. Develop a school radio station. (Find out more about this on the Internet at www.radiowaves.co.uk/.)
Knowledge and understanding	Take a music quiz made by the teacher using short extracts from CDs, or by getting the children to play different musical instruments for identification. This could be done with a tape recorder.
	Record pupils' own sound quizzes about different kinds of music and musical vocabulary. This could be done as an aural quiz or as part of a multimedia presentation.
	Use an **electronic keyboard** (or several if they are available) to provide the basic notes or a drone for other children to accompany with percussion instruments. There are several virtual keyboards online, which could make this easier to demonstrate. A good example can be found on www.bgfl.org/bgfl/custom/resources_ftp/client_ftp/ks2/music/piano/organ.htm, which also provides a variety of instrument sounds in order to vary the timbre.
	Use **digital music software** to create motifs for pupils' dance, as well as music to accompany their paintings and the work of other artists.
	Explore musical rhythms from other cultures on African Polyrhythms (www.ancient-future.com/africa.html).
	After a performance at a local concert or theatre, send a collective **e-mail** or **word-processed** letter to the artist explaining what the pupils most enjoyed about the performance.
	Create visual presentations and animations to go with a piece of music they enjoy.
Breadth of study	**Music software** can be used to explore the dynamics of music. Listening to a wide range of musical cultures and traditions will help to widen pupils' experience and musical vocabulary.
	Digital recordings of music can be used to enhance the learning experience in many subjects, such as art, literacy, dance and drama, as well as when learning about cultures from the past or in other countries.

Children compose great tunes in fun landscapes

Figure 27.1

28 Physical education

Much of the essential knowledge for this area of learning will come from direct teaching and discussion. However, useful information can be gained from first-hand experience recorded digitally, whether by film or sound recording and through secondary sources, such as the Internet and e-mail.

Skills can be developed using digital film and video to record and analyse personal and group performance. The graphing of scores, in circuit training for example, can aid reflection and the target-setting process. Focused searches on the Internet can help pupils find information, check its accuracy and look at the ways that sports issues are presented by different viewpoints in the media. Films and video recordings of dance gymnastics and other sports-related activities, to suit children of all tastes and skills levels, can stimulate them to choreograph both individual and collective work and inspire a new generation of artists and athletes.

The use of ICT in PE supports literacy, through digital communication; supports science, through data-logging and health education; supports maths, if spreadsheets are used to analyse results and plan physical exercise programmes; as well as the arts, through digital video and sound recording of both pupil and professional performances. Through writing, drawing and creating podcasts, e-zines and presentations, pupils can communicate electronically with a range of audiences to express their ideas on issues that affect their physical fitness, health and well-being.

Table 28.1 *Physical education KS1: Knowledge, skills and understanding*

Acquiring and developing skills	Use **digital photos** and films of pupils' PE skills and movements and use these to identify ways to improve their control and coordination.
	List the rules for games they know, using a **WP** program to make them readable for everyone else.
Selecting and acquiring skills, tactics and compositional ideas	Watch **video** clips, e.g. from YouTube/teacher's TV, that show successful tactics and strategies for sports and games.
	Create, with the teacher's help, a class keep-fit plan on the **IWB**. Record PE times and after-school opportunities to keep fit, and look at ways to keep fit at playtimes. List local opportunities such as swimming and sports clubs.
Evaluating and improving performance	Take **digital photos** of themselves and add labels to say what they are good at and the ways they would like to improve.
	Use digital photos and films of their PE skills and movements and use these to identify ways to improve their control and coordination.
Knowledge and understanding of fitness and health	Reorder lists of daily activities on a **template** prepared by the teacher to cover all aspects of personal hygiene. Discuss the importance of each.
	Annotate an outline child on the **IWB** to show what needs to be done to keep each body part clean and healthy.

Sort household items on an interactive screen into those that are safe and those that are dangerous, e.g. bleach, pills, cleaning fluids, cigarettes, alcohol, foods and drinks.

Use an art program to make a poster about dangerous substances.

Keep Ben alive and healthy on www.bbc.co.uk/schools/scienceclips/ages/6_7/health_growth. shtml.

Drag pictures of foods to create a balanced meal on an **IWB**.

Follow simple recipes found online to prepare healthy meals.

Breadth of study	Create lists of games and activities to develop physical fitness at playtimes. Word-process and laminate them for outdoor use with small apparatus. Use a **Wii** to gain experience of unfamiliar sports such as tennis/bowling.
Dance activities	Use **Wii dance mats** to motivate and give confidence to less confident pupils who are familiar with them in a home setting. Watch **video** clips of different dances to inspire similar activities.
Games activities	Add explanations/reasons to a word-processed set of rules for class activities and games. Watch **video clips**, e.g. from **YouTube**, to inspire and improve their performance. Type out games rules and display as posters in the class/changing room. Use a **graphics** program to design fitness trails/potted sports activities that will develop stamina and flexibility.
Gymnastic activities	Record their work in gymnastics, dance or Tai Chi on **digital film** or photos. Use these to identify areas to improve.

Table 28.2 *Physical education KS2: Knowledge, skills and understanding*

Acquiring and developing skills	Invent their own games and make posters of the rules for others to share. Follow links from www.bbc.co.uk/northernireland/schools/4_11/uptoyou/weblinks.shtml, which has activities and animated stories about keeping healthy through diet and exercise.
Selecting and acquiring skills, tactics and compositional ideas	Use a **table** in a **WP program** to help plan a keep-fit-and-healthy diet routine. Include a column for reflective notes to aid progress. See Figure 28.1.
Evaluating and improving performance	Measure pulse with **data-logging equipment** and compare the effect of different forms of exercise on the pulse. Use **digital timers** to monitor performance in sprints and races. View the watch-again facility on the BBC website/clips on YouTube so as to watch extracts of sports fixtures and identify movements that pupils might be able to incorporate into their dance sequences. Use **digital film** to record their dances to review and improve them.
Knowledge and understanding of fitness and health	Use **WP** to create advice leaflets and rules sheets for games they know/have invented. Learn about the dangers of drugs, tobacco and alcohol using one of the **CD-ROMs** on the market. Test their knowledge about drugs and alcohol at http://kidshealth.org/substance_abuse_Quiz.jsp?lic=1. Find recipes online that include favourite, but healthy ingredients (www.bbc.co.uk/food/recipes/ and http://recipefinder.ninemsn.com.au/). Create a **database** of simple, healthy meals. Use to create a weekly menu. Use a **spreadsheet** to compare content of different foods. Take one type of food, e.g. breakfast cereal, and compare the protein, fat, sugar and salt content. Use to inform cereal or snack choice. See Figure 28.2. See how alcohol and tobacco can affect the body at: www.nick.com/ads/asklistenlearn/kids/body/index.jhtml and www.smokingstinks-aaco.org/tobacco.htm. Use the BBC **CD-ROM** on drugs education (Drug, alcohol and tobacco education whiteboard active **CD-ROM**). Use heart-rate monitors or **personal digital assistants (PDAs)** to ensure pupils are working within their target heart-rate zones.
Breadth of study	Use a **spreadsheet** to compare the number of calories used doing different exercises. Get information from a site such as www.diet-i.com/health/calories-burned.htm, which shows how much energy is used per hour for a range of activities. Use it to work out how long it would take, with different exercises, to use the energy in a biscuit, an apple or a bag of crisps.

Dance activities	Use **pulse sensors** to show how heart rates increase when the body is exercised. Talk about the ways this helps people keep fit. Record notes and diagrams for dance/gymnastics routines pupils have invented. Use copy and paste facilities for sequences that are repeated. Watch film clips from YouTube and the websites of theatres such as the Royal Opera House to inspire pupils' own performances. Use graphics software to record visual representations of dance motifs in order to devise new dances; see Figure 28.3, for example. Pupils should decide on their own ways to represent each step, using Autoshapes and arrows to indicate movements.
Games activities	Add targets to class **wiki**/diary about improving performance. Use **spreadsheet** to record scores/performance where appropriate. Chart results and use to inform target-setting.
Gymnastic activities	Watch digital clips to help improve techniques. Video footage of expert athletes or gymnasts in action can be used to inspire, to demonstrate correct techniques and to develop pupils' understanding and knowledge. Take digital films of gymnastics, dance and games skills and techniques in the class, which can be used to teach other children. They can also be used as coaching exemplars by teachers. Put them together using **Windows Movie Maker**. Use iPods, Nanos and Nike Sensor to motivate pupils to improve their fitness (Google these to find out more).
Swimming activities and water safety	Use a computer to create safety posters for a range of contexts, such as water safety, e-safety and road safety.
Athletic activities	Keep a spreadsheet showing performance in a variety of events. Challenge the children to use ICT to devise a decathlon of events.
Outdoor and adventurous activities	Google 'education outdoors safety' for simple ideas to stay safe outdoors.

Figure 28.1

	Exercise plan	**Diet**	**Comments**
Monday	Gym club at school	5 a day	Need to eat more veg
Tuesday	Circuit training in playtimes	5 a day	Did this 2/3 playtimes
Wednesday	Football practice	5 a day	Must practise left foot passes
Thursday	Jogging after school with friends	5 a day	Ran 3 miles with Tom and Jerry
Friday	Football game	5 a day	Won 3/2

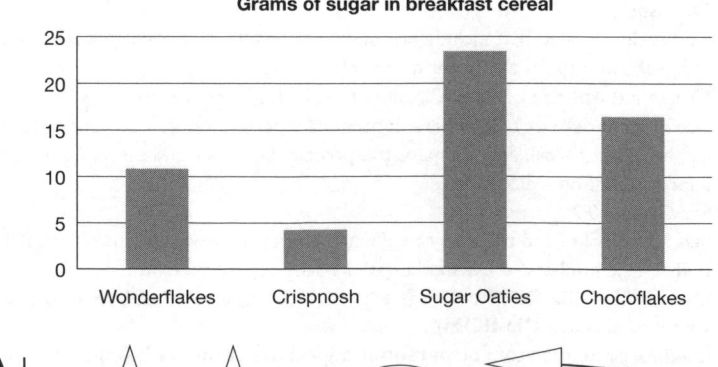

Figure 28.2

Grams of sugar in breakfast cereal

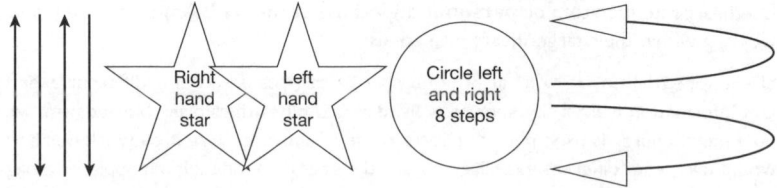

Figure 28.3

29 Religious education

When developing an understanding of religious ideas, pupils need information from a range of first- and second-hand sources. The use of ICT enables pupils to record examples of first-hand information, such as interviews with local religious leaders, and take photos of sacred buildings and artefacts, as well as search for second-hand information. Pupils can then process and present information about their learning using a range of digital formats. Interrogating CD-ROMs and specific sites on the Internet is a good way to acquire basic information to supplement first-hand experience.

Much of the work will involve discussion of ideas, as pupils search for the meanings and values of a religion and come to understand the diversity of each, as well as the sense of identity a religion bestows on its adherents. Some of this work could be reinforced by recording such discussions and creating aural texts about what they learn.

Much of the work in this area will be oral, but editing and refining questions that the children wish to explore can help to frame them accurately. Word processing is one way to do this. A database might be used to gather, compare and analyse a range of information, ideas and viewpoints about different religions. Simple presentation programs or more complex multimedia packages can be used to present pupils' findings and express their ideas and feelings. A computer can help them to organise their enquiries, and templates might be used to help pupils evaluate and reflect on their learning.

Visits to local holy buildings can be recorded both visually and aurally using digital formats, and the material can be integrated into presentations or simply used to relive an experience. Tables and charts can be used to compare ideas and data in themed studies. Appropriate specialist vocabulary can be checked using an online dictionary or thesaurus. Differentiated templates should include specialist vocabulary, so that it becomes a standard form of expression in this context; for example, when pupils are writing about a religious building, the key terms can be provided ready for use. There is good advice from Becta on using a computer suite to enhance religious education (http://schools.becta.org.uk/index.php?section=cu&catcode=ss_cu_ac_rel_03&rid=7249).

Curriculum progression

The ideas suggested in each table below are intended to complement other activities and contribute to investigations and design activities in each area of learning. The examples given in each section are intended as a starting point, not an exhaustive list of activities that must be undertaken. Ideas suggested in one section may be just as applicable in other areas. Practical experience and investigation are essential at every stage of learning. ICT can be used to support, extend and reinforce learning or substitute for experience, if practical investigation is not possible for reasons of safety or practicality.

Although there is no section in the National Curriculum on religious education, the teaching of RE is compulsory for every class. The areas of learning below come from the discarded New Primary Curriculum (2010). Words in **bold** can be found in the glossary.

Table 29.1 *Religious education KS1*

Objectives	Examples of ICT use that will support other learning activities in religious education
Explore a range of religious and moral stories and sacred writings and talk about their meanings	Read **CD-ROMs** of religious stories using the keywords facility to link to a glossary. Listen to online texts found by the teacher that are moral texts or sacred writings (www.bibleforchildren.org/languages/english/stories.php and www.hindukids.org/stories/index.html). Take **digital photos** of freeze-frame moments in dramatisations of religious stories. Discuss the key points to aid understanding and use photos in their writing to show understanding of a story.
Name and explore a range of celebrations, worship and rituals in religions or beliefs, recognising the difference they make to individuals, families and local community	Search suitable **Internet** sites for up-to-date information about religious festivals. Use **paint/draw programs** to make pictures about festivals and celebrations. Add text to explain what is happening in the pictures. Individual pictures and captions could be put together to make one long story on the wall, e.g. a story about the creation. Take photos/make films of religious celebrations in school or the local community, perhaps in a church, mosque or temple if allowed. Add text to explain and make into posters and booklets.
Identify and suggest meanings for religious symbols, using a range of religious and moral words and exploring how they express meaning	Use the **IAWB** board to share posters of religious pictures or symbols. Annotate using a range of religious and moral words where appropriate or sort to show which symbols some religions have in common and which are specific to one religion. Listen to sacred music and discuss how it makes them feel. Use the site www.reonline.org.uk/ks1/topiclist.php to find out about the symbols of different religions.
Recognise the importance for some people of belonging to a religion or holding special beliefs, in diverse ways, exploring the difference this makes to their lives	Use a speech bubble **template** (see p. 55) for children to explain what they have learned about different aspects of a religion. See Figure 29.1. Ask parents to help make **digital videos** of particular acts of worship such as *puja*, prayer and baptism ceremonies, which can then be shared with classmates in school. Use a **word bank** with unfamiliar vocabulary specific to a religion to help them write about it, e.g. the characteristics of Judaism/the importance of the Torah to Jewish people.
Communicate their ideas about what matters most, and what puzzles them most, in relation to spiritual feelings and concepts	Use **WP** and **drawing programs** to make a poster to show the main characteristics of a religion. Create simple **concept maps** to show their ideas about love, wonder, thankfulness, joy and sadness. The advantage of using ICT is that the text boxes are easily moved to space out ideas as they are added. Add clip art symbols where appropriate. Record question and answer sessions with local spiritual leaders. Use to revise the answers or add to a simple multimedia presentation.
Reflect on how spiritual qualities and moral values relate to their own behaviour	Word-process a short list of guidelines for class or personal behaviour. Make up stories about moral issues such as forgiveness and record them on tape or with a **digital microphone**. Use speech bubbles and photos of the children or clip art for pupils to explain ways in which they can help others, e.g. I share my ball, I listen to friends when they have problems.

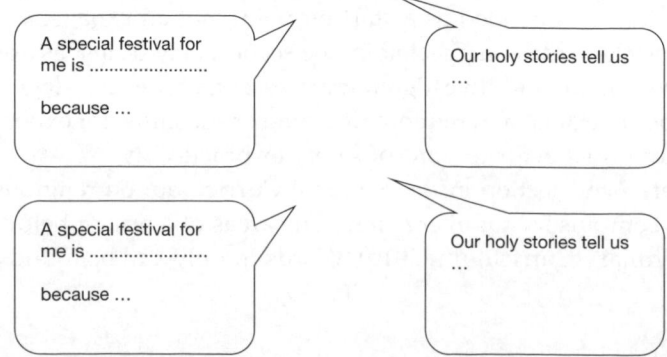

Figure 29.1

Table 29.2 *Religious education LKS2*

Objectives	Examples of ICT use that will support other learning activities in religious education
Explore and discuss some religious and moral stories, sacred writings and sources, placing them in the context of the belief system	Use text boxes and speech bubbles to tell stories from the religion being studied. Add clip art or hand-drawn pictures afterwards. Use a **digital camera** to record the acting out of faith stories. Use these pictures to help tease out the meanings behind the stories and the ways characters involved may feel. Retell a religious or moral story using a **multimedia program**. Pupils write a few sentences on each screen and add pictures, music and photos of artefacts where appropriate. **Word** and **picture banks** would help to differentiate this activity.
Investigate and suggest meanings for celebrations, worship and rituals, thinking about similarities and differences	Use a **CD-ROM** or website to look round sacred buildings: a synagogue, www.hitchams.suffolk.sch.uk/synagogue/index.htm; a mosque, www.thebcom.org/mosquetour/index.htm; a Hindu temple, 360°; www.willpearson.co.uk/virtual_tours/chennai/chennai-005. php?format=fpp; a Christian church, http://stmaryswoodbridge.org/tour.htm. Use a **table** to compare similar rituals and beliefs between religions, e.g. naming and birth ceremonies, or similarities between religious services with different names, such as Mass, Eucharist, Communion and the Lord's Supper. Use **presentation software** to share text and images related to worship and celebrations. Pupils can annotate the screens with questions or highlight key words.
Describe and interpret how symbols and actions are used to express beliefs	Use **paint/draw programs** to record religious symbols. Add text boxes to explain their significance. Use puppets to tell religious stories where this is acceptable to the religion, such as those in the Hindu tradition. Scripts can be word-processed, and the stories can be filmed. Use NGO and charity websites to see how they respond to problems around the world: Global Gang, www.globalgang.org.uk; Christian Aid, www.christianaid.org.uk; Muslim Aid, www.muslimaid.org.
Recognise that people can have different identities, beliefs and practices, and different ways of belonging, expressing their interpretation, ideas and feelings	Use a **branching database** or table to record differences and features common to a range of religions. Use a **WebQuest** to explore the ways religion can affect our understanding of ways to respond to poverty, e.g. about caring for others (http://WebQuest.org). Use digital media to create Diwali/Christmas/birthday cards, rangoli patterns or invitations to religious celebrations.
Reflect on questions of meaning and purpose in life, expressing questions and opinions	List questions that they would like to discuss. Print in large speech bubbles and use to stimulate class discussions. Create **multimedia presentations** of stories or factual accounts of learning about any religion. Add text, images and sound files to create an engaging presentation. Photos can be inserted, as well as scanned images of the children's artwork. Use **e-mail** to ask questions of local religious leaders.
Investigate questions of right and wrong in life, expressing questions and opinions	Watch a short film from teacher's TV to introduce moral issues (selflessness, charity, stealing and more). Redraft stories from the Bible or other religious traditions, using a **word processor**, to tell them from another viewpoint. This could help pupils consider issues of right and wrong and express questions and different opinions.

Table 29.3 *Religious education UKS2*

Objectives	Examples of ICT use that will support other learning activities in religious education
Describe and discuss some key aspects of the nature of religion and belief	Make a film about a visit to a religious building, e.g. a Hindu temple. Create a **multimedia presentation** about the faith they are studying. Images of people, holy buildings and objects can be interspersed with religious music and texts to help make the concepts learned more interesting and engaging for the class. Children should be given adequate time to focus on the text and images used, and sensitive discussion should be encouraged to help them explore the ideas covered. Useful advice on ways to do this can be found at: http://schools.becta.org.uk/index.php?section=cu&catcode=ss_cu_ac_rel_03&rid=8630. Use **concept-mapping software**, e.g. **Kidspiration**, or just text boxes and arrows, to explore ideas that are common to two religions and ideas that are different.
Investigate the significance and impact of religion and belief in some local, national and global communities	Use **e-mail** to communicate with pupils in a culturally different area about their religion. Use NGO and charity websites to see how they respond to problems around the world: Global Gang, www.globalgang.org.uk; Christian Aid, www.christianaid.org.uk; Muslim Aid, www.muslimaid.org; Hindu Aid, www.hinduaid.org/aboutus.php. Search local newspapers online to see what charitable work is being carried out in the locality and whether it is by religious or non-religious groups. Check out sites such as: Oxfam, www.oxfam.org.uk; SightSavers, www.sightsavers.org; Médicins Sans Frontières, www.msf.org/.
Consider the meaning of a range of forms of religious expression, identifying why they are important in religious practice and noting links between them	Some parents and pupils might be able to record worship at home for their peers to see using digital film or photos. These can be shared back in school on an **IWB**. Annotate plans of religious buildings on screen to show what they have learned from a trip/lesson about them. Watch films with a data-projector and large screen about Indian dance, Buddhist meditation, creating Arab calligraphy or Sikh *sewa* (service).
Reflect on the challenges of belonging and commitment both in their own lives and within traditions, recognising how commitment to a religion or personal belief is shown in a variety of ways	Make **podcasts** to record their learning about worldwide faiths. This would be especially relevant when interviewing faith leaders and practitioners. The podcasts can be published on the school intranet or website or shared between classes. This can be done through Podium to create, edit and publish their podcasts, which is available from SoftEase (www.podiumpodcasting.com). **Audacity** is free, open-source software for recording and editing sounds. It can be downloaded from SourceForge (http://audacity.sourceforge.net). Create a cartoon strip or storyboard using a computer **template** that explains the traditions and commitments which are important to a particular religion/set of beliefs.
Describe and begin to develop arguments about religious and other responses to ultimate and ethical questions	View a **CD-ROM** that has specially prepared material about religious and moral issues, e.g. 'Interactive moral issues' (**CD-ROM**), to find out what Jews, Muslims and Christians think about life after death. Use two websites to work on a response to the question: What do Buddhists and Christians, for example, believe about what happens after we die?
Reflect on ideas of right and wrong and apply their own and others' responses to them	Use **digital animation** (e.g. with a **Digi-blue** camera/**Kar2ouche** software) to tell a story with a moral dilemma. Make more than one ending to aid reflection about ideas of right and wrong. Use **PowerPoint** with **hyperlinked** pages to write stories with moral dilemmas, where the reader has a choice at the end of every page about what the character should do next in response to problems encountered.

Part 4
Using ICT in cross-curricular topics

This part looks at ways to use ICT appropriately and imaginatively in a selection of cross-curricular topics. Each of the spreads below has a topic web on the left-hand page, with generic suggestions for using a range of hardware and software in different subject areas. There are ideas for using ICT with literacy and numeracy on every spread, and plans for other subject links, which differ according to the topic. For instance, 'A look at the past' has many ideas for ICT in the study of history, whereas the section on a 'Fabrics and bags enterprise project' has more of an emphasis on DT. We have not tried to include every idea that could be followed up with each topic, and have only included suggestions for the use of ICT that seem appropriate. Of course, there will be many activities of great value that do not involve the use of any IT equipment, and these should also be carried out with each topic. The ones suggested aim to show some of the great variety of ways digital technology can add interest and value to the teaching and learning process.

As each topic heading covers a generic range of skills and activities, the right-hand page looks at ways these might be adapted for Key Stage 1, Lower Key Stage 2 and Upper Key Stage 2 classes. Not all the suggestions will be appropriate for every level of learning. The ideas can be integrated into the school's regular medium-term plans with other, non-ICT-based activities. Some spreads cover ideas for quite a wide range of related themes. For example, the 'Robots, monsters and superheroes' section suggests the development of skills that could be adapted to several different projects. It is not expected that a cross-curricular project on, for instance, plants would use all the suggestions listed here. Teachers might want to add ideas of their own or leave out some of the IT suggestions entirely. It is unlikely that pupils will have unlimited access to a computer suite to pursue all the activities outlined, so teachers may need to plan small-group activities that can be carried out by pairs or groups of pupils on a rota basis, perhaps just using a couple of standalone computers or a few laptops, during sessions where other pupils are engaged in similar hand-based activities.

When planning a topic, teachers should aim to include elements from each of the four aspects of ICT study that extend through all key stages to provide coherence. These are:

- finding things out;
- developing ideas and making things happen;
- exchanging and sharing information; and
- reviewing, modifying and evaluating work as it progresses.

Teachers will, of course, have their own ideas for using the range of digital technologies available to them in their school. They should also consider the expertise available to them from other teachers, TAs and even parents in the school. When planning a topic, try to look at the full range of digital tools that might enhance your teaching and learning. Here are some that are currently available; others will, no doubt, be added to the list soon. Information about each of these can be found elsewhere in this book.

Software/hardware

1	Word processing
2	Spreadsheet
3	Database
4	Branching database
5	Data logger
6	Digital camera
7	Digital movie camera/camcorder
8	Photocopier
9	Digital microscope
10	Visualiser
11	Paint/draw program
12	Simulation software
13	Control technology
14	Turtle/Pixie/Roamer
15	Digital audio recorder
16	Hand-held PDA
17	Multimedia authoring program
18	E-mail
19	CD-ROM
20	Internet access

In addition to thinking about the IT tools, teachers should also consider the techniques and approaches that IT can support and enhance. A list of suggestions is offered below.

Techniques to consider using		
Animation	ID cards	Poem
Article/report	Interactive/multimedia	Puzzles and games
Audio tour	Hyperlinked presentation	Quiz
Blog	Invitation	Questionnaire
Brochure	Labels for displays	Slideshow presentation
Cartoon	Labelled diagram	Soundscape
Concept map	Letter	Story
Digital diary	Map	Survey
Film	Newspaper-style report	Table
Flyer	Photo	Template
Game creation	Picture	Timeline
Graphs and charts	Podcast	Treasure hunt
Hyperlinked story	Poster	Wiki

Topics for adaptation with subject focus

The table below lists ten topics to which IT can make a strong contribution. Lack of space in this publication prevents a more comprehensive coverage of the curriculum, but you might find these ten double-page spreads stimulate your ideas for using IT in other topics.

Topic	Subject focus
1 Fabrics and bags enterprise project	Science, DT, art and design, enterprise education
2 Looking into the past	History, art and design, music
3 Our community	Geography, RE/PHSE
4 Learning about animals	Science, art and design
5 Plants and growing	Science, art and design, DT
6 Famous people	Art and design, music, history
7 Healthy me	Science, DT, PE, MFL
8 Sports/Olympics/World Cup	Geography, art and design, MFL
9 Robots/superheroes/monsters	Science, DT, history
10 Caring for our planet, recycling and conservation	Geography, DT, PHSE

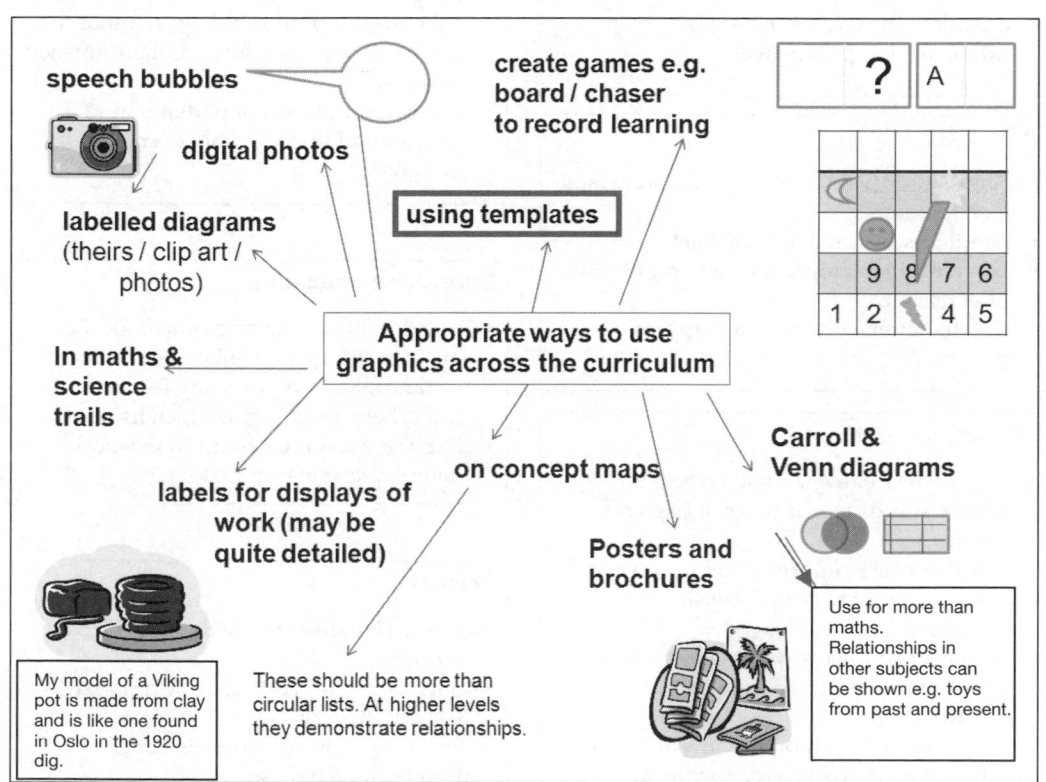

Topic 1
Fabrics and bags enterprise project

Numeracy

- Create nets for bag pattern-making in a **graphics program**.
- Compare the area and capacity of bags on a **spreadsheet**.
- Calculate the cost of materials with a **calculator** or **spreadsheet**.

DT

- Assess user needs with a **word-processed** questionnaire.
- Graph results on a **spreadsheet**.
- Use a **design template** on a **computer** to plan design.
- Create pattern pieces in a **graphics program**.

Literacy

- Use a **word bank** to create labels for fabrics and different types of bag on a display.
- **Word-process** reports on tests/consumer research as if for *Which?* consumer magazine.
- Organise and list instructional writing about the stages in bag-making in a **WP document**.
- Carry out research on the **Internet** about types of bags worldwide to inform designs.
- Write sales promotion and advertising material in a **WP document**.
- Plan and redraft text in a **WP document** for oral presentation about the project to parents in assembly.
- Create a multimedia presentation in **PowerPoint** to summarise learning on the project.
- **E-mail** Accessorize shop to get information about where its bags are made.

Art and design

- Designs for bag decoration: use a **paint program**.
- Create logos: use a paint/graphics program.
- Take **digital photos** of bags familiar to pupils, as well as photos of their finished designs.
- Use **digital photos** of patterns in nature/buildings/people to create designs.

Enterprise education

- Use the Internet to find out about the thirteen enterprise skills used by, for instance, Rotherham ready (www.rotherhamready.org.uk/13skills.html).
- Use the **ActiVote** system to develop democratic decision-making skills.

Science

- Use a **visualiser** to see the structure of fabrics.
- Sort fabrics on **IWB** using Venn and Carroll diagrams.
- Sort and identify materials using a **branching database**.
- Use **data-logging** to see which materials are the best insulators.
- Test to see which materials are waterproof/strongest/softest/most resistant to wear etc. and record the results and graph on **spreadsheets**.
- Record testing procedures with a **digital camera** and add photos to reports and presentations.
- Use **investigation templates** on the computer to plan and report on practical investigations.

Topic 1: Fabrics and bags enterprise project

Enterprise projects are an excellent way to involve skills learned in many areas of the curriculum in one project. The skills listed here do not include the practical ones, such as those needed to design, cut, sew and make prototype bags in paper, before using more expensive fabric. Some of the tasks suggested could be done without the benefit of ICT, but ICT offers increased accuracy and the opportunity to draft and redraft with ease, until the pupils are satisfied with their work. Enterprise projects that can be carried out at any age typically involve pupils working with a small amount of money to make a profit, and so spreadsheets and calculators can help with working out profit and loss and checking estimates. All age groups would benefit from using a visualiser to compare the structure of different fabrics. Design templates for planning the project can be used in both key stages, with keywords or more extensive prompts provided for those who need them. Digital cameras can be used by all year groups to collect ideas for designs and record activities for later evaluation.

Key Stage 1

At this stage, pupils will be involved in simple calculations that can be done in their heads. These would also benefit from being checked on a calculator. Younger pupils would find it easier to get information from CD-ROMs or a single website found by the teacher. Although they may not be attempting some of the more advanced features of word processing, children at this age would find it useful to be able to drag words from a word bank in a WP program to help them write about the fabric they use and investigate. Labels with background information could be made for a range of fabrics and bag samples as part of a class display. The IWB can be used as a follow up to practical sorting activities when the correct fabric names are sorted on a Venn diagram.

Lower Key Stage 2

Older pupils would benefit from more complex data-handling, with the aid of a spreadsheet from which charts can be made to help analyse the data. They can sort using Carroll diagrams on the IWB to help compare the properties of materials. Using a binary branching database with increasingly sophisticated questions would be useful to analyse the properties of different fabrics. Pupils should be starting to find relevant information from a limited number of given websites and, as part of a project on using e-mail, could contact shops for information about how and where their bags are made. Some pupils might like to use graphics programs to create nets to help them design their bags.

Upper Key Stage 2

Older pupils would benefit from practising their research skills using keywords and the AND, OR and NOT functions of a search engine. Ethical issues to do with fair trade could be followed up. More advanced graphical packages should be used to create designs and decorations for their bags. Some pupils will be able to use drawing programs to create templates for the pattern pieces. If digital voting systems are available, they could be used to vote on task allocation, materials and designs, as children learn about the democratic process. All age groups will benefit from seeing their teacher present ideas on the IWB, and more capable children could create multimedia presentations about their work.

Topic 2
Looking into the past

Numeracy

- Create **databases** of facts about people/places/inventions.
- Use **spreadsheets** for budgeting, e.g. WWII coupons.
- Use **spreadsheets** to show the variety of jobs people did and how these have changed over time.
- Use **calculators** to compare weekly budgets from past with present.
- Create a timeline using a **table** or **spreadsheet**.
- Use **calculators** to check sums involving people's lives and inventions.

Literacy

- **Word-process**, using **word banks** where necessary, diaries, articles, stories, poems and reports about the period studied.
- Research information from **CD-ROMs** and the **Internet**, with focused questions and keywords.
- Create film script and make a **digital film** about a story from the period, e.g. the lives of Henry VIII's six wives, each giving their point of view.
- Write a **blog** as if a character from the past, e.g. a WWII soldier.
- **Twitter** in the voice of a character from the period.
- Create a **multimedia** presentation to summarise learning on the project.
- **E-mail** museums/people who were alive in the period studied/other relevant sources of information.
- Write and record a **podcast** as if recording at the time or a news report in historical period.
- Create labels and information leaflets on a **word processor** for a museum of created/collected artefacts to share with parents.
- **E-mail** places of historical interest visited to thank them for the visit and ask further questions.

Art and design

- Take **digital photos** of pupils in period costume to use in artwork/**multimedia** presentations.
- In **graphics** programs, create wanted posters of famous people.
- Create own clip art from **digital photos** taken on visits. Erase backgrounds in a **paint program** and add new ones to represent the period studied.
- Use a **paint program** to create pictures of the period.
- Use a **draw program** to create cartoon characters of the period and add speech bubbles to create a comic strip about stories from the time.

Music

- Create **digital soundscapes** to represent different places or events for the periods of time studied.

History

- Use a **visualiser** to see details on historical artefacts, e.g. medals or documents.
- Use the **Internet** and CD-ROMs to search for information about key events and people.
- Use the **Internet** to search census information.
- Use the **Internet** to find information about streets and shops through online resources such as Kelly's Directory.
- Fly through ancient cities in **simulations**.
- Find old photos/maps on the **Internet**: the Ordnance Survey site is good for this. Compare with modern maps online and **digital photos** taken by pupils at the same location.
- Look at civilisation-/period-specific **websites**.
- Use a **digital camera** when visiting local sites.
- Visit online museums on the **Internet**.

Topic 2: Looking into the past

These ideas can be adapted to many historical topics, from ancient civilisations to invaders and settlers to life in Grandma's time. At all stages, it is useful to be able to use timelines to help develop a sense of chronology, and there are many useful ones to be found on the Internet. There will be many other activities undertaken in connection with historical projects that are not listed here, as they do not require the use of ICT. Although forms of communication such as blogs, Twitter, e-mail and films are suggested, younger pupils may need to be reminded that people in the past did not have access to such facilities. The range of fonts available on some computers can add a motivating, period touch to a child's writing in a historical context. Try YouTube for interesting animations, especially of the Bayeux tapestry (www.youtube.com/watch?v=bDaB-NNyM8o).

Key Stage 1

One way to encourage relevant writing for young pupils is to get them writing labels for a museum or exhibition of the artefacts they have, both old and recently made by themselves. More able children will be able to write explanatory labels with some detail, while their peers use just a few words. In either case, the task will be more authentic and professional if the labels are word-processed. Pupils in KS1 are able to create quite sophisticated stop-frame animation films, using either plastic figures or plasticine ones modelled by themselves. A digital camera can create resources to label or manipulate in an instant, and this is a good way to record events on class trips, especially those that involve dressing up or using historical artefacts.

Lower Key Stage 2

Databases can take a long time to assemble before they have enough data in them to be useful. A historical database started in Year 3 could be added to throughout the time a class spends in the school, if it is copied to the next class along with their other digital records. This would help pupils to build on prior knowledge and make connections across several periods of history. It should be remembered that databases and spreadsheets are not ends in themselves, and that enough time to analyse and evaluate the data they display needs to be built into the busy timetable. Using the Twitter technique of a message in just 140 characters is good for reluctant writers, as well as those who need to sharpen their writing to say as much as they can in as few words as possible. At this age, pupils should be able to communicate by both letter and e-mail, and letters of thanks, perhaps with a further enquiry, to places visited are both good manners and relevant.

Upper Key Stage 2

By Years 5 and 6, children should be examining historical records with increased criticality and analysis. A visualiser helps to share details of maps, pictures and historical artefacts simultaneously with a whole class, without fear of damage to the originals. A project on World War II might use a spreadsheet set up by their teacher to help pupils realise the problems with budgeting (albeit without a spreadsheet to help at the time!). Clothing items should be listed in column 1, with the numbers of coupons required in column 2. (See www.fashion-era.com/utility_clothing.htm#Limited Coupons To Spend for this information). In the third column, pupils can type the number of items they want to buy. A formula in the cell at the bottom of this column can add up the number of coupons used and subtract it from the total allowed (sixty-six a year for clothes). They will quickly run out of coupons and be unable to buy all the new clothes they want.

Topic 3
Our community

RE/PHSE

- Use the **Internet** to find out about local religious buildings and services in the area. Where is the nearest church/mosque/temple? (Do this even if your immediate locality does not have these facilities.)
- Use **digital photos** and **WP** to create a church/synagogue/other brochure.
- Write a story of a local saint or hero using a **cartoon template** on a computer to help plan this.
- Create **digital films/animations** about local moral issues, e.g. littering, vandalism, racial issues.
- Record interview **digitally** with local councillor/religious figure/character about their experiences and ways to develop community cohesion. Edit to create a **podcast**.

Literacy

- Use a **word bank** to create a local brochure.
- **Word-process** reports on local events; create a newspaper/news-sheet for the local community and walk-to-school posters.
- Create a **multimedia presentation** of the local area as a holiday destination using **WP** and **graphics programs**.
- List and organise local facilities in a **WP document** using a **table**.
- Research the local community on the **Internet**.
- Create a **concept map** to show community links.
- Use a **word bank** to create a poster to advertise the area.
- Draft and redraft lyrics to sing about the area/a particular community in it.
- Update the **Wikipedia** entry about the local area/community.
- Write a **blog** about local news for the school website.
- **E-mail** the local council about local issues/facilities. (This can be to praise as well as complain.)
- Use a **WP document** to write about local ghost stories/traditions.

Numeracy

- **Graph** surveys and a summary of census figures from 2001.
- Create a **database** of local facilities and distances to them or of local buildings and materials used to build them.
- Use a **spreadsheet** to record and chart traffic census or local opinions about proposed developments.
- Compare prices with a digital **calculator**.
- Create a **pictogram** of the ways pupils travel to school/how far parents travel to work.

Geography

- Use **data-logging** to find the quietest/darkest corners of the school/grounds and record results on a spreadsheet.
- Use **data-logging** to record local weather, sunny/shady areas (light/temperature), measure noise pollution.
- Create a **multimedia presentation** about the local area or community to send to link a school in another country.
- Use **WP** and local maps to help write directions from one location to another.
- Sort local statistics/digital photos on **IWB** using Venn and Carroll diagrams.
- Use **GPS equipment** to trace a path around the school/local area.
- Use **Roamer/Turtle** to reinforce the direction and compass points on a map of the school grounds/local area.
- Use a **visualiser** to magnify features of maps/rock/soil/plant samples.
- **E-mail** local facilities for information.
- Annotate **digital photos** to show developments proposed by pupils. This can be done on IWB, as well as individual computers.
- Create an interactive map of the local area or park or a specific building using **hyperlinks** in **WP** or **multimedia** software.

Topic 3: Our community

For young children, this project might involve just the school and its immediate locality. For older pupils, a wider local study, or one comparing two British localities, might be more appropriate. Ideas from the 'Looking into the past' topic might be appropriate to use with a local study as well. Much information for both topics can be found on the Vision of Britain website, including maps, statistical trends and historical descriptions (www. visionofbritain.org.uk/relationships.jsp?u_id=10002369&c_id=10001043). The Mouseprice website (www.mouseprice.com/) uses data from the 2001 census. The area guide tab has useful local information, including demographic data. The Office for National Statistics has some parish records as recent as 2001.

One aim of any local study should be to develop community cohesion. Starting with looking at the diversity of people who help in the school, perhaps through questions planned by the pupils (WP can help to get this right), to audio recording interviews with them, which are edited to create podcasts for the school website, pupils can be helped to see that we all have a role to play. In my school, the crossing lady was so thrilled with the digital painting one pair of pupils did of her, as well as the article they wrote about her, that she asked for a copy.

Key Stage 1

Coming to school starts with the journey, so this is a good place to start looking at statistical data. It should be more than a car versus walk activity though, and, in the interests of road safety and health education, pupils might be helped to create advice leaflets and posters to encourage walking to school. Roamers can be used to negotiate local streetplans, and these skills can be developed later on logo programs.

Lower Key Stage 2

Working on community cohesion necessitates looking at community faiths. Even in an area where there is little religious diversity, the Internet can help to locate the nearest mosque, temple or synagogue, even if the distance is great, and a religious leader from that community can be invited by pupils to visit the school and talk about other ways of life. Children can be helped to find a range of ways to record the visit and then e-mail, text, fax or write a letter to thank the visitor. The pros and cons of each method could be discussed. Data-logging at this stage would be useful to make a record.

Upper Key Stage 2

To further develop community cohesion, young people need to understand about civic responsibility and perhaps get involved with their local council, helping to clear litter and plan local facilities. Using the Internet to find out about recycling and conservation activities is a practice they could take into later life. Redesigning part of the school grounds or a local park can be done in a graphics program, where several versions can easily be drafted. Becoming aware of local facilities, including sports, libraries and creative opportunities, their times and prices, through electronic sources, can provide a life skill, so that boredom and apathy do not become endemic.

Topic 4
Learning about animals

Literacy

- Use a **word bank** to write about animals and create pet/minibeast/other passports or swap cards.
- **Word-process** care leaflets for pets or minibeasts.
- Research animals on the **Internet**/CD-ROMs.
- Create a multimedia presentation in **PowerPoint** to summarise learning on the project.
- **E-mail** schools in other areas to compare information about local animal life.
- Use a **WP/graphics** program to make wanted posters describing animals and their habits.
- Organise and list features of animals in a **WP document** using a **table**.
- Plan and redraft text in a **WP document** for an oral presentation about the project to peers/parents.
- Use **speech bubbles** and **digital photos** to help reluctant writers explain what an animal might want to tell us.
- Prepare text and record digitally for a **podcast**.

Art and design

- Use a symmetry tool available in some **paint programs** to design new minibeasts.
- Take **digital photos** of animals and use as clip art/labelled diagrams.
- Use **digital photos** of patterns in nature/buildings/people to create designs.
- Use a digital photo of themselves in a **paint program** to turn themselves into an animal/bird.
- Take **digital photos** on school field trip and edit/alter in paint program to create special effects.
- Keep **digital photos** of models made in arts and crafts and add to digital presentations and records.
- Use a **paint program** to provide background for clip-art minibeasts.
- Use a **graphics/paint program** to create pictures for labelled diagrams.

Numeracy

- Use a **spreadsheet** to compare features/distribution of animals.
- Create **pictograms** or use tables to compare features of animals.
- With a **calculator**/spreadsheets work out relative weights, sizes, distances travelled.
- Use a **calculator** to work out inconceivable comparisons, e.g. how many spiders/mice/sparrows would equal the length/weight of another animal, such as an eagle or whale.
- Use a **spreadsheet** to create times-table programs of minibeast legs, e.g. a beetles times table (6 times), a starfish (5 times/7 times) or octopus (8 times).
- Use a **calculator/spreadsheet** to work out the cost of caring for different pets to help decide which one to buy.

Science

- Create a **database** about features of animals.
- Use a **visualiser** to see live specimens in more detail, *for a very short time*, or dead ones.
- Sort pictures/names of animals on an **IWB** using Venn and Carroll diagrams.
- Sort and identify animals using a **branching database**.
- Use **data-logging** to see light and temperature conditions preferred by animals in different habitats. Use movement sensors to see what the class fish/guinea pig/hamster does at night.
- Use **investigation templates** on the computer to plan and report on practical investigations.
- Test to see which conditions/foods animals/birds prefer and graph on **spreadsheets**.
- Record investigations with a **digital camera** and add photos to reports and presentations.
- Create flowcharts in a **graphics program** to show lifecycles.
- Label diagrams/digital photos in **WP** or a **graphics program**.
- Find **YouTube** clips to show examples of camouflage, migration, pupation and metamorphosis.
- Use a **webcam** to study the school bird table/bird-box.

Topic 4: Learning about animals

The ideas in this section could be adapted for a number of projects, including minibeasts, pets, African animals, birds or fish, depending on the age and other topics the class are studying. If a local study is being undertaken, then some of these techniques could be used to study birds and minibeasts and other local wildlife. Care should be taken not to upset or injure any animals studied, so webcams and data loggers should not be used intrusively, and live minibeast specimens studied with a visualiser should only be placed there for a few seconds, as the strong light could be distressing or damaging for them. Dead specimens can be studied at length and in greater detail.

Key Stage 1

Pets are often the first animals young children study, as they are likely to be familiar to them and tolerant of handling. It is appropriate that they should learn how to care for other living things at an early age, and the variety of pets provides useful information for data-handling and graphical interpretation. Interrogating CDs is a useful way to develop finding-out skills in a very safe environment, before they progress to Internet research. Paint programs are a good way for pupils to learn mouse control while creating pet pictures, or, if a graphics tablet and stylus are available, they could use these. They will enjoy using their own digital art as a basis for stories, poems and labelled diagrams. Hand-drawn art could also be scanned in and used in a similar way.

Lower Key Stage 2

Minibeasts, if not studied before, provide a useful progression in scale and complexity. Pupils who are still at the early stages of writing may enjoy creating fact-file cards, which can be printed and awarded as prizes and swapped like football cards under class rules. Digital photos of larger animals can be used to illustrate their work and give it a professional touch. In Years 3 and 4, speech bubbles and also tables with clear headings are motivating and structured ways to encourage pupils to write succinctly. Templates can also structure recording activities, and, if keywords required are given, then greater independence is possible for the budding writer.

Upper Key Stage 2

By this stage, pupils should be taught the skills they need to make effective Internet searches to find out about animal care and animal cruelty. If children are involved in personal projects on pets, then the RSPCA site has advice on how to care for a range of animals (www.rspca.org.uk/home). If they research the cost of buying and caring for different animals, they are in a better position to decide which, if any, pet would be appropriate for their circumstances. Calculators, spreadsheets and their charts are useful to help analyse the data and so make a decision. Calculators are also useful for working out inconceivable comparisons, such as whether a man, flea, kangaroo, frog or grasshopper is the best jumper, taking into account its size and the height it can jump.

Topic 5
Plants and growing

Art and design and design and technology

- Design a school/class garden in a **graphics program**, having surveyed user needs and graphed results on a **spreadsheet** to help analyse data.
- Design plant containers for a garden centre using a **graphics program** to help with nets and planning.
- Use a **paint program** to design garden accessories.
- Take **digital photos** of plants and use to create designs for collage, montage and printing.
- Use a **paint program** to illustrate the parts of a plant. Copy to a WP program to add labels.
- Create animated **digital film** about plant life cycles.
- Use **scanned** or **photocopied** images of plants as a basis for artwork.

Science

- Create a **database** about plants.
- Use a **visualiser** to see details of different flowers, leaves, bark, seeds and stems.
- Sort pictures/labels of plants on an **IWB** using Venn and Carroll diagrams.
- Sort and identify plants using a **branching database.**
- Use **data-logging** to record light levels in different habitats favoured by plants. Compare with plant types on a **spreadsheet**.
- Test to see the effect of water, light and fertilisation on plant growth and graph on a **spreadsheet**. Use a **WP** to help with reports.
- Record testing procedures with a **digital camera** and add photos to reports and presentations.
- Use **investigation templates** on the computer to plan and report on practical investigations.
- Use **simulations** to experiment on virtual plants in speeded-up timescale.
- Use YouTube clips to see germination and seed dispersal with time-lapse photography.
- Use **palmtops** with **GPS** and built-in keys to identify wild plants and trees.

Literacy

- Use a **word bank** to create plant-care leaflets and reports on plant investigations.
- **Word-process** a guide to local plants.
- In a **graphics program**, create a concept map to show relationships between local plants and their habitats.
- Use **tables** in a **WP** program to compare features of different types of plant.
- Organise and list plans for enterprise activities of growing and selling plants/ growing projects in a **WP document**.
- Carry out research on the **Internet/CD-ROMs**.
- Plan and redraft text in a **WP document** for an oral presentation about the project to peers/parents.
- **E-mail/word-process** letters to a local garden centre for advice about plants.
- Create a **multimedia presentation** in **PowerPoint** to summarise learning on the project.
- **E-mail** schools in other areas to compare information about local plants.

Numeracy

- Create **graphs** and **pictograms** of plant growth and seed germination.
- Use a **spreadsheet** to compare the number of plant types in different locations and record test results.
- Calculate planting costs for a class garden with a **calculator**.
- Use a **calculator** to find out the number of seeds in a seed-head.
- Measure and record in a **table** the tallest plants and leaves with the largest area found. Do the tallest plants in a species have the largest leaves?

Topic 5: Plants and growing

This is another topic where the suggestions given may be integrated with other topics, such as 'Our community' and 'Caring for the planet'. The IWB should be used to maximum benefit to show speeded-up film of plant germination and growth, which can seem slow and dull in real-time. If it is possible to show excerpts from David Attenborough's *Plants* series, then the almost sinister growth of brambles, the scramble of climbing plants and the many ways plants flower and disperse their seeds can be appreciated. Comparing localities with different plant types can be fascinating, whether on different sides of the same hill or through e-mail exchange with a school in another locality, or even another country. Make sure that data-handling and graph-drawing results in data interpretation and the drawing of conclusions, and that the charts are not thought of as ends in themselves. At any age, growing and selling plants and plant products can become an enterprise activity, where budgeting and cooperative skills can be practised. Advice from local growers or garden centres could be sought by e-mail or traditional post. Investigation templates can be used at all ages, with differing amounts of support to plan and record practical tests.

Key Stage 1

Young children with poor manual-dexterity skills can create complex artwork by laying arrangements of plants on a digital scanner. The resulting photos can be coloured and manipulated in a paint program. Just inverting the colours can produce a magical effect, which might then be used as part of a collage or framed in its own right. Ferns, oats and other grasses are especially effective when used in this way. Black and white photocopies of plants can be coloured with crayon, pastel, paint or inks to give interesting effects. These in turn can be scanned into the computer and enhanced digitally.

Lower Key Stage 2

At this age, pupils will enjoy creating their own clip art, whether through digital photos of plants or by creating them in a paint program, perhaps in an art session, for later labelling of the parts in a science session. Simulations are useful to see quite rapidly the effects of different light, water and temperature conditions on seeds and plants. They enable tests to be done without waste or harm to living plants. Playing 'Twenty questions' is a useful starter activity when teaching children how to use or construct a branching database, so that they understand the yes/no options that help to narrow down the possibilities at each stage.

Upper Key Stage 2

Once used to a branching database, pupils are in a good position to understand how digital keys work, and these can be a great help when identifying plants on field trips. Older pupils should be able to construct one to help identify plants in their school grounds or local park. If children become interested in identifying wild plants, it can provide them with an interest for life that turns every outing into a treasure hunt. When trying to identify plants in the wild, they should be encouraged to take digital photos of specimens with a hand or coin in the shot, to show relative size. The specimens can then be identified at a later date. Pupils should not be collecting much living plant material, especially of unknown or rare species.

Topic 6
Famous people

Art and design

- Create **digital animations** using artwork to illustrate poems.
- Use **digital photos** of instruments, books/other relevant artefacts to create designs.
- Use **paint and draw programs** to create artworks, logos and cartoons.
- Edit and add to **digital photos** of people to show their characters in a **paint program**.

Literacy

- Use a **word bank** to create stories, poems, biographies and articles.
- **Word-process** questionnaires and reviews about peer habits in reading, art and musical preferences.
- Order instructions in a **WP document** for creating a digital film/podcast.
- Use **e-mail** to share story writing with pupils in another school. Compose in a **WP document**.
- Create an anthology of poems/gallery of favourite pictures in a **hyperlinked presentation**. (Sort entries according to subject/artist.)
- **E-mail** to get information about a living artist/writer/musician.
- Create an alphabet of technical terms for art/music in a **table** in a **WP document**.
- Assemble an alphabet of ideas for music/art/writing; e.g. A is for allegro, B is for Bach, C is for chord. This is most easily done in a two-column **WP table**, where one column is used to give information about the terms used.
- Use **paint** and **draw programs** to create a poster about an exhibition, book, school concert.

History

- Carry out research on the **Internet/CD-ROM** about famous writers/musicians/artists.
- Use a **spreadsheet/draw program** to create a timeline showing which famous people were contemporaries and which could have used the telephone, ridden in a train/car/plane, ridden a bike or used a camera.
- Create a **table** to show which countries have produced famous writers/artists/musicians. Why are some countries more prolific than others?

Music

- Create ringtones using **musical software**.
- Use **digital sound files** and music clips to create soundscapes for pictures and poems, with **music software** and free digital clips from the **Internet**.
- Record a **digital** soundtrack for a story.
- Create a **podcast** about a famous person that uses musical audio clips, speech and sound effects.
- Compose a jingle with **sound files** to advertise a book/play/art exhibition.
- Use **digital photos** of instruments to create labelled diagrams of each.

Numeracy

- Fill or use a **database** with facts and figures about the lives of artists, musicians or writers. Use to compare longevity, publications and genres.
- Use a table/**spreadsheet** to create a timeline.
- Use a **calculator** to compare book/CD/other costs associated with genre studied.

Topic 6: Famous people

The ideas in this section could be used in many projects about writers, musicians, artists or other categories of famous people. They might be adapted for work with sports personalities, film stars, inventors or great religious or humanitarian leaders. Some sections are obviously more suited to musical or artistic people, but the ideas here could be adapted. Practical work with paint, collage or real musical instruments should not be replaced by ICT versions, merely supplemented by them.

You may use the sound effects on this website (www.pacdv.com/sounds/index.html) free of charge in your video, film, audio and multimedia productions (but do not resell them or post on a website for download). See the subject sections for other musical and artistic software sites. Look at www.youtube.com/watch?v=nUDIoN-_Hxs&feature= related for a wonderful short film showing the history of art through women's portraits.

Key Stage 1

Soundtracks made at this level can use musical instruments and household items to create sounds that are then recorded on tape or with a digital audio recorder. Some professional writers will share a story-writing challenge with a class, swapping contributions through e-mail. See http://primary.naace.co.uk/curriculum/communications/email.htm for Trevor Millum's account of shared writing projects, starting with pupils in Key Stage 1. If you cannot afford a professional, even the class teacher might act as a mystery writing partner.

Lower Key Stage 2

Older pupils should be able to start combining sound files to create soundscapes to illustrate stories and poems or as part of a podcast. It takes a lot of practice, trial and error to create a useful questionnaire that does not ask questions with yes/no answers. Using a word processor is a good way to draft and redraft such work, possibly with the teacher acting as amanuensis for the class using the IWB.

By this age, pupils should be using timelines to assist in their understanding of chronology. There are several ready-made ones online, but it may be more useful for children to create their own, either using a two-column table, with dates in column 1 and events in column 2, or a spreadsheet, with dates in row A and events and lives in the rows below, overlapping where necessary to show which figures were contemporary.

Upper Key Stage 2

By Years 5 and 6, pupils will be developing personal tastes in art, poetry and music, and so making personal digital anthologies and galleries of professional artists' work in a hyperlinked presentation could be a project done by the whole class, or one that each individual starts now and takes with them to secondary school and beyond. Contacting professional writers, musicians and artists through their websites can often produce a motivating response.

Topic 7
Healthy me

Literacy

- Use a **word bank** to create leaflets and posters about handwashing, taking exercise and healthy eating.
- **Word-process** reports and quizzes about health issues and body functions.
- Research on the **Internet/CD-ROM** about local facilities for keeping healthy and taking exercise, as well as healthy eating.
- Organise and list in a **WP document** instructions for tooth care/hair care and exercise routines.
- Write recipes for healthy eating in a **WP document**, in card or booklet form, which they can take home.
- Plan and redraft text in a **WP document** for oral presentation about the project to peers/parents.
- Create **multimedia presentation** in **PowerPoint** to summarise learning on the project.
- **E-mail** food companies to get information about including more oats/pulses/fruit and vegetables in their diets.

Numeracy

- Compare heights and weights of pupils at different ages to show growth on a **spreadsheet** with a scattergram.
- Calculate food intake and calory values with a **calculator** or **spreadsheet**.
- Create a **database** about foods.
- Use **spreadsheets** to compare food values of cereals/yoghurts/crisps/vegetables.
- Use a **spreadsheet** to record achievements in athletics and potted sports over a term.

PE

- Use **data-logging** to measure pulse and temperature with exercise.
- Use **simulations** to see how different exercises affect pulse and heart rate.
- Test pupils' fitness and record results and graph on **spreadsheets**.
- Use **digital photos** and **film** to improve personal performance.
- Use **GPS** to help with orienteering activities.

Design and technology

- Design new bread/biscuit/muesli recipes in response to a class survey on food preferences. **Word-process** questionnaire and recipes. Chart results of survey using a **spreadsheet**.
- Use **design templates** to plan new, healthy-eating salads.
- Design a school fitness trail on the computer, using a **graphics program** to annotate a **digital map** of the school.
- **Word-process** instructions for each part of the trail, to be laminated and put on boards at each point in the trail.
- Create healthy-living leaflets on a **word processor.**
- Create healthy-living **digital films** and **podcasts**.
- Use **WP** and **graphics** to design board games with a sports theme, based on snakes and ladders, monopoly or dominoes.

MFL

- Look up words for body parts and food on the Internet. Hear how they sound on sites such as www.audiofrench.com/.
- Run a healthy-eating café in an MFL, with menus and ordering in the appropriate language.

Science

- Use an **IWB** to see pictures of healthy and diseased lungs/other organs in relation to smoking/drug abuse and obesity.
- Sort foods on an **IWB** using Venn and Carroll diagrams to identify the healthier food options.
- Use **digital photos** or pictures created in a **paint program** to create labelled diagrams of body parts.
- Use a **visualiser** to show X-rays, if available, as well as to compare details of pupils' hands, milk teeth, if available, and hair.
- Record testing procedures with a **digital camera** and add photos to reports and presentations.
- Use **investigation templates** on the computer to plan and report on practical investigations.
- Use a **digital camera** to record and evaluate sports achievements.

Topic 7: Healthy me

With the rise in obesity and the increase in free time that many people have, it is becoming quite urgent that health education is taught regularly in schools. Of course, care must be taken not to embarrass those who are overweight when collecting data and making charts, and so it may be useful to use data from a 'virtual class' record prepared by the teacher, so that children can draw appropriate conclusions about appropriate weights for different heights. Ideas for this topic could be linked with a sports topic to celebrate an occasion such as the Olympic Games.

Key Stage 1

Children need to become aware of their diet at an early stage, and learning to adapt recipes and make healthy choices may be crucial to later eating habits. Once practical experimentation has taken place, even young pupils could be helped to make recipe cards to take home, if they are given a word bank of ingredients and terms with which to compose their recipes. Instructions for hand-washing, teeth and hair care can be word-processed to get the order right, before being turned into posters and leaflets for school display. Children love to record their sporting achievements in graphs, and using a spreadsheet for this is a quick way to chart progress. They should be encouraged to reflect on what their chart shows and to explain why a performance may have improved (with practice, for example) or deteriorated (the pupil had a cold that week).

Lower Key Stage 2

Calorie counting can be a discouraging and onerous task with the large numbers involved. Using a spreadsheet that simply divides the calories of a food and the ideal calorie intake for a person by 100 gives a simpler points system to work with. Many food and sports companies respond generously to e-mails with requests for information about their products, and this can give writing a real purpose. Data-logging pupils' temperature as they exercise will bring the surprising result that the skin appears cooler when the child feels hotter. This is because perspiration evaporates from the skin, and this cools it and lowers its temperature. Ask the children to predict the temperature change and then to try to explain it themselves, before being given an explanation. Help them to devise further tests with the data logger, such as checking the amount of protection given by different sunglasses or working out how sensitive their hearing is to different sounds.

Upper Key Stage 2

Graphing the different components of foods such as cereals, sweets and biscuits can give a very dramatic indication of which are highest in salt or sugar or fat, so that it is easy to see which are the healthier options. Each pair of pupils could be responsible for collecting and charting one food per food type to help with this work.

If pupils create a fitness trail for playtimes, then advice about the exercises to be done at each station should be word-processed, laminated and available for all breaks. Devising a quiz is a good way to revise learning: this could be a word-processed document taken home to challenge parents and carers, or a hyperlinked electronic one designed to check on peer learning or, perhaps, posted on the school's website for all to enjoy.

Topic 8
Sports/Olympics/World Cup

Literacy

- Use a **word bank** to create information sheets and sports cards, which can be kept or swapped like football cards.
- **Word-process** reports on sports events around the world/in school.
- Use a **WP document** to write a sports quiz.
- Research on the **Internet** about sports personalities and events, including the history of the event.
- Organise and list facts about sports in a table in a **WP document**.
- Create a concept map with a **graphics program** to show major facts about a range of sports.
- Create a **multimedia presentation** to explain why a local town should be host for the next World Cup.
- **E-mail** sports clubs/embassies to get information about teams and training.

Art and design

- Create country flags in a **paint program**.
- Design sports logos in a **paint program**.
- Plan a design for a sports trail/village in a **draw program**.
- Use **digital photos** of sports stars to create photo collages of them, either paper-based or digitally in a **Photoshop**-type program.
- Use a **paint program** to illustrate sports events and to add to written work about them.
- Film and edit a school sports event to create a programme for the school **website**.
- Use **digital animation** to tell the story of a person trying to improve at a sporting event.
- Use a **WP** and **graphics** to create posters for sports events.
- Use **digital photos** to record personal performance and edit in a paint program to create special effects.

MFL

- Use **Internet** sources to find out how to greet and congratulate in the language of competing teams.
- Use the **Internet** to research traditions and cultures of competing teams.
- **E-mail** schools in twinned countries to ask about sporting traditions.

Numeracy

- Compare scores, averages and performances on a **spreadsheet**.
- Calculate inconceivable comparisons with a **calculator** to show how long pupils or the fastest person/animal/bird in the world would take to travel from Land's End to John o' Groats. Compare highest-jumping animals and people.
- Create a **database** about sports clubs/personalities.
- Use a **spreadsheet** to compare equipment costs for different sports. How much does it cost to get kitted out for each one?

Geography

- Use a **branching database** to create a quiz to identify different sports.
- Annotate a digital map in a **paint/draw program**, with arrows and text boxes to give team information.
- Use **spreadsheets/calculators** to compare populations/land area with medals or goals achieved by different countries. Does the country with the largest land area/highest population get the most medals?
- Use a **visualiser** to share maps or details on sports cards.
- Use the **Internet/CD-ROM** to find out about lifestyles and sports in countries worldwide.

Topic 8: Sports/Olympics/World Cup

Projects on topical sporting events can be run almost every year, with the cycles of World Games, Olympic Games, World Cup and other international events. Ideas here can be linked with the 'Healthy me' and 'Famous people' topics. It is increasingly common for schools to be linked with schools in other countries. The Comenius project is one of the organisations that facilitate this type of cultural exchange. Pupils can devise their own mini games or potted sports and chart their progress in each activity.

Key Stage 1

Mouse control can be developed in young children with the creation of simple graphics, such as national flags and logos. Word banks can be used to create simple texts that are adapted as posters for a variety of uses. Branching databases and Venn and Carroll diagrams are all useful ways to learn to sort data, especially if used in conjunction with an IWB.

Lower Key Stage 2

Tables are a useful way to organise and simplify a lot of data. As they can be filled with text, numbers or graphics, they can be made visually attractive and can contain brief comments on different personalities and their sports. Tables can be used to record team scores or list countries, flags and a few basic phrases, as well as to compare equipment or distances for different sports and events. Once pupils realise the range of ways in which they can be used, they may choose to use them when they need to organise information in many subjects.

Upper Key Stage 2

Concept maps are a useful way of recording learning, if before and after versions are created at the start and completion of a project. They can also show relationships, in this case between countries, sports and other cultural traditions, depending on the interests of the pupils. Digital photos can be used, not only to see how a gymnastic performance, for example, might be improved, but also as materials for an arts-based project that uses special effects to improve the photos artistically. Digital collages can be fun to create in programs such as Photoshop. Although this is quite a complex program, only a few basic skills are required to do this. Budgets can be organised with spreadsheets or a calculator and a table.

Topic 9
Robots/superheroes/monsters

Music

- Use **music simulation software** to create themes for superheroes or monsters.
- Use a **digital audio recorder** to record robotic music, using percussion and body percussion.

Numeracy

- Create a **database** about characteristics of different types of robot/superhero/monster/dinosaur.
- Use a **spreadsheet** to chart and compare sizes of creatures studied.
- Make a robotic calculator with a **spreadsheet**.
- Use **floor turtles** disguised as robots or robotic pets to explore directions and control technology.
- A **branching database** can help to identify a mystery monster from data already inserted.

Science

- Sort materials for making monsters on an **IWB** using Venn and Carroll diagrams.
- Use a **graphics program** to make circuit diagrams for use in robot construction.
- Sort and identify superheroes/properties of materials using **branching database**.
- Test to see hardness/strength of different materials and record results and graph on **spreadsheets**.
- Record testing procedures with a **digital camera** and add photos to reports and presentations.
- Use **investigation templates** on the computer to plan and report on practical investigations.

Literacy

- Use a **word bank** to create stories, based on *The Iron Man* or other sci-fi stories.
- **Word-process** poems in the shape of a robot or monster (concrete poetry).
- Use a **table** with speech bubbles to create a comic strip-type story.
- Organise and list attributes of superheroes in a table in a **WP document**.
- Carry out research on the **Internet** about the development of robots and create a timeline in a **spreadsheet** or a table to record this.
- Use a **WP** to place instructions in the best order to create a robot.
- Plan and redraft text in a **WP document** for oral presentation about the project to peers/parents.
- Create a **multimedia presentation** in **PowerPoint** to summarise learning on the project.
- **E-mail** to get information about the use of factory robots, e.g. in the making of cars.
- Use the **Internet** to find out about robot and monster artists, such as Eric Joyner, Roger Dean and Clayton Bailey.

DT

- Use a **design template** on a **computer** to plan a design for a pupil-made robot/monster that uses pneumatics or cams.
- Use a **digital camera** to record model-making and finished models.
- Use a **recording template** on a computer to evaluate finished models.

Topic 9: Robots/superheroes/monsters

This topic has ideas that are adaptable to a number of topics, even including the old favourite of dinosaurs. Not every idea would be suitable for a robot or superhero topic, but most could be adapted in some way and could be used with other, non-ICT-based techniques to provide a challenging and creative project.

Key Stage 1

Programmable floor turtles are useful for work on estimation, direction, angles, spatial awareness and control technology. They can facilitate group work and group investigations. Older pupils should do similar work with screen turtles, which can take on many guises.

Lower Key Stage 2

As this is often an age when pupils are learning to use e-mail, it would be motivating for them to create stories, with either professional writers or partners in other schools, through e-mail.

Design and recording templates are a useful way to plan and adapt designs as work progresses. They can remind pupils about points such as success criteria and collecting adequate resources and tools before starting work. They should help to evaluate so that successes are celebrated and points for further development are noted.

Upper Key Stage 2

A robotic calculator can be made with a single line from a spreadsheet that uses a simple formula to calculate a sum: e.g. $x + y = z$. Cell z has an IF/THEN formula in it that calculates the answer to the sum and then says either 'well done' or 'try again' (=IF(C5+E5=G5,"well done","try again")). Pupils can alter the function of the machine to add, subtract, multiply and divide. They can paste this into a graphics drawing, so that only the numbers show and the whole appears as a monster machine. Even pupils who are poor at maths enjoy testing themselves on their times tables using a machine they have made for themselves.

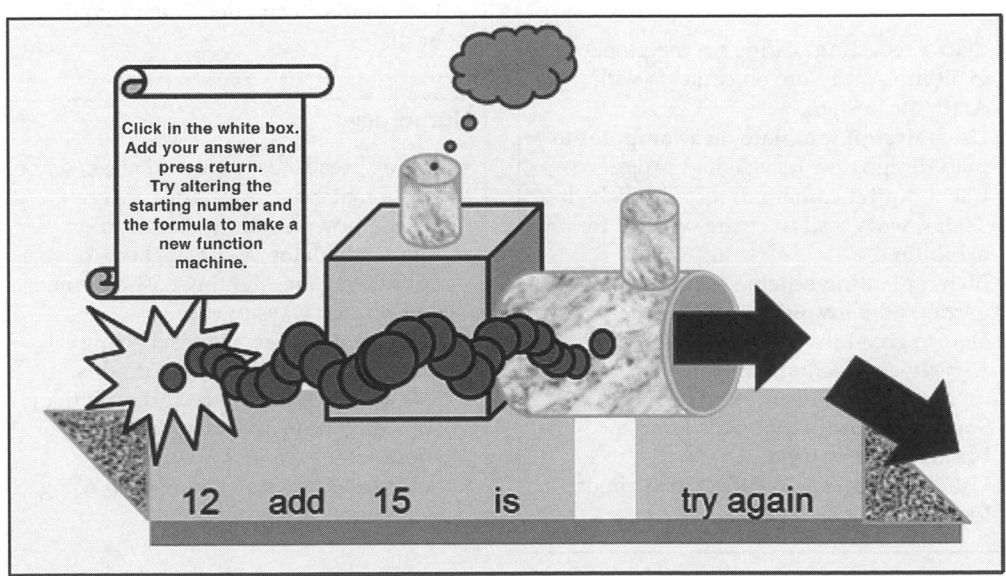

Topic 10
Caring for our planet

Geography

- Carry out research on the **Internet** about environmental issues, as well as local penalties for littering and antisocial behaviour.
- Use **data-logging** to record noise pollution around the school.
- Take **digital photos** of local areas that could be improved and contact the council about them through e-mail or a WP letter.
- Take part in local litter-clearing projects. Make posters to advertise them and record weight of materials/types of litter on a **spreadsheet**.
- Annotate local **digital maps** to highlight areas where littering/graffiti are a problem.
- Make a **podcast** about a local environmental issue and post on the school website.
- Make a **digital film** about an environmental issue, e.g. littering/growing plants.

DT

- Plan a recycling/caring for the planet exhibition and vote on contents with **ActiVote** system.
- Use a **design template** on a **computer** to plan designs for recycled art projects.
- Use a **digital camera** to record finished design work and to create pictures for an exhibition.
- Plan a planting scheme for the school garden on a **graphics template**.
- Devise green inventions for a *Dragon's Den*-style presentation. Plan notes for this on a **word processor**.
- Sort and identify materials using a **branching database**.
- Use **data-logging** to collect data about local noise pollution.

Literacy

- Use a **word bank** to create posters and information leaflets about environmental issues.
- **Word-process** reports on a newspaper template about caring for the planet.
- Organise and list ways to recycle in a **WP document**.
- Write a letter to a local MP in a **WP document** about local environmental issues.
- Plan and redraft text in a **WP document** for oral presentation about the project for school assembly.
- Create a multimedia presentation in **PowerPoint** to summarise learning on the project.
- Use **e-mail** to find out about local allotments/swap shops and recycling facilities.

PHSE

- Plan information for debates using a **WP** to organise ideas.
- Find out about living conditions and recycling in developing countries and how tourism can affect them for good or ill.

Numeracy

- Use a spreadsheet to record class/school waste materials in weight per week. Decide how this can be reduced.
- Use a **calculator** or spreadsheet to work out heating and lighting costs for the class and discuss ways to save.
- Create a **database** about recycling materials and best ways to do this.
- Use a **spreadsheet** to record growth of sprouting bean shoots in different conditions.
- Sort waste materials on an **IWB** using Venn and Carroll diagrams.

Topic 10: Caring for our planet

There are many school projects that can look at environmental issues; weather as part of a local study; a project on materials; one with a geographical and weather focus; or one on inventions or improving lifestyles. The ideas here focus on obtaining and presenting data, as well as recording test results, and evaluating both test results and factual information obtained from a variety of sources. Pupils should be encouraged to look critically at the data they collect, as well as information found in books and on the Internet. They should discuss ways to develop sustainable living for all, and how what they do may affect people in other countries. Many science activities could be planned as part of this topic as well.

Key Stage 1

Pupils in KS1 can look at very local or school environmental issues to do with littering, healthy eating and caring for the environment, including developing its biodiversity. A school garden can be a great help here, and budgets for this can be managed with the help of a child-friendly spreadsheet. A good way to record learning might be through filming the pupils in practical activities and adding scanned pictures and examples of them talking to the camera about their ideas.

Lower Key Stage 2

When sorting materials, either practically or on the whiteboard, they could consider those that are recyclable, as well as those that are biodegradable or those with hazardous properties, such as glass and metal. They could look at the local water company's website to see ways to reduce their water use and record their learning as a comic strip. A spreadsheet could be used to add up water wastage from different places in school or at home. Noise pollution, whether from traffic, machinery or just pupil voices, is easily charted with data-logging, and such work could lead to discussions in PHSE sessions about the use of car radios and music in the street.

Upper Key Stage 2

Members of Parliament are very good about responding to children's requests for information. A response on House of Commons headed paper can feel very exciting to a young writer. The Internet has information on eco-footprints, global warming, recycling issues and vegetarian living.

Pupils can calculate their carbon footprints on sites such as www.carboncontrol.org.uk/teachers_and_parents/default.aspa and look at ways to live a greener lifestyle. The IWB could be used to display items of environmental interest from around the world each day, as pupils arrive in school.

Appendix I
Attainment targets

Attainment targets for ICT can be found at: http://curriculum.qcda.gov.uk/key-stages-1-and-2/subjects/ict/attainmenttarget/index.aspx (last accessed 21 July 2010).

Level I
Pupils explore information from various sources, showing they know that information exists in different forms. They use ICT to work with text, images and sound to help them share their ideas. They recognise that many everyday devices respond to signals and instructions. They make choices when using such devices to produce different outcomes. They talk about their use of ICT.

Level 2
Pupils use ICT to organise and classify information and to present their findings. They enter, save and retrieve work. They use ICT to help them generate, amend and record their work and share their ideas in different forms, including text, tables, images and sound. They plan and give instructions to make things happen and describe the effects. They use ICT to explore what happens in real and imaginary situations. They talk about their experiences of ICT, both inside and outside school.

Level 3
Pupils use ICT to save information and to find and use appropriate stored information, following straightforward lines of enquiry. They use ICT to generate, develop, organise and present their work. They share and exchange their ideas with others. They use sequences of instructions to control devices and achieve specific outcomes. They make appropriate choices when using ICT-based models or simulations to help them find things out and solve problems. They describe their use of ICT and its use outside school.

Level 4
Pupils understand the need for care in framing questions when collecting, finding and interrogating information. They interpret their findings, question plausibility and recognise that poor-quality information leads to unreliable results. They add to, amend and combine different forms of information from a variety of sources. They use ICT to present information in different forms and show they are aware of the intended audience and the need for quality in their presentations. They exchange information and ideas with others in a variety of ways, including using e-mail. They use ICT systems to control events in a predetermined manner and to sense physical data. They use ICT-based models and simulations to explore patterns and relationships, and make predictions about the consequences of their decisions. They compare their use of ICT with other methods and with its use outside school.

Level 5
Pupils select the information they need for different purposes, check its accuracy and organise it in a form suitable for processing. They use ICT to structure, refine and present information in different forms and styles for specific purposes and audiences. They exchange information and ideas with others in a variety of ways, including using e-mail. They create sequences of instructions to control events and understand the need to be precise when framing and sequencing instructions. They understand how ICT devices with sensors can be used to monitor and measure external events. They explore the effects of changing the variables in an ICT-based model. They discuss their knowledge and experience of using ICT and their observations of its use outside school. They assess the use of ICT in their work and are able to reflect critically in order to make improvements in subsequent work.

Appendix 2
Creating templates

How to create a template

1 Create the document in Word, Textease, Excel or any other program that will allow the creation of a template (with Macs, it is called stationery).
2 Use 'save as' and choose the template option (Figure A2.1). It is sometimes necessary to scroll down in the document type box if your computer works like this (see Figure A2.2).
3 Make sure the file name is in the format you want: you might add the word *template* to the file name to make this clear; e.g. 'Y4 Science Ch. Of State template'.
4 Choose the location for the template. Do not let the computer store it in the templates folder, or you may never find it again. It is better to create and use your own templates folders, with sub-folders for different subject templates.
5 Save and close the template without further saving.
6 To use: locate the template and open it.
7 Save the used template to an appropriate location. Pupils should be taught to save the work to their own folders, with a file name that clearly identifies it. Ideally, this will include the child's name or initials (in case they save it to the wrong folder) and the date, as well as a name for the work; e.g. 'JJ Ghost story May 3' or 'Jack King DT costs 6 Nov'.

Examples of templates

A blank planning template to be used by groups of pupils in a DT session is shown in Figure A2.3.

An example of the completed template is shown in Figure A2.4. The teacher can add comments in italics to show the work has been read and discussed with the pupils. The finished work can be saved to each pupil's folder, and a copy can be printed for a wall display, if appropriate. To get all the explanations of ideas, there will be several drafts, as the result of feedback given by the teacher.

Other examples of template use

An example of a template for young children to use with a sewing activity is shown in Figure A2.5. If the clip art were changed, it could be adapted for a different DT challenge.

Figure A2.6 shows a template to help plan a science investigation. This can give the work a clear structure and ensure consideration is given to each stage of the work.

Templates can be used for recording as well and can be differentiated by the amount of help, e.g. keywords, that are given.

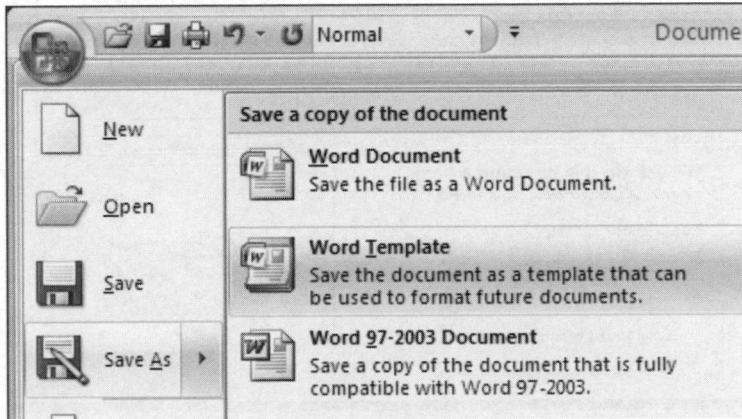

Figure A2.1

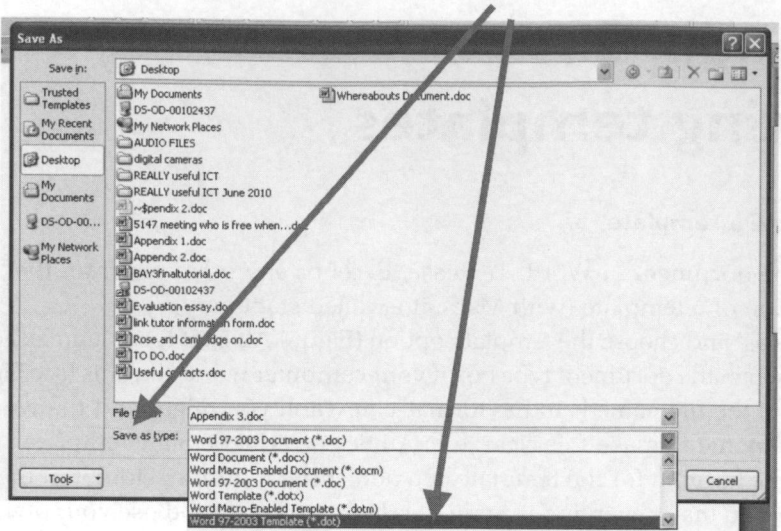

Figure A2.2

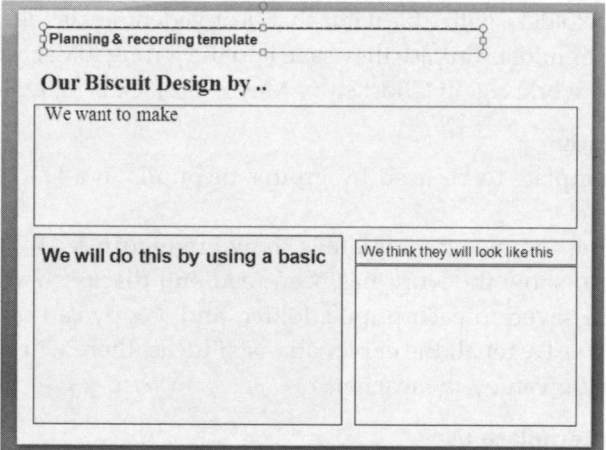

Figure A2.3

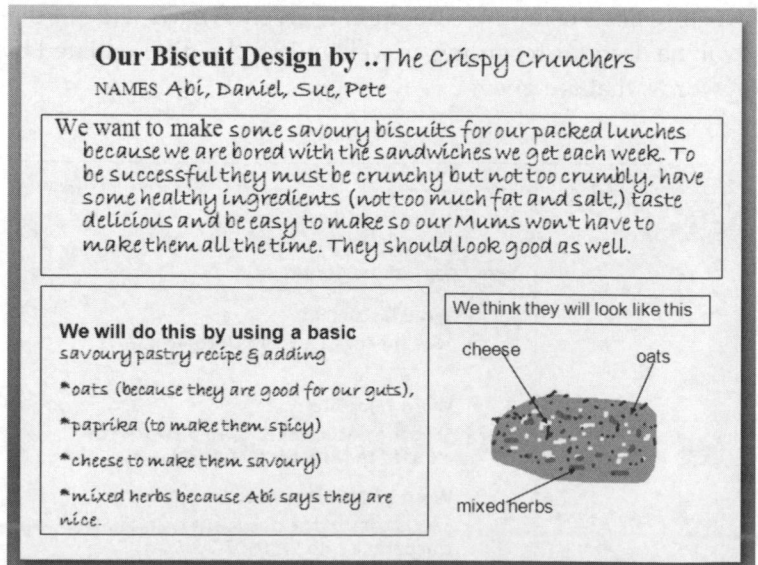

Figure A2.4

Figure A2.5

Figure A2.6

Appendix 3
Instructions for creating a hyperlinked PowerPoint presentation

1

To make basic presentation

- Each group of children creates 3/5 screens about their topic area, depending on their ability. They should use clear headings such as

- Viking Homes
- Viking Food
- Viking Clothes
- Viking Travel

Each screen should have on & back buttons from Insert menu.

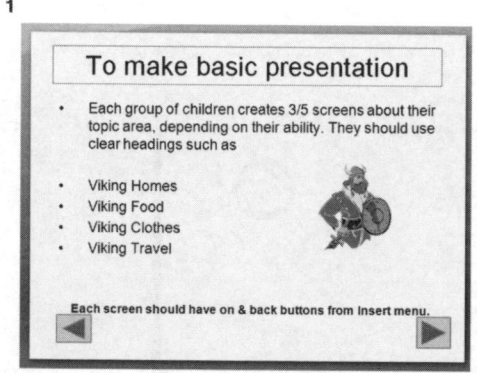

2

To link the presentations

1. Open a new page at the start of the presentation using the title only layout. Call it Introduction.

2. Copy and past all the presentations after the title page.

3

Link each section

- Add links to the first page in each section.

- Insert a Home button at the end of every mains section to return to the Introduction page.

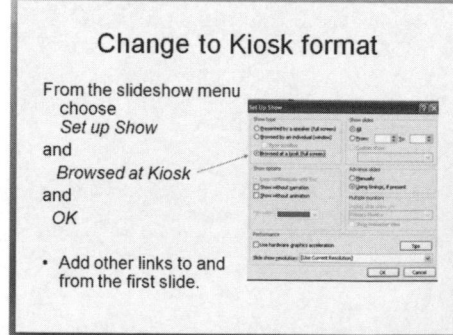

4

1. On slide 1 *Introduction* use the text box tool to create 4 boxes called

| Homes | Food | Clothes | Travel |

2. Click on the first label   Homes
3. and from the Insert menu choose Hyperlink.

4. Choose Place in this document

5. Choose the page to which you want to link (the Homes page)

6. Click OK

7. On a full screen check your link and   ESC   to escape

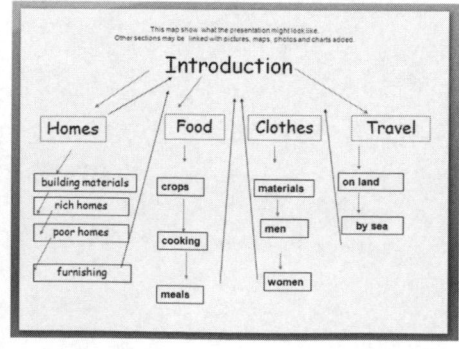

5

Change to Kiosk format

From the slideshow menu
   choose
    Set up Show
and
    Browsed at Kiosk
and
    OK

- Add other links to and from the first slide.

6

This map show what the presentation might look like.
Other sections may be linked with pictures, maps, photos and charts added.

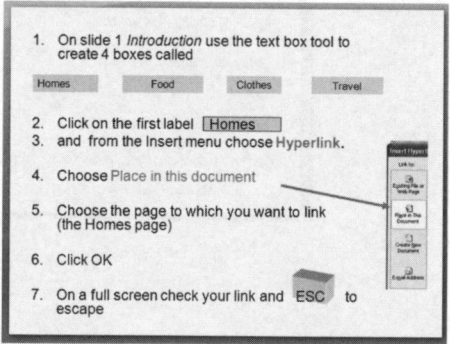

Appendix 4
E-safety

Although the Internet can be an excellent place to find out information, share ideas and photos, and communicate with friends, not everyone out there has children's best interests at heart. Without being alarmist, teachers have the responsibility to make sure that every child is aware of possible dangers and about responsible Internet use. It is particularly important that children never reveal personal details about themselves that would give unwanted access to strangers. Many children have suffered from cyber-bullying by people they know, who post unkind or even offensive material about them on social networking sites. Children who would not consider themselves to be playground bullies may do this for a laugh, but cause immense hurt. Therefore all pupils need training in appropriate use of social networking sites and how to communicate responsibly. There are several good online sites to help with this.

The sites www.thinkuknow.co.uk and www.kidsmart.org.uk have sections for children, parents and teacher trainers. The Directgov site has advice on cyber-bullying on computers and mobile phones, social networking sites, downloading and file sharing illegal material, and online gaming: www.direct.gov.uk/en/Parents/Yourchildshealthandsafety/Internet safety/index.htm. This site suggests three simple rules to help children stay safe:

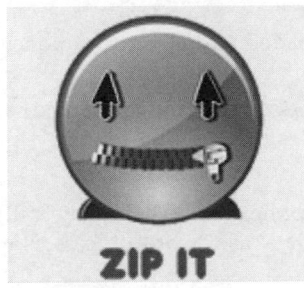  

- Zip it – keep your personal information private and think about what you say and do online.
- Block it – block people who send you nasty messages and don't open unknown links and attachments.
- Flag it – flag up with someone you trust if anything upsets you or if someone asks to meet you offline.

The Child Exploitation and Online protection Centre (CEOP) www.ceop.police.uk provides an online facility for reporting inappropriate online activity.

Children should be encouraged to use a nickname instead of their real name in chat rooms or on instant messaging services. To stop people accessing their online accounts, encourage them to keep their passwords secret, and to change them regularly. They should not open any attachment from an unknown source as it may contain a virus and be aware that much Internet information is not free for them to copy without either permission or acknowledgement, otherwise they could be accused of stealing someone else's work.

Pupils need to learn the 'netiquette' rules of behaviour and this may be done on the school's virtual learning platform, if they have one, or on an educational networking site such as Learning Landscapes for Schools, SuperClubsPLUS or in the virtual world of Club Penguin, which uses penguin avatars to teach about safe Internet communication. Internet safety posters can be downloaded and printed for free from sites such as www.free-for-kids.com/internet-safety-posters.shtml.

Appendix 5
Glossary

2Simple	A brand of software that makes child-friendly versions of most types of popular software, e.g. 2Create A Superstory, 2Draw, 2Animate, 2Publish.
Activote	Hand-held devices that interact with Promethean whiteboard software to allow individuals in a class to choose from a number of options. Teachers can assess the understanding of an individual child or an average for the class.
Animations	A moving image, often in cartoon style, that demonstrates a procedure or activity on-screen.
Audacity	Free audio editing software can be downloaded from http://audacity.sourceforge.net/.
Autoshapes	Ready-made shapes in Word that can be moved, resized and coloured. Some have text added to them.
Binary database	See branching database.
BlackCat	A software supplier that offers a full range of applications. The bundle called SuperTools comprises cut-down spreadsheet, database, word-processor and drawing packages.
Blog	Blog is an abbreviation for weblog. This allows users to write, edit and share an online journal.
Branching database	A database such as Branch for TextEase sorts items using a series of yes/no questions. It has many of the features of an identification key. Also known as a decision tree.
CAD	Computer-aided design programs, which often supply ready-made graphics to be moved and resized.
CD-ROM	A plastic disk sandwiching a metal layer that stores digital information. It has a read-only memory.
Clicker	A suite of software by Crick. One of its more popular items is a package that helps children with word banks and phonics.
Compress (compressed file)	Large files can be compressed, with some loss of picture quality, to take up less room on a computer or data stick. Loss of quality will not be noticed on websites and most documents.
Concept-mapping software	Inspiration software, SmartDraw and ThinkBuzan are some of the companies that offer concept-mapping and flowchart applications. Also known as graphical organisers.
Correl Draw	Graphic-design software.
Dance mat	A dance mat is a mat with pads that operate pressure switches. These interface with the computer allowing the dancer to respond to instructions. The software controls the speed at which the dancer has to respond. Easiteach is one supplier.
Data-handling package	Data carry information. They can be handled by spreadsheets and databases that combine to form a data-handling package.

Data-logging/ data logger	Sensors such as thermometers, light meters and sound measuring devices can be plugged into a buffer box. This box protects the computer from damage and allows information from the sensors to be recorded using a software package. One supplier of this hardware and software is Data Harvest.
Database	A database stores information in a series of records. Each record consists of several fields. For instance, each child in the class might have a record, and fields could include height, shoe size and eye colour. Several software suppliers, e.g. BlackCat, supply databases suitable for use by primary children.
Dazzle	A drawing and paint package suitable for young children.
Decision tree	See branching database.
Desktop publishing	Word processors are very effective at presenting text but, for special effects, the easy placing of images and flexible design features, a desktop-publishing package is essential. Adobe, Quark and Microsoft publisher are aimed at adults, whereas PawPrints is the desktop-publishing element of the BlackCat suite of programs.
Digi-blue	Stop-motion and video clips can be made using these blue digital cameras. These cameras are supplied by the company Digital Blue.
Digital animation	Stop-motion video recording in the style of Wallace and Gromit allows children to create animated sequences.
Digital camera	A camera that stores the images using electronic circuitry rather than film.
Digital film	See digital video.
Digital music software	Music can be recorded digitally. MP3 files are used to record digital sound. MP3 players, such as Apple iPods, are used to play the files.
Digital photos	These are images recorded in a digital format.
Digital poster	A multimedia poster that incorporates images, text, sound and video. Glogster.com is one supplier of these.
Digital sound files	Digital sound files are stored in MP3 format.
Digital sound recorder	Also referred to as an MP3 player.
Digital sound recording	A sound recording stored digitally, often using MP3 files.
Digital video	Digital video relies on images stored electronically rather than on analogue tape.
Draw program	Draw programs allow the user to draw on-screen using shapes, lines and imported images.
DTP	Desktop-publishing applications contain WP and page-layout options to help create newspapers, dairies, reports and other presentation formats.
E-books	E-books are books that are held as digital files. They can be viewed on standard computers or on dedicated readers, such as Amazon's Kindle.
Electronic keyboard	An electronic keyboard for music can also be called a digital keyboard. It is an electronic instrument that can be connected to a computer to aid composition and the digital recording of music. Many come with inbuilt rhythms and a selection of instrumental sounds.
Electronic voting system	See ActiVote.
E-mail	A means of communicating through the Internet. E-mails can have attachments such as photos, sound fields and video clips.
E-zine	Any magazine that is distributed electronically; often this is a web page, or it may be an e-mailed newsletter.
Fax	A fax machine can communicate through the phone lines with another fax machine. It can only send relatively simple images.
Floor turtles (including Pixies and Roamers)	A floor turtle is a small robot that can be programmed to move forward for a specified distance. It can turn right or left and, using these simple movements, it can move through a maze or navigate round part of a classroom.
Function machine	A program that makes calculations in response to a user's input. These are easily set up in spreadsheets, where pupils can change the numbers supplied, as well as the calculation to be carried out.

GIS	Geographic information systems use digital maps linked to a database of information. See Mapzoneto find out more (http://mapzone.ordnancesurvey.co.uk/mapzone/giszone/english/).
Google Earth	A site on the Internet where maps and images of locations are stored and can be viewed.
GPS	Global positioning system: devices that use GPS rely on the signal from an array of satellites to fix their position to within a few metres.
Graphical model	This is a way of looking at the future, using graphs to predict probable events.
Graphical organiser	See concept-mapping software.
Graphics applications/ program	The simplest graphics applications are draw programs on computers. These include Microsoft Draw. Paint and photo-processing software such as Photoshop are also graphics applications.
Group/ungroup	Graphical objects can be grouped by clicking on each shape, holding shift, right clicking and choosing 'Group' (PC). On a Mac, use a sub menu to do this. Items can be ungrouped as well.
Hardware	This term covers all the items, such as screens, printers and keyboards, as opposed to software, which encompasses computer programs.
Help	Advice that is built into the computer or can be accessed online. Press F1 or the Help icon in any program (the Apple key on a Mac).
Hyperlinked	Where two locations in a document are linked electronically they are hyperlinked. Often these links are shown by text that is a different colour or has been underlined.
HyperStudio	An application that allows the user to mix video, text, images and sounds.
Internet: good practice	The Internet is a wonderfully varied and fun place, but children should be taught how to stay safe. The Byron Report on Internet safety is a sensible set of guidelines for anyone working with children (www.dcsf.gov.uk/byronreview/).
Intranet	Within large institutions, there is frequently an intranet, which is like a mini Internet, available only to people within that institution.
ITP	Interactive teaching program can be found online at: http://nationalstrategies.standards.dcsf.gov.uk/search/primary/results/nav:49909.
IWB	Interactive whiteboards use images projected on to a live whiteboard. The images can be drawn over, added to, deleted and coloured.
JPEG	A graphics file format commonly used for saving photos.
Kar2ouche	A suite of programs that allows students to compose role play, storyboards, movies and animations on-screen, using drag and drop commands.
Kidspiration	A suite of programs that use strong visual images in presentations and learning (see also concept-mapping software).
Light sensor	A data-logging sensor that is light sensitive and can be attached to a computer through an input device to record light levels.
Listening stations	A set of headphones that can be used by a number of children simultaneously.
Logo	A program that uses simple commands to move objects (often a screen turtle) on-screen. Commands such as forward, back and turn can be repeated with variations to produce complex and beautiful patterns.
MFL	Modern foreign language.
Mobile phones	Portable cordless phones that connect to a cellular network owned by a mobile network operator. They may support texting and be able to take photos or even connect to the Internet (smart phones).
MP3	This is a file format for recording music, with CD tracks reduced to around a tenth of their normal size without a significant loss of quality. This makes it practical to download music over the Internet, as download times have been cut. MP3 strips out a lot of the information recorded in a song that our ears are not able to hear.
Multimap	A website that allows you to browse maps and directions. It is also possible to see aerial photos of specified places.

Multimedia presentation	A presentation that makes use of a number of different ways of presenting information. This might include moving images, sound, hyperlinks and text.
Multimodal texts	Texts that may use words, diagrams, graphics, sound and varied layouts to present information.
Music software	Programs that enable the user to create musical compositions using a simulated keyboard and a selection of pre-recorded sounds.
NPC	A non-player character, frequently known as an NPC, is a character in a computer role-playing game that is not controlled by a human. Typically, NPCs are only neutral or allied characters and not enemies of players.
Paint program	These programs allow the user to achieve images using the computer that are similar to paint effects. They include brush strokes and easy colour fill.
PaintShop Pro	A graphics program that is useful for manipulating digital photos, as well as creating pictures using paint software.
Palmtops	These are small computers that typically hold diary, telephone book and other simple functions. PDAs or personal digital assistants are also palmtops. PDAs have computing, telephone, fax, Internet and networking features.
Photoshop	A program that allows the user to alter digital photos in a wide number of ways. For instance, the exposure can be changed, sections of the photo can be removed, and features can be added.
Podcast	A podcast is a number of MP3 files linked together. Podcasts are typically downloaded from a broadcaster. They can be saved and listened to at any time using an MP3 player. Educational institutions frequently publish lectures as podcasts.
PowerPoint	A Microsoft program that links screens of text, pictures, charts, moving images and sound. Internet links can be added as well. PowerPoint presentations are frequently used in teaching or pitching product ideas.
Presentation packages/ document	See PowerPoint. Hyperstudio, 2Simple software and BlackCat all have presentation programs suitable for pupils to use.
Promethean	A brand of interactive white board (see IWB, above).
Raster image	A grid of pixels also known as a bitmap image. Each one can be a different colour. A bitmap image is good for photos and details, though they use a lot of memory and may appear jagged when zoomed in on.
Rising Stars	A publisher that has a range of simulation CDs suitable for pupils in KS1 and KS2.
Roamer	A type of floor turtle.
Scanning	A document can be scanned, using a scanner, and the types of written text can be digitised and made available as electronic text.
Screen turtles	See Logo, above.
Sensors (digital)	Devices that detect sound, light, temperature, movement or pressure. These are frequently used in data-logging applications (see above).
Sibelius	A brand of musical software, mainly used to write scores.
Skype	This is a software application that allows users to make voice calls over the Internet.
Sound sensor	A data-logging sensor that is sound sensitive and can be attached to a computer through an input device to record sound levels.
Soundscape	A combination of sounds that arise from a locality. Pupils can create an audio recording that is intended to represent an area or an occasion. They can record sounds using percussion and musical software to represent particular locations, both real and fantasy.
Spreadsheet	A spreadsheet is an array of boxes into which data are inserted. The data can be sorted and manipulated using mathematical formulae.
Stop frame/ stop motion	This is a type of animation where a photograph is taken of a model. The model is then moved, and a further photograph is taken. This operates in a similar way to flick books, in that the images produce the appearance of movement.

Table	A set of cells that can be filled with data. In WP documents, tables allow the user to set out text and sort items easily.
Talking book	An actor's reading of a book can be made available as an MP3file.
Template	This is a file, such as a WP document, that can be altered and, when saved, it saves the new version, leaving the original untouched. This is a form of 'save as', but it takes place automatically, thus avoiding unintended saves that overwrite the original.
Temperature sensor	A data-logging sensor that is temperature-sensitive and can be attached to a computer through an input device to record temperature levels.
Textease	A suite of programs aimed at primary children. The programs include a word processor, spreadsheet, database and branching database.
Texting	The use of a mobile phone to send a short item of text to another phone.
Turtle (screen)	See Logo, above.
Video camera	A camera that records moving images digitally.
Video-call (see Skype)	A phone call where sound is supplemented by a live video image of the person being spoken to.
Video-conferencing	A phone call involving more than two participants, with live video images of all involved.
Visualiser	A piece of hardware, connected to a computer, that produces an image of anything placed under the lights of the visualiser. Magnified images can be viewed, and many teachers use the visualiser to project images of items such as books, cloth, shells and small mechanical objects.
VLE	These initials stand for virtual learning environment. VLEs normally allow registered users to use the tools and content within the VLE. Many schools have created their own VLEs to help with aspects of homework and communication with parents, e.g. http://laughtonallsaintsvle.com/.
Web 1.0 (WWW)	The term Web 1.0 refers to sites that have very limited interactivity and where information flow is one way.
Web 2.0 (use) personal websites, blogs, podcasts, photo and video sharing	The term Web 2.0 is usually associated with web applications that facilitate interactive information sharing and collaboration. A Web 2.0 site allows its users to interact with each other as contributors to the website. Examples of Web 2.0 include web-based communities, hosted services, web applications, social-networking sites, video-sharing sites, wikis and blogs (see Wikipedia for definitions of these).
Webcams	A video or still digital camera that is connected to the Internet. Many of the images are free to view, but some involve sites where there are admission costs.
WebQuest	This is a site where learners collaborate to solve problems. Learners can, in some situations, play the role of researchers or experts.
Wii	A video-game console that is interactive and wireless controlled.
Wiki	A wiki is a website that allows the easy creation and editing of any number of interlinked web pages. Wikis allow anyone to contribute. The most famous wiki is Wikipedia.
WildKey	Palmtop technology from Wild Knowledge that enables users to record field data and, with the use of Wild Keys, to identify plants and animals. Some systems have GPS and digital-camera facilities as well.
Windows Movie Maker	A program that allows users to build, edit and delete movies shot on a digital movie camera.
Word	The Microsoft Office word processor. This can be made user-friendly for pupils through the use of templates.
Word bank	Contains words that are already typed and can be dragged and dropped into a learner's text.
Word-processed	A document that has been created using a word processor has been word-processed.
Word-processing (WP) program	There are many WP programs, ranging from primary-school programs such as Textease to full-featured professional word processors such as Word.
Word processor	A program that allows users to type and edit text. Some basic word processors, such as BlackCat's WriteAway!, include a word bank.

Bibliography

Alexander, R. (ed.) (2009) *Children, their world, their education: final report and recommendations of the Cambridge Primary Review*, London: Routledge.

Allen, J., Potter, J., Sharp, J. and Turvey, K. (2007) *Primary ICT, knowledge, understanding and practice*, Exeter: Learning Matters.

Assessment Reform Group (2002) 'Assessment for learning' (available at: www.assessment-reform-group.org/CIE3.PDF).

Balanskat, A., Blamire, R. and Kefala, S. (2006) *The ICT Impact Report. A review of studies of ICT impact on schools in Europe*, European Schoolnet.

Ball, B. (2003) 'Teaching and learning mathematics with an interactive whiteboard', *Micromath*, 19 (1): 4–7.

Barber, D., Cooper, L. and Meeson, G. (2007) *Learning and teaching with interactive whiteboards*, Exeter: Learning Matters.

Barrett, H. (2006) 'Using electronic portfolios for classroom assessment, learning, engagement and collaboration through technology', *Connected Newsletter*, October, 13 (2): 4–6.

BBC Weather website: www.bbc.co.uk/weather/world/city_guides/results.shtml?tt=TT000180.

Becta CD-ROM: *Teaching and learning using digital video*. This free CD-ROM contains information about using digital video in teaching and learning. It includes ideas on how to get started, how to choose suitable technology and software, plus hints and tips, FAQs and other advice and resources. The CD-ROM also contains the findings from Becta's digital video pilot, plus films of pupils using this technology and examples of their work. Order your copy by sending an email to: dvcdrom@becta.org.uk.

Becta (2003) *What the research says about interactive whiteboards*, London: Becta (available at: www.Becta.org.uk/research).

Becta (2003) *What the research says about using ICT in English*, Coventry: Becta.

Becta (2003) *Becta digital video pilot project* (available at: http://partners.becta.org.uk/index.php?section=rh&rid=11258UTH; last accessed 20 March 2010).

Becta (2006) *Teaching interactively with electronic whiteboards in the primary phase* (available at: http://publications.Becta.org.uk/display.cfm?resID=25918).

Becta (2007) *Human rights controversies* (available at: http://research.becta.org.uk/upload-dir/downloads/page_documents/research/visualisers.pdf last accessed 3 June 2010).

Becta (2007) *Test bed project* (available at: http://research.becta.org.uk/index.php?section=rh&catcode=_re_mr_tb_03&rid=13547; last accessed 20 September 2010).

Becta (2009) *Evidence on the impact of technology on learning and educational outcomes*, Becta.

Becta (2010) *Inspiring learners*, Becta.

Becta (2010) *Digital literacy: teaching critical thinking for our digital world*, Becta.

Bracegirdle, P. (2009) 'Embedding ICT across the curriculum. Using a visualiser in the primary classroom', *The Dig IT 2009 project. A Key Stage 2 writing project* (available at: www.segfl.org.uk/files/Projects/casestudies/reportvis09.pdf; last accessed 12 September 2010).

Brennan, G. (2010) 'Curriculum – Pens down, camera up, look ahead', *TES Magazine*, 5 March.

Byron, T. (2008) *Safer children in a digital world*, DCSF Publications.

Carter, A. (2002) 'Using interactive whiteboards with deaf children' (available at: www.bgfl.org/bgfl/activities/intranet/teacher/ict/whiteboards; retrieved 23 March 2004).

Chandler, P., O'Brien, A. and Unsworth, L. (2009) 'Challenges in the development of a multimedia authoring pedagogy'. Paper presented at the Australian Association for Research in Education, Canberra, Australia.

Davies, D., Howe, A., Fasciato, M. and Rogers, M. (2004) 'How do trainee primary teachers understand creativity?'. Paper presented at BERA Conference, University of Manchester, at the *Creative teachers for creative learners* symposium.

DCSF and QCA (2010) *New Primary Curriculum* (last accessed from www.dcsf.gov.uk/primarycurriculumreview/).

Deadman, G. (1997) 'An analysis of pupils' reflective writing within a hypermedia framework', *Journal of Computer Assisted Learning*, 13: 16–25.

de Bono, E. (1976) *Teaching thinking*, London: Penguin Books.

DfEE and QCA (1989) *National Curriculum*.

DfEE (1997) *Connecting the learning society* (publication that introduced the National Grid for Learning).

The Education and Training Inspectorate (2005) *ICT in primary schools*, The Education and Training Inspectorate.

Hall, D. (2010) *The ICT handbook for primary teachers*, Fulton.

Harrison, C. *et al.* (2002) 'ImpaCT2: The impact of information and communication technologies on pupil attainment', *ICT in Schools Research and Evaluation Series*, No. 7 (available at: www.becta.org.uk/page_documents/research/ImpaCT2_strand1_report.pdf).

Hayes, T. and Ge, X. (2008) 'The effects of computer-supported collaborative learning on students' writing performance'. Proceedings of the 8th International Conference on the *Learning Sciences*, Utrecht, the Netherlands, Vol. 1: 335–41.

Higgins, C. (2005) *Interactive whiteboards in primary schools pilot study*, Becta.

Higgins, C. *et al.* (2005) 'Embedding ICT in the Literacy and Numeracy Strategies: Final Report', UK: DfES, University of Newcastle, Becta (available at: www.Becta.org.uk/page_documents/research/univ_newcastle_evaluation_whiteboards).

Independent ICT in School Commission (1997) *Stevenson Report* (available at: http://rubble.ultralab.anglia.ac.uk/stevenson/ICTUKIndex.html).

Jarvis, G. (2003) *Using ICT in primary humanities teaching*, Exeter: Learning Matters.

John, P. and Wheeler, S. (2008) *The digital classroom*, David Fulton.

Karchmer, R. (2001) 'The journey ahead: thirteen teachers report how the Internet influences literacy and literacy instruction in their K-12 classrooms', *Reading Research Quarterly*, 36 (4): 442–66.

Latham P. (2002) 'Teaching and learning mathematics: the impact of interactive whiteboards – results of the North Islington Education Action Zone RM Easiteach Mathematics Project'. BEAM Education, London.

Long, S. (2001) 'What effect will digital technologies have on visual education in schools?', in A. Loveless and V. Ellis (eds), *ICT, pedagogy and the curriculum: subject to change*, Routledge.

Loveless, A. and Thacker, J. (2005) 'Visual literacy and ICT: I'm only looking . . .', in S. Wheeler (ed.), *Transforming primary ICT*, Exeter: Learning Matters.

McCormick, R. and Scrimshaw, P. (2001) 'Information and communications technology, knowledge and pedagogy', *Education, Communication and Information*, 1 (1): 37–57.

Matthewman, S. and Triggs, P. (2004) '"Obsessive compulsive font disorder": the challenge of supporting pupils' writing with the computer', *Computers and Education*, 43: 125–35.

Mumtaz, S. (2001) 'Children's enjoyment and perception of computer use in the home and the school', *Computers and Education*, 36: 347–62.

Mumtaz , S. and Hammond, M. (2002) 'The word processor revisited; observations on the use of the word processor to develop literacy at Key Stage 2', *British Journal of Educational Technology*, 3 (33): 345–7.

NACCE (1999) *All our futures: creativity, culture and education* (NACCE report), DfES.

Ofcom (2006) *Media literacy audit*, The Stationery Office (available at: www.cyberethics.info/cyethics2/UserFiles/Ofcom_MediaLiteracyAuditAdults_Report_2006.pdf).

Potter, P. and Darbyshire, C. (2005) *Understanding and teaching the ICT National Curriculum*, David Fulton.

Prensky, M. (2007) 'How to teach with technology: keeping both teachers and students comfortable in an era of exponential change', in *Emerging technologies for education*, Vol. 2, Becta.

QCDA (2004) 'Creativity: find it, promote it' (available at: http://orderline.qcda.gov.uk/bookstore.asp?Action=Book&ProductId=9781847211002).

QCDA (2009) National Curriculum poster DfEE (available at: http://curriculum.qcda.gov.uk/uploads/ELL%20Poster%20A3_tcm8-18062.pdf; last accessed 7 November 2010).

Rose, J. (2009) *Essentials for learning and life* (available at: qcda.gov.uk/curriculum).

Rose, J. (2009) 'Independent review of the primary curriculum' (available at: http://webarchive.nationalarchives.gov.uk/tna/+/http://www.dcsf.gov.uk/primarycurriculumreview/; last accessed 24 September 2010).

Rudd, A. and Tyldersley, A. (2006) *Literacy and ICT in the primary school*, London: David Fulton.

Rudd, A. *et al.* (2009) 'Harnessing Technology Schools Survey 2008' was conducted on behalf of the National Foundation for Educational Research (NFER). Becta.

Smith, H., Higgins, S., Wall, K. and Miller, J. (2005) 'Interactive whiteboards: boon or bandwagon? A critical review of the literature', *Journal of Computer Assisted Learning*, 21: 91–101.

Somekh, B. *et al.* (2007) 'Evaluation of the Primary Schools Whiteboard Project'. Report to the Department for Children, Schools and Families, Becta, Manchester Metropolitan University.

Thomas, A. (2003) 'Little touches that spell success', *TES Magazine*, 23 May.

Wheeler, S. (2005) *Transforming primary ICT*, Exeter: Learning Matters.

Wood, C. *et al.* (2006) 'Children's use of mobile phone text messaging and its impact on literacy development in primary school'. Becta report (available at: http://partners.Becta.org.uk/upload-dir/downloads/page_documents/research/reports/childrens_use_of_mobile_phone_text_mess aging.pdf; last accessed 21 July 2010).

Index

animations 96, 100, 119, 142, 154, 163, 164
Appleworks 27
AREST acronym 8
art and design, using ICT in 62–4
assessment, use of ICT in 46
assessment of ICT work 39–44
  individual pupil record 42, 43
  points to consider 41–4
  problems 40
  reasons 39–40
  strategies 41
  whole-class records 42, 44
  year-group portfolios 44
attainment targets 39, 198
Audacity 112, 167, 174
audio equipment *see* digital audio equipment

back up 48
bar charts 70–1, 140
BBC 32, 73, 108, 130
Bebo 32–3
bitmap files 101
Black Cat 51, 53, 60, 66, 69
BlockCAD 102
blogs 13, 27, 33, 54
bookmarking 31
brain trainers 132
branching databases 80–3
  foreign language lessons 144
  history lessons 148
  maths lessons 133
  religious education lessons 173
  science lessons 139, 142

CAD (computer-aided design) 9, 102, 157, 160
calculators 132, 133, 135, 137
Caring for our Planet topic 196–7
Carroll diagrams 133, 135, 142
CD-ROMs 28
  art and design lessons 163
  English lessons 129
  geography lessons 152, 153
  history lessons 145, 146
  religious education lessons 172, 173, 174

science lessons 138, 139, 140, 141, 143
  storage of digital photos on 89
Celestron 95
charity websites 174
charts 56–7, 132
  spreadsheets and displaying information in 70–1
Children's Message Board 32
classroom, using ICT in the 15–38
Clicker 139, 153
clip art 9, 18, 102, 133, 139, 142
Comenius project 131
computer suites 23, 24–5
computer viruses 31
computer-aided design *see* CAD
computers
  hand-held 117–18
  standalone 23, 25–6
concept maps 10, 13, 102, 172
connections, making 9–10
control technology 110–11
  design and technology lessons 160
  science lessons 143
Corral Draw 102
creativity, and ICT 7–14
cross-circular topics, using ICT in 175–97

data, manipulating of and spreadsheets 71–3
data-logging/data loggers 38, 84–6
  design and technology lessons 158, 160
  geography lessons 154
  physical education lessons 169
  science lessons 138, 140, 141, 142
databases 69, 76–9
  branching *see* branching databases
  design and technology lessons 158
  geography lessons 152, 154, 155
  history lessons 148
  maths lessons 136
  National Curriculum requirements 77
  physical education lessons 169
  progression in 79
  religious education lessons 171
  science lessons 139, 141, 142

ways of helping children 77
ways of helping teachers 77–8
Dazzle 101
decision-tree program 136
design and technology, using ICT in 157–61
desktop publishing 102
  geography lessons 152, 154, 155
Digi-blue cameras 90, 164
digital audio equipment 112–16
digital audio recorders/recording 112, 113
  English lessons 126, 128
  history lessons 146, 148
  music lessons 166
  science lessons 140, 143
digital cameras/photos 11, 47, 87–94
  advantages 87
  art and design lessons 162, 163
  creating films 90–1
  design and technology lessons 158
  English lessons 126
  foreign language lessons 144
  geography lessons 51, 152, 153, 154
  good practice when using 89–90
  history lessons 146
  maths lessons 137, 139
  and National Curriculum requirements 90
  physical education lessons 168
  points to consider when choosing 88–9
  power supply 89
  progression in using 92–4
  religious education lessons 172, 173
  science lessons 138, 139, 140, 141, 142, 143
  storage media 89
  use of outside school 38
  ways of helping children 91
  ways of helping teachers 91
digital divide 65
digital microscopes 95–9
  religious education lessons 172
  science lessons 138, 140, 141
digital music composition 113–14, 166
digital photos *see* digital cameras/photos
digital recording *see* digital audio
      recorders/recording
digital sound files 112–16, 138, 165
digital timers 169
digital videos
  art and design lessons 163
  history lessons 146, 148
  religious education lessons 172
discussion boards 32
draw programs 101–2
  art and design lessons 162, 163, 164
  design and technology lessons 159
  religious education lessons 172, 173
  see also paint programs
dyslexic pupils 23, 31

e-books 144
e-mail 34–5
  foreign language lessons 144
  geography lessons 152, 154, 155

religious education lessons 173, 174
  science lessons 141
e-mail distribution lists 32
e-palling 35
e-zines (electronic magazines) 34, 131
editing text 52
electronic bulletin boards 32
electronic keyboard 167
electronic portfolios 12, 26–7, 41
English, using ICT in 125–31
equals sign 71
e-safety 203
Excel 66

Fabrics and Bags Enterprise Project 178–9
Facebook 27, 32–3
Famous People topic 188–9
Flickr 27, 32–3
floor turtles 12, 47, 134, 152, 163
foreign languages, use of ICT in 144
formatting text 54–6

games, ICT 36
geography, using ICT in 151–6
GIS (Geographic Information Systems) 151, 155, 156
glossary 204–8
Google 30
Google Earth 139, 151–2, 154
Google Picasa 102
Google SketchUp 102
GPS (global positioning system) 37, 132, 142, 154
graphical organisers 102
graphics programs 12, 100–6
  art and design lessons 162, 163, 164
  design and technology lessons 157, 159, 160
  geography lessons 152, 155
  maths lessons 136
  National Curriculum requirements 103
  physical education lessons 169
  progression in 104–6
  science lessons 142, 143
  types of 100–2
graphs
  and data loggers 84, 85
  and spreadsheets 71

hand-held devices 117–18, 141
handwriting 56
Healthy Me topic 190–1
history, using ICT in 145–50
hyperlinked presentations 27, 54, 130, 202
hyperlinks 18, 26, 29, 143, 160
Hyperstudio 119, 137, 155, 164

Ictopus site 129
iMovie 90, 113
interactive teaching programs (ITPs) 132, 133,
      134, 135, 136
interactive whiteboards *see* IWBs
Internet 9, 27–36
  art and design lessons 164
  background information 28–9

benefits of 29
design and technology lessons 158, 159, 160
English lessons 129
finding information from 29
foreign language lessons 144
geography lessons 152, 154
history lessons 146, 148, 149
maths lessons 135, 136, 137
physical education lessons 168
problems on the 31–2
religious education lessons 172
safety issues 29, 33
science lessons 139, 140, 141, 142, 143
searching on 29–31
IWBs (interactive whiteboards) 15–23, 46, 47,
  125
  advantages 15–17
  art and design lessons 162
  design and technology lessons 160
  English lessons 126, 127, 129, 130
  features 17–18
  geography lessons 155
  history lessons 146, 148
  maths lessons 133, 135, 136
  music lessons 165, 167
  physical education lessons 168, 169
  points to consider when using 18
  religious education lessons 174
  science lessons 139, 140
  and special educational needs 22–3
  use of in different parts of the lesson 20–2
  ways of helping children 19–20
  ways of helping teachers 23

Kar2ouche 130
keyboards 65
  electronic 167
  overlay 65
keywords 30
Kidspiration 10, 102, 103, 142, 174
Kindergarten Karaoke 165

laptop suites 25
laptops 37
layouts, text 54–6
Learning about Animals topic 184–5
lesson plans 45
line graphs 71, 135
listening stations 126
listserv 32
Logo program 110, 163
Looking into the Past topic 180–1

malware 31
mathematics, using ICT in 132–7
media cards 89
memory sticks 89
microphones 112
microscopes, digital *see* digital microscopes
Microsoft Picture manager 102
Millennium Village Simulation 108
mind maps 148

mobile phones, and texting 34
modern foreign languages (MFL) *see* foreign
  languages
Motic Digiscope 95
Movie Maker *see* Windows Movie Maker
movies, digital 88, 89, 90–1
MP3 files/players 112, 113, 166
Multimap 151, 154
multimedia programs/presentations 119–22
  English lessons 127, 130, 131
  geography lessons 155
  history lessons 149
  music lessons 167
  religious education lessons 173, 174
music, using ICT in 165–7
music composition, digital 113–14, 166
music software 12, 166
MySpace 27, 32–3

NACCE report (1999) 7
National Curriculum requirements
  branching databases 81
  control technology 110
  data loggers 85
  databases 77
  digital cameras/photos 90
  digital microscopes and visualisers 96
  digital sound files 114
  graphics programs 103
  hand-held devices 117
  multimedia presentations 120
  simulations 108
  spreadsheets 67
  word processors 53
Nintendo 36

Ollie's Island Educator 139
Our Community topic 182–3
overlay keyboard 65

paint programs 100, 101
  art and design lessons 162, 163, 164
  design and technology lessons 157, 159
  foreign language lessons 144
  maths lessons 135
  religious education lessons 172, 173
  see also draw programs
palmtops 37–8
  geography lessons 154
  science lessons 141, 142
parents
  contact with 47–8
  involving in learning 36
Pattern Builder 166
Pawprints 138
PebblePAD 26, 27
personalised learning 35–6, 113
photo-editing software 102
photos 56
  of pupils work 47
  see also digital cameras/photos
physical education, using ICT in 168–70

pie charts 70
Pinpoint 69
Pixies 47, 110–11, 134
plagiarism 32
planning, use of ICT in 45, 46
Plants and Growing topic 186–7
podcasts/podcasting 13, 113
  English lessons 128, 130
  history lessons 148
  music lessons 167
  religious education lessons 174
portfolio technologies 27
portfolios
electronic 12, 26–7, 41
year-group 44
PowerPoint 12, 21, 27, 113, 119
  art and design lessons 163, 164
  creating hyperlinked presentations 202
  geography lessons 155
  history lessons 149
  religious education lessons 174
  science lessons 138, 141

questioning 8–9

RAISEonline 47
record-keeping 46–8
  and databases 77
  and spreadsheets 74
reflection 12–13
religious education, using ICT in 171–4
residential visits 37
resources, organising 48
Roamers 110–11, 134, 152, 160
Robots/Superheroes/Monsters topic 194–5

saving, successful 25
scattergram 139
school trips 37–8
science, using ICT in 10, 138–43
screen turtles 134, 136, 160, 163
search engines 30
Sibelius 166
SimCity 12, 108
SIMS 47
simulations 12, 107–9
  design and technology lessons 158, 160
  English lessons 128
  geography lessons 151
  history lessons 149
  science lessons 139, 140, 142, 143
social networking sites 32–3
sound clips 56–7
sound files *see* digital sound files
special educational needs
  and IWBs 22–3
  and podcasts 113
speech bubbles 55–6, 172, 173
spelling checkers 54, 130
split screens 57
Sports/Olympics/World Cup topic
  192–3

spreadsheets 12, 66–75, 76
  advantages 67
  design and technology lessons 158, 159, 160
  geography lessons 152, 154, 155
  history lessons 148, 149
  maths lessons 132, 134, 135, 136, 137
  National Curriculum requirements 67
  physical education lessons 169, 170
  progression in 75
  science lessons 139, 141, 142
  and templates 74
  ways of helping children 67–73
  ways of helping teachers 74
standalone computers 23, 25–6
Stevenson report (1997) 28

tables 56
  geography lessons 151, 152, 154, 155
  history lessons 145, 148
  maths lessons 136
  physical education lessons 169
  religious education lessons 173
  science lessons 142
  see also spreadsheets
talking books 126, 129
teaching, use of ICT as aid to 45–6
teaching assistants (TAs) 41
templates 26, 45, 56, 125
  creating 199–201
  design and technology lessons 157, 158,
    159, 160
  English lessons 127, 130
  history lessons 145–6
  maths lessons 135
  physical education lessons 168
  religious education lessons 171, 172, 174
  science lessons 138, 139, 140, 141
  and spreadsheets 74
  word-processing software 65
Textease 9, 53, 60, 66, 102, 119, 139, 145, 153
texting 34
Think.com 32–3
turtles
  floor 12, 47, 134, 152, 163
  screen 134, 136, 160, 163
Twitter 11, 33–4
2Simple 53, 60, 66, 102, 119, 166
typing skills 65

Venn diagram 133, 134, 142
video games 36
video-conferencing 19, 32, 96, 128, 151, 156
videos 57, 128, 168, 169 *see also* digital
    videos
virtual learning environments (VLEs) 35,
    36
Virtual Puppeteers 155
visual literacy 87, 100
visualisers 95–9
  design and technology lessons 158, 160
  history lessons 146, 148
  science lessons 138, 140, 141

webcams 11
    English lessons 128
    geography lessons 154, 156
    science lessons 142
WebQuest 173
websites 31–2
    school 34
'What if?' question 11, 67
Wii 169
Wikipedia 32, 33, 129
wikis 27, 33
wild card symbol 30
Windows Movie Maker 90, 96, 113, 141, 155, 170
wizards 102
word banks 53, 59, 60, 139, 146, 151, 172
word processors 12, 13, 51–65
    benefits to writing development 51–2
    design and technology lessons 159
    English lessons 126, 127, 128, 129, 130
    features 59

foreign language lessons 144
geography lessons 151, 152, 153, 154
history lessons 146, 149
National Curriculum requirements (2009) 53
physical education lessons 168, 169
problems with 65
progression in 60–3
religious education lessons 172
science lessons 138, 139, 141, 142
templates 65
types of 60
ways to help children 52–8
ways to help teachers 58–60
word-processed documents, reading 65
worksheets 45
WWW (World Wide Web) 29, 125

Xbox 36

YouTube 129, 142, 149, 164, 169